An Oxfordshire Market Gardener

Joseph and Ann Turrill with their children in the garden of Fern Cottage, *c.* 1890. This is the only authenticated likeness of Joseph Turrill

An Oxfordshire Market Gardener

The Diary of
JOSEPH TURRILL
of Garsington 1841–1925

Edited
by
E. Dawson and S.R. Royal

ALAN SUTTON

OXFORDSHIRE BOOKS

First published in the United Kingdom in 1993 by
Alan Sutton Publishing Ltd
Phoenix Mill · Far Thrupp · Stroud · Gloucestershire

Oxfordshire Books · Oxfordshire County Council
Department of Leisure and Arts · Central Library · Westgate · Oxford

First published in the United States of America in 1993 by
Alan Sutton Publishing Inc.
83 Washington Street · Dover · NH 03820

A catalogue record for this book is available from the British Library.

ISBN 0–7509–0327–9

Library of Congress Cataloging in Publication Data applied for

Typeset in 10/11 Bembo.
Typesetting and origination by
Alan Sutton Publishing Limited.
Printed and bound in Great Britain by
The Bath Press, Avon.

Contents

Acknowledgements   vii

Maps   viii

Introduction   xi

Family Trees   xvi

Diary: March 1862 to June 1867   1

Notes   143

Glossary   159

Some People and Families in the Diary   161

Index   172

One of Joseph Turrill's daughters at home in Fern Cottage

Acknowledgements

The transcription of the diary was originally shared between five members of the Garsington Local History Group, viz. Eve Dawson, Joan Newby, Flora Pickering, Shirley Royal, and Mollie Witcomb. Afterwards the editors collated, checked, and revised this material. The notes and all other ancillary material have been compiled by Eve Dawson; Shirley Royal has helped with the research, and the maps were drawn by Patricia Macartney. Photographs not listed below are from the Garsington Local History Group.

The editors would like to thank the following: David Vaisey, Ann and Henry Hardy and Jean Cook who saw the transcript of the diary and gave helpful advice and encouragement; Jan and John Paling, of Fern Cottage, for the loan of the Turrill photographs (pp. ii, vi, 10, 34, 38, 42, 47, 71, 75, 81, 85, 88, 101, 142); Malcolm Graham, Head of the Centre for Oxfordshire Studies, who found other appropriate photographs in his collection (pp. xviii, 2, 12, 22, 55, 56, 61, 66, 91, 93, 127) and also suggested some alterations and corrections to the notes; the Bodleian Library for permission to reproduce the pictures on p. 23; Heather Green for the photograph on p. 10; Raymond Dawson who helped with and advised on preparing the text for publication and also wrote the introduction; and all others who helped with queries, including members of the staff at the Centre for Oxfordshire Studies and the County Record Office. Responsibility for errors or inaccuracies remains with the editors.

Garsington
March 1993

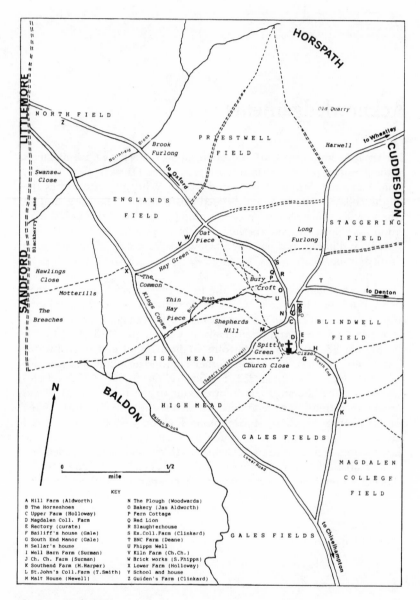

KEY

A Hill Farm (Aldworth)
B The Horseshoes
C Upper Farm (Holloway)
D Magdalen Coll. Farm
E Rectory (curate)
F Bailiff's house (Gale)
G South End Manor (Gale)
H Sellar's house
I Well Barn Farm (Surman)
J Ch. Ch. Farm (Surman)
K Southend Farm (M.Harper)
L St.John's Coll.Farm (T.Smith)
M Malt House (Newell)
N The Plough (Woodwards)
O Bakery (Jas Aldworth)
P Fern Cottage
Q Red Lion
R Slaughterhouse
S Ex.Coll.Farm (Clinkard)
T BNC Farm (Deane)
U Phipps Well
V Kiln Farm (Ch.Ch.)
W Brick works (S.Phipps)
X Lower Farm (Holloway)
Y School and house
Z Guiden's Farm (Clinkard)

Garsington in the 1860s

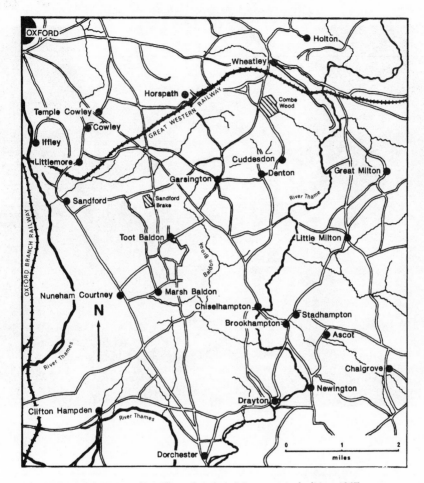

Garsington and the surrounding villages (based on OS map, revised edition, 1867)

Fern Cottage, taken in 1975

Introduction

The name of Garsington has become well known in the twentieth century, but only in relation to the manor-house where Lady Ottoline with her husband, the Liberal MP Philip Morrell, entertained her literary and artistic lions between 1915 and 1928. Now this diary gives a brief glimpse into village life in nineteenth-century Garsington. Joseph Turrill was eighty-four when he died in 1925, only three years before the Morrells left the manor. During his long life many changes affected the village, whose history has been much influenced by the proximity of a great university city. As Oxford expanded so the village increasingly supplied its inhabitants with food, and in more recent times both the size of the village and the nature of its population have changed with the growth of the motor-car industry at Cowley. Nevertheless it has managed to retain its independence from Oxford and much of its beauty.

Although Joseph lived to see many changes, his diary-writing took place in the 1860s when he was a young man with a taste for girls, and he did not foresee that what was meant for his eyes alone would be scrutinized with such diligence and presented to the world by residents of Garsington of a later age. The reader will be amused at the Victorian double standards which he applied to himself and his eventual bride Ann Harper of Southend Farm, not that he can bring himself to commit to writing everything that went on between them at the trysting-stile. For this was an important period in Joseph's life, when he was confiding to these secret pages the trials and tribulations of courtship. It was also, as we shall see, a time of importance in the history of the village. Living at the Red Lion, where he helped his mother who was the licensee, he was well placed to accumulate gossip.

The diary was written in the blank pages of old rate books, which were found in a wall-cupboard in Fern Cottage, Garsington, where Joseph, Ann, and the children lived after they moved out of the Red Lion. When he was writing the diary the cottage belonged to the brewers, Hall and Tawney, who also owned the Red Lion, and he was using its garden to grow additional produce. It is not clear when Joseph became the owner, but in about 1880 the building was refaced with local bricks and given a Victorian appearance. The cupboard was discovered under several layers of wallpaper when the cottage was being renovated in the 1960s. A bundle of mouldy photographs was found with the rate books and these had to be carefully separated and dried out. Most of them dated from the last two decades of the nineteenth century, when Joseph was the village photographer. Many of the best ones were copied, and these can be found in the Centre for Oxfordshire Studies together with the photocopied pages of the diary.

Joseph started writing irregular gardening notes in 1861 after he had rented an allotment from F.J. Morrell, Philip Morrell's grandfather, who was at that time owner of the North Manor Estate in Garsington. Gradually the notes became interspersed with a variety of other information but still included much detail about his work in the garden, the effects of the weather, and what he had sent to market in Oxford.

Joseph emerges from the pages of the diary as an energetic young man, better educated than might be expected and with a lively interest in the world around him. He regularly read the *Oxford Chronicle*, which covered national and international news in some detail as well as local affairs, and he contributed reports on Garsington cricket matches and Feasts to that paper. Although he had to work hard both at the Red Lion and also in his market garden, where he often turned out to work by moonlight, he frequently visited Oxford and villages round Garsington, sometimes on foot, and sometimes by cart or wagon with the cricket teams. When the new railway line opened in 1864, it became possible to go to Oxford by train from Wheatley and he says in the diary that he was the first person from Garsington to use the new line. Journeys further afield by train took him on a memorable trip to Malvern (accompanied by two girls), as well as to Banbury and other places in the locality.

Joseph took up photography in the 1880s. He had his equipment in an outbuilding and took studio portraits, wedding pictures, local views for postcards, and of course photographs of his own family. Some of his work has been used to illustrate this volume. After Joseph's death his daughters are said to have used his large collection of photographic plates as cloches in the garden. Certainly all traces of his equipment disappeared. His three surviving children all remained unmarried. The two daughters, known as Hettie and Lin, died in the house in 1954 and 1958. They are remembered as being 'well-spoken', since they did not have the usual local accent. Lin was in service in Oxford for some years and is described in her old age as rather eccentric looking, wearing black with her hair twisted up on top of her head. The son, who was known as Harry although baptized Arthur, took over from his father as a market gardener, and it seems that he was for a time bailiff to Philip Morrell.

The relative prosperity of the Turrills and the cheerfulness of the diary in comparison with some contemporary accounts of rural life, may give the reader a false impression of nineteenth-century Garsington. As elsewhere the enclosure of common land early in the nineteenth century had meant that most farm workers were entirely dependent on their wages, for they no longer had grazing rights for animals or enough land to supply themselves with food. After the publication of the Garsington Enclosure Award there was a survey of farms in 1824 to assess tithe contributions. It is significant that the surveyor's remarks on the entire parish were damning: 'The occupiers are men without capital and spirit and farms, with trifling exceptions, are very badly managed.' Later, in

One of Joseph Turrill's photographs, possibly of the Yeates family at the Brick Works, Kiln Lane

December 1848, a letter in the *Oxford Chronicle* painted a picture of a community full of poverty, ignorance and vice, with 'complaining farmers', 'discontented tradesmen', and 'turbulent, reckless and demoralised' poor.

In the following January a coroner's inquest on a thirteen-year-old girl who had died of cholera in Garsington criticized the conditions in which she and her family were living and the lack of attention to hygiene. In 1854 eight deaths from cholera were recorded and although the diary shows that determined efforts were made to combat the smallpox epidemic ten years later, no great improvement in conditions could have taken place by then. The arrival of a new official, the Public Health Inspector, is mentioned in the diary, but the school log-books continued to record epidemics of measles, scarlatina, and other diseases; and the school was closed at intervals because too many pupils and staff were away ill.

The mid-nineteenth century is referred to by agricultural historians as a period of 'high farming'. Markets were expanding and prices were rising as city populations grew while labourers' wages remained low. The bigger farmers in Garsington were sharing in the general prosperity, as is indicated by Joseph's observations on their farming practices, including their use of steam power. But it is also clear from the diary that many of his more enterprising friends were leaving the village to find work in Oxford, London and elsewhere, while others were emigrating. This drift away from the countryside accelerated towards the end of the century when farmers were hit by the effects of the importation of cheap grain and refrigerated meat and by several successive years of poor harvests. However, market gardeners and small farmers within easy reach of Oxford were able to supply the demand for fresh fruit and vegetables for the increasing populations. By 1891 there were nine market gardeners in Garsington and early in the twentieth century there were fifteen. (Now there are none.) Later, in the 1890s, the Parish Council applied to colleges and other landowners for some of their land so that this could be rented out as allotments to help labourers who wanted to grow cheap food.

Some knowledge of the historical background is bound to increase one's admiration for Joseph Turrill. Both he and Ann Harper had each lost no fewer than six siblings at the time when the diary was written. Familiarity with death and disease had given Joseph and his friends a fatalistic attitude to the sadder aspects of rural life in the 1860s. Although suffering is there, it does not obtrude so much as in the pages of parsonical diarists like his exact contemporary Francis Kilvert, who had to take a professional interest in human misery and also saw the situation of the poor from an upper-class viewpoint. There was still much to enjoy, and Joseph gives us a glimpse of Garsington at a time when it was just beginning to be embraced by the modern world.

The diary came to the attention of the local history group as an obvious source from which to extract material on the nineteenth-century history of the village. Its transcription proved to be an arduous task since some of the writing was very tiny, many of the words were difficult to decipher, and in some places the ink had faded badly. But although some nineteenth-century diaries are too voluminous for their editors to give more than a taste of the material, this is not the case here. It has been possible to reproduce virtually the whole of the book, with a series of dots indicating the few short passages which remain totally illegible. Square brackets have also been used to indicate words which need to be supplied in the interest of comprehension.

One of the difficulties in interpreting the diary is that many people are referred to only by their initials. These have been filled out where possible by inserting the rest of the name in square brackets. It has not been felt necessary to spell out A.H. (Joseph's frequent way of referring to his girl-friend) or Q, since this uncommon initial always refers to Quartermain. Joseph's own spelling and style have been left unaltered, although the former is often inconsistent and the latter awkward, but his punctuation is inadequate so some has been added to assist the reader. Sometimes dates are too confused to disentangle, e.g. on pp. 4–6.

Raymond Dawson

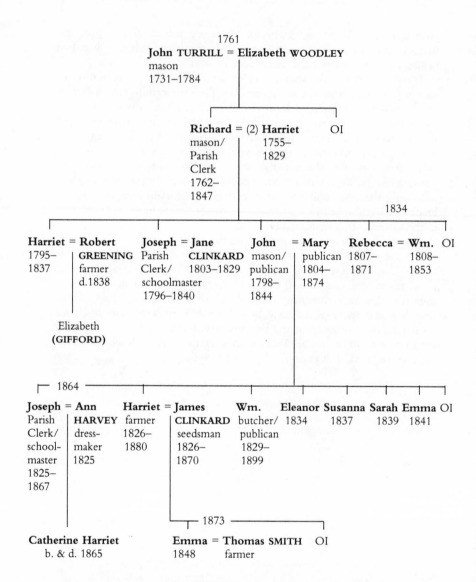

Dates of baptisms, marriages and burials are from the parish registers.

OI = other issue

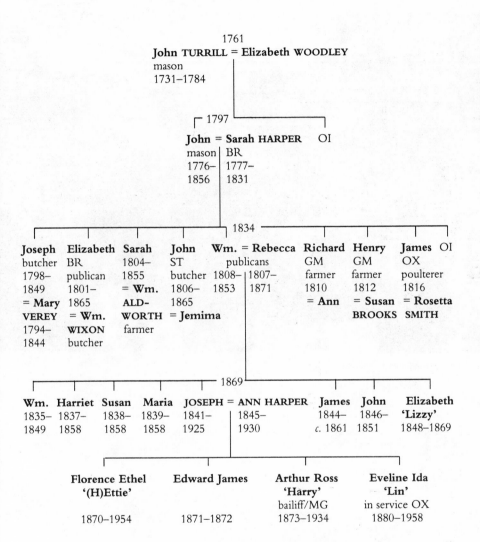

1761
John TURRILL = Elizabeth WOODLEY
mason
1731–1784

┌─ 1797 ─┐
John = Sarah HARPER   OI
mason | BR
1776– | 1777–
1856 | 1831

1834

Joseph	**Elizabeth**	**Sarah**	**John**	**Wm. = Rebecca**	**Richard**	**Henry**	**James** OI
butcher	BR	1804–	ST	publicans	GM	GM	OX
1798–	publican	1855	butcher	1808–|1807–	farmer	farmer	poulterer
1849	1801–	= **Wm.**	1806–	1853 | 1871	1810	1812	1816
= **Mary**	1865	**ALD-**	1865		= **Ann**	= **Susan**	= **Rosetta**
VEREY	= **Wm.**	**WORTH**	= **Jemima**			**BROOKS**	**SMITH**
1794–	**WIXON**	farmer					
1844	butcher						

1869

Wm.	**Harriet**	**Susan**	**Maria**	**JOSEPH = ANN HARPER**	**James**	**John**	**Elizabeth**
1835–	1837–	1838–	1839–	1841– | 1845–	1844–	1846–	**'Lizzy'**
1849	1858	1858	1858	1925 | 1930	c. 1861	1851	1848–1869

Florence Ethel	**Edward James**	**Arthur Ross**	**Eveline Ida**
'(H)Ettie'		**'Harry'**	**'Lin'**
		bailiff/MG	in service OX
1870–1954	1871–1872	1873–1934	1880–1958

Dates of baptisms, marriages and burials are from the parish registers.

BR = Brookhampton   OI = other issue
GM = Great Milton   OX = Oxford
MG = market gardener   ST = Stadhampton

Military parade in Broad Street, Oxford, 1874

1862–63

The main diary began on 17 May 1863 but there are some earlier notes from which the following have been extracted:

March 18th 1862   Sold 6 Hen Pheasants and 2 Cock Pheasants to Captain Sandeman of Westfield Lodge, Hayling Island, Havant, Hants. Sent them off this morning at 8 o'clock in a candle box with Partition in. Bored and burnt holes in all round and tied tight with strong string (cord) – 3d. worth. Got to Oxford at 20 minutes past nine too late for the 9 o'clock train. Sent them off by the 2 o'clock train – arrived quite safe. Had Post Office Order on Saturday morning for £7. 5s. 0d. for birds and box. Gave agent Mr James Ash, Stadhampton, Nr. Wallingford, Oxon., one pound for commission to Mr Sandeman's keeper – name Mr James Eborn. Had Mr W. Harper's pony and cart. Gave A. Harper 2s. for it and expences 1/9.

Sunday, April 26th 1863   Had a walk with W. and A. Harper to Oxford to see the Militia go to Church. It was a most beautiful day – Warm and sunny – a splendid spring day everything fresh and green and still. Started at half past 1 o'clock and got there at St Mary's Church at 10 minutes to 3. Saw the Militia meet in Broad Street about 800 strong with band playing and then march to Church. We went in and stood inside the Church and heard the Service and the beautiful organ. Came out again at 10 minutes to 5 and went down St Aldates to a public house and had a quart of Beer and Biscuits and then down alongside the river to Sandford. A beautiful walk. The river was clear and still as it rolled·on; the grass in the meadows almost knee high, the cowslips and wild flowers all in bloom, the sun setting like a ball of fire over the top of Bagley Wood, very few boats on the water. Went and saw Sandford Lock and the Monument to two young Gentlemen who were drowned there 20 years ago.[1] It is a fearful, grand and beautiful fall and you can hear the roar half a mile off. A very pretty view just round there. Went to the Public house at Sandford ferry and had a Quart and Biscuits and started home up through Sandford and across the fields by Sandford Break home. Whilst opposite

Littlemore Asylum I heard the Cuckoo for the first time this year. It was about half past seven and he was singing near the Asylum. The sun had set and it was just getting dusk but mild and clear. Saw no game at all coming home. Got home about 8.30. Waited upon the Cricketers. W., A. and Mrs Harper came up to supper and then we went the fields way home with them to hear the nightingales. Heard them singing beautifully at eleven o'clock, the Moon shining bright and all calm and clear.

Sandford-on-Thames weir and monument, *c.* 1875

1863

Building of railway between Wheatley and Oxford – frosts in July damage crops – J.T. begins serious courting – he and A.H. meet and go for long walks.

Sunday, May 17th 1863   Very fine day indeed but cold nights and mornings. It's trying to threaten rain now. Went down the Common gardens, then into the Cricket Common and looked at the Cricket Players; an immense number of persons there and some good play. I just missed viewing the eclipse. It was just over when I thought of it last Sunday. H., Mrs H. and I took a walk to Baldons and looked at Church etc. A beautiful day got back about 9.

Monday   I went to Oxford and bought some Ginger Beer bottles. Gave nine pence per dozen for them and some cups at 3/6 per doz., also some cream of tartar at 1s. 8d. a pound and Ginger at 1/- per lb. Lemons at 4 for 5d. . . .

Tuesday   Started to Stokenchurch this morning about 8. Most miserable wet day it rained all the way there and the wind was rough. Stopped at the Three Pigeons on our way there and back. 5 carts went and 20 persons from here. Began Cricket at 1 o'clock but very rough and cold. Our side went and got 151 and Stokenchurch got 41 with 3 wickets down and then it rained so fast they was obliged to give in. It soon cleared up but the Stokenchurch men would not come on the ground to time and the Umpire decided the game in favour of Garsington. There were some hard words in consequence but it was soon all over and we enjoyed a very tidy evening. But I was so cold and it was so wet that it made it very dull indeed. The supper was badly managed and the beer very bad. Got back about 20 minutes to 12 and glad enough I was. It is a beautiful county in fine weather.

Wednesday   Hoed potatoes and earthed the peas up – don't grow fast so cold and frosty nights and mornings.

Thursday   Cleaned Ginger Beer bottles.

Friday   Made Ginger Beer.

Saturday   Tied Lettuce in, in gardens and moulded Kidney Beans up in the Common and stuck them – looks very yellow. Cabbage want cutting and Lettuce wants pulling. Played for a cheese at skittles and got 9 and Rogers got 10 and won it and then Spring won it with 9 again. A beautiful clear starlight night but intensely cold and a sharp white frost in the morning. Too cold for Nightingales. The blight among the Gooseberry trees is about again but not very bad at present, it is too cold. Had a swarm of Bees on Monday but it was very warm in the morning and they wanted to swarm before but the weather was so bad. Swarmed on a little gooseberry tree in front and went in the hive the first time very tidy and warm.

Sunday   Beautiful morning the sun shone bright but it clouded over at 2 o'clock and now looks quite missly (5 o'clock). Shot a pigeon this dinner time in Elm tree against the Privy. There was two but the gun smoked and so I only had one. Did not go to church. Mrs Wilgress died last Friday and Joe Ruffles was married the next day. Tomorrow is Whit Monday and likely to be wet. The plum, apple and damson trees seem set well and everything wants sun and warm weather. Planted 6 rows cabbage on Wednesday last May 20 1863. The peas at bottom of Lower Piece just coming up. Sharpened sticks for them.

May 21st   Gathered some apricots off the tree but they was too old ought to have been got after the job.

Friday, 22nd May   Moulded potatoes in Com[mon] some time ago. Ted Watson wrote to me on Tuesday May 19th '63. Made a cucumber bed on May 27th and planted 3 little plants from Ben Hanks. Peas in garden growing well. Mrs Wilgress buried May 29th. Cream of tartar 1s. 8d. per pound. Budded roses on Friday June 26th. Dug first potatoes up on that day – yielded very tidy considering it being first lot . . . Hoed the carrots among the cabbage same day. All the cabbage and lettuce gone now.

June 27th   Parsnips are blighting – peas are looking uncommonly well and onions. There is a good prospect of Apples, Plums, Black currants and Potatoes. Rather dull weather now but fine. It rains now a little.

June 24th   Wednesday went to the Oxford Volunteer Rifle Review today.[2] It rained in the morning a little but cleared off afterwards and was a warm nice day. Went in Howards cart and came back in Harper's. Got there about 11. Went and got a Skittle Ball and Tyre Rod and had dinner and then to the review. It began about 3 and ended at 6.30 there were 8500 troops engaged with 250 cavalry and 6 guns 26-pounders and 4 18-pounders. The reports from the big guns was distinctly heard 24 miles off and shook the houses at Garsington and Baldon making the windows rattle whilst the musketry firing could be plainly heard it was calculated there were 60,000 persons present. General Russley was the commanding Officer.

June 27th   Put the slab down in front of skittle alley. Kidney Beans just out in bloom. Ripe fruit coming in – raspberries, gooseberries, currants, strawberries etc. Apples on standard are large as a child's fist. Heard Cuckoo today . . .

July 7th   Shallots nearly ripe and fruit ripening very fast – very hot dry weather indeed now – everything drying up for want of rain. Took young thrushes in garden on July 8th. Planted mangolds on Friday and watered them on July 3rd. The weather has been most brilliant up to now, July 20th and no sign of rain. It was a most extraordinary sharp frost in the morning of Sunday last July 19th – it cut the potatoes and Kidney Beans up quite black and shrivelled.[3] Never was known such a frost it did not hurt anything else as I could see.

Aug. 1st   The weather still continues very fine and warm and now, 11 o'clock, the Moon is shining very bright and not a cloud to be seen. I was down the Common last night just finished gathering K[idney] B[eans] when the Church clock struck nine but it is getting quite dark now at that time. J. Tromp was fined 30s. and to forfeit his gun today. W. Druce is at work today all right. Had the first ripe plums today. Wheat now gathered. Walnuts for pickling ourselves today. Sowed cabbage seed today about half an ounce but did not water it – sowed it in drills. Gathered first Apricots today in the lower tree – about a dozen. Tried the potatoes in the Com. on Friday June 12th but would not do – too small. Nearly all the Cabbage and Lettuce gone. Harpers took up their potatoes – good ones, 2½ bushel – on Friday and Sunday 14th. He had a swarm of bees on the Sunday got stung. Gathered the bottlers on Thursday 11th – ¾ of a bushel – showery weather. Mother paid me for 11 dozen of Ginger Beer on Saturday June 13th 16s. 6d. – 5 dozen left.

July 17th   Beautiful dry weather very warm and sunny but sadly wants rain – it has been fine for a long time now and very hot. Was not very well yesterday – felt sick and giddy – better today. The Apples and Apricots fall very much and the fruit is going off very fast indeed ripe. The potatoes are all wasting up and my shallots are quite ripe – the Kidney Beans are looking well. Played the return Match at Cricket on Tuesday 14th July on the Magdalen Ground Oxford with the St Clements Eleven and beat them with 8 wickets to go down. A beautiful day. Went to the Circus at night and got home at half past 12 – only two of the Clements men to dinner. Haymaking all over now and the cornfields are looking quite ripe in places – a splendid wheat year but middling bean year.

July 21st   It began raining today and it looks like wet. I went down the Common and gathered my Peas and it rained nearly all the time – it is a nice gentle rain just what we wanted.

July 22nd   It still keeps raining with occasional sunshine. Went to Harpers and fetched some Cauliflower plants and planted them where early potatoes, lettuce was.

July 23rd   It is a beautiful day – it has not rained since yesterday morning – ranting tea meeting today.[4] Gathered Kidney Beans first lot Tuesday. 1 Quarter and measured the cuks [cucumbers] today. Inspection at Wheatley yesterday. Did not go and did not know of it.

July 29th   Very hot and close with cold frosty mornings still. Had a little misty rain on Saturday but it soon went off and now there is no signs of rain. James Humphries was caught trespassing near the copse last Sunday took to Oxford by the police. Brought up next day and dismissed till Saturday. It was the G.W.R. W.& O. Fete yesterday at Nuneham Park.[5] A beautiful day. Mother and Lizzy went by Harper's cart with Mrs and Anne Harper enjoyed themselves much and got home about 9 o'clock. Thinned carrots out (Whites) on Friday last – wants hoeing down there now. Watered mangolds yesterday and budded some roses last Saturday. Apricots ripening fast – Currants nearly over.

July 30th   No rain up till now. The bother about William Druce being lost – he was missing from 5 till 12 o'clock. Found wandering about up again the Brakelane. Bought Cabbage seed of Sellar. One ounce for 1/0. Hoed carrots etc. yesterday.

August 4th   It has been raining all the afternoon. Began about 1 o'clock and rained gently till 7. Was gathering peas etc. down the Common and got wet through and caught a cold. Had a supper that night – leg of mutton – about clearing T. Aldworth's pond out – 10 of us to supper. In the morning about 7 o'clock W. Druce made an attempt to cut his throat with a drawing knife. He did not cut it much though and is going on very well.

August 5th   It has been fine today and the reapers have been on today. Reaping became general in this parish last Monday but some had begun before.

August 6th   Took dung down the Common today. It has rained early this morning and is very cloudy today. W. Druce is better. Trained the apricot trees yesterday. Had brewers in today.

August 7th   Pruned upper Apricot trees today fine all day.

August 8th   Fine weather still. Going to do the Pump.

August 9th   Fine weather still and very warm. We sweat indoors sitting still. No skittling of any kind occurred last Saturday night. Cabbage seed come up well.

August 10th   Fine but gloomy still. W. Druce is very violent this morning – suppose they must send him to an asylum now. Jack Godfrey's just gone up to help look after him. Did not go to church yesterday. Richard Clinkard is going to carry some wheat or corn today. Peas nearly over – my last row looks uncommonly well though. Gathered first lot – about a peck of it – on Saturday last.

August 12th   Glorious weather still and no signs of rain all the wheat cut and oats and some of the wheat is carried. All the farmers have carried some and Richard Clinkard is thrashing some wheat with steamer [steam thresher] today. W. Druce was took to the Asylum Littlemore on Monday last. He went very quiet and has been so ever since. First saw the Potato Complaint down the Common yesterday but saw no bad potatoes. Put some more buds in roses yesterday. Sowed some turnip seed down the Common in among the Parsnips yesterday. Everybody very busy at harvest work now.

August 17th   Glorious harvest weather still no rain except just enough to lay the dust yesterday for about five minutes. Oat Piece just finished mowing – everybody carrying today rather cloudy and windy but very drying. Taylor had a most extraordinary escape from being killed on Saturday night by falling down the shaft of Railway, but only shook himself and hurt his knee a little and he worked till 8 o'clock on Sunday morning.[6] This happened at 12 o'clock on Saturday night. Rubbed Lettuce seed out today. Fanny Watson down here now – came on Saturday. Most splendid crops of corn this year some 5, 6 and 7 quarter to the acre. Richard Clinkard winnowed some new wheat and sold it on Saturday last for £12 2s. 6d. per load at 6 qrs to the acre. Seed Peas are ripe – gathered all the Apricots on Friday – have had no rain for a long time now and the ground is very dry.[7] Nobody at cricket scarcely on Sunday last. Went stripped out all last week.

August 19th   It rained a little yesterday with occasional sunshine – sowed the Lettuce seed yesterday. Harper took up his bees yesterday. Today it has rained. Mizzly all the day but no regular showers and now (9 o'clock night) it is clear and bright and very cold more like a frost. It has checked harvest operations for a time. First saw Fanny Watson tonight. Rather short, stout, fairish looking girl, very sensible too. Hoed the Cauliflower plants today and shaped the rose stems. John Druce went down to the Asylum to see W. Druce; he is about the same. Tremendous lot of Blackbirds about the garden now – shot some today.

August 23rd   With the exception of a little mizzly rain, about enough to lay the dust, it has been no rain. Gathered my seed peas and shifted dung on to the ground yesterday – Fraser Wards peas. Found a few bad potatoes. Sowed turnip seed among the Cauliflowers yesterday. Rather cloudy today. Finished gathering Apricots on Friday. Took bees up on Thursday last. 3 stocks very tidy ones too better than any we have had for a good time – did not get stung. Went to Church this morning. Bells chiming now. Gathered about half a bushel of seed peas yesterday. Most of the white corn cut and carried now and bean reaping begun now. Market very low. Plums ripen very bad – not sun enough with frosty mornings. Fanny Watson is here now and it has been raining a little but it now appears to be fine.

August 30th   Went to church this morning. It is fine now but looks cloudy. It has been raining on and off ever since the 23rd and it rained nearly all day on Tuesday, Wednesday and up to Thursday night. I should think that some of the corn is growed as it is so warm. The ground is thoroughly well soaked now and things look quite fresh again now. The Lettuce Seed is come up well now but it has been in a long time. The Cabbage plants look well now. Went to Oxford yesterday and bought some Bedford cloth for trousers and waistcoat cost about 30/- and a new hat for 5/- but I do not like the hat – paid for it. Was measured for new shoes last Tuesday. Had a walk by moonlight with Fanny Watson and Lizzy to Baldon last Monday. Met her [A.H.] in Oxford yesterday went to . . . with her and back to Carfax then parted and came home to the Club Funeral of James Young at Cuddesdon about half past five o'clock. It has rained all morning and it is threatening now. Saw some ground oats on Gales farm last night. Jack White caught in old Bradons bedroom last night for the purpose it is supposed of stealing his money and took off to Oxford by the Policeman. Boots want mending. Gathered some Lettuce seed today but it is very wet and shedded a good deal it has rather more the appearance of being fine now. Cricket match at Stadhampton. Serious illness of Mrs Wixon Jun. Brookhampton Marriage of Young Squire Hall last Thursday. Gathered some Peas on Saturday. Turnip seed in Cauliflower some up.

Sept. 3rd   It has rained little missly rain on and off all the week but warm with it. The barley and other white corn is unmistakably damaged now. Saw Holloways carrying barley today. Got the tops off Potatoes today. Put a rosebud in on Tuesday last . . . Had new shoes home last night costs £4 0. 0.[8] Had new hat 6/8 last night.

Sept. 16th   The weather has been very wet all last week but it [cleared?] up on Sunday last and although it has been fine since and today the sun is shining bright (11 o'clock) the farmers have been very busy this week and all the corn will be carried today I think in our parish. Took my potatoes up on Monday last and onions. Had 5½ sacks of good potatoes and I had sold 4½ sacks to J. Aldworth at 6s. 6d. per sack and he fetched them off the ground and 3 sackfuls of onions up. Took Harpers up next day and gathered basket of damsons afterwards. Meeting here last night about a barrell of Beer for Feast 46 shillings down and 86 names down. They are going to have 11 of Half and Half and 11 of Ale, with Cricket Match races etc. Sent account to Chronicle office today about it. Went to Great Milton through Stadhampton to Uncle Henrys to meet Lizzy. Got there just as they were coming out of church. Went inside and looked at the church – a very fine church and old tomb inside.[9] Harpers went to the Bull and had some Beer and I went to Henrys to tea. Got home 7.30 rather tired. Went to the railway the Sunday before and into the tunnel to Littleworth, the brickfields and to Wheatley Bridge and home through Cuddesdon. Sent Bedford cord the next day to Chalgrove to be made up. Had the two pair of trousers back last Monday but no waistcoat. Dug potatoes up in garden last week. Had money for potatoes.

Sept. 19th   Feast Monday. It was fine all the morning but a thunderstorm about noon and after. It was a very good Feast this year there was racing, steeplechase for a pig and a barrell of beer on the ground and another at night.[10] They were all pretty well and quiet. At the Feast we had a fight on Monday night but it did not last long and on Wednesday we had the finishing up of the barrell and dancing again on the hill. There was 2 stalls, dancing indoors, a photographic gallery and cuff boxing and on Saturday night there was a stall on the hill again which was the first time in the memory of any man. There was a little quarrelling among the dancers on Saturday night but it all went off alright. There was not much cricketing on Monday. The prizes consisting of hats, smocks, braces were presented to the winners in the Slaughter house at night which was closed at [two?] o'clock.

Garsington Feast on the village green

Sept. 23rd It has been gloomy all the week and now it rains quite fast and looks like it. Autumn appears to be coming very fast now. The trees etc. are getting yellow and the walnut trees leaves are falling fast and the early fruit trees are nearly bare.

Sept. 26th Cuddesdon and Baldon played the conquering Match at Cricket. Cuddesdon beat in one innings. Next day young Taylor and I planted Cabbage plants – 25 rows – a beautiful day.

Sept. 30th It has rained tonight all night. Gathered Lemon Pippins and Ripstons and Blenheims – trees behind cart hovel today.

Oct. 1st Got ground ready for plants and limed it as the grubs are very troublesome this year. Took Ginger Beer bottles down the Garden House today. Terrible fires in Oxford a week ago last Sunday morning burnt Grimbly Hughes premises down and two men killed.[11]

Oct. 3rd It has been gloomy and dull for the last 2 or 3 days but not much rain and the glass is rising. Gathered the best Blenheim tree today – it took me all day and a very fine lot there was, they was quite ripe. Planted Cabbage plants in garden yesterday. Swallows are getting very thin now and everything is looking like Autumn. The woods are looking quite brown and yellow – a good many blackberries this year. Cricketing down the Common over – last Sunday there was none for the first time. Sold last K.B. on Wednesday last. Sent Garsington Feast account to the paper last Tuesday – it is in. Had a Rabbit cooked for our skittles tonight. Rogers won it with 8. Walnuts want backing, they fall very much. First Saturday night I have had nothing from Market. Potatoes keep very bad this year after they are up. Joseph Clarke married last Saturday, Abingdon. W. Harper caught a polecat in a trap last Saturday morning. We had it at night fighting a dog. Joe Boswells killed it at last. Had letter from London last Sunday morning. It was lost I suppose. Turned the settle round today but had a fire in washhouse although it was very mild today and is so tonight – a good lot there now. Missionary meeting last Tuesday night at School. Mary Holloway is better yesterday. New policeman came on Feast Monday and lodges at Robert Druces.[12] A most remarkable shock of an earthquake was felt in different parts of this county on the morning of Tuesday last about 8 o'clock lasting about half a minute.[13] It was not felt in this Parish at all as far as I can hear but Cooper felt it at Oxford. It was not very violent, merely a trembling motion from W. to N.

The ruins of the fire at Grimbly Hughes and Dewe, Cornmarket Street, Oxford, September 1863

Oct. 14th It has rained all the morning and all day yesterday. It was a fine day on Monday last and showery on Sunday. Set my lettuce plants on Monday and went down today to see if the grubs had hurt them. Only found 3 among the Cabbage plants and I pulled two rows of peasticks up and gathered the strings off them and all the others. I finished getting my seed peas on Monday last. On Tuesday (yesterday) we had a windup supper for the Cricketers – we expected 24 and had 32 for dinner. We had a spare rib and another small bit of pig meat baked and a leg of mutton boiled, about 5 quarters of potatoes and some turnips. Everything was eat up and the bones scraped. We had a very pleasant and merry evening and finished up about 2 o'clock next morning. Cleaned the parlour up today . . . The grubs have not hurt the plantation Garden at all. Cooper has not scarce any of his potatoes up. Heard that Jane Clinkard and the keeper at the Break felt the earthquake. The beagles are expected to go out tomorrow. The meat for the supper came to 14s. 10d. Been some skittling these last few nights and today I played Tom Harper and beat him 5 to 1. Some walnut trees are bare of leaves and the leaves are falling very fast. J. Aldworth has done with R. Quarterman today and he has been drinking about all day. Went with A.H. to Baldon on Sunday last, got home about 5 o'clock, never met anybody. Put faggots in the dry today. Have had a good deal of thunder and lightning since the earthquake and it lightens strong tonight but no thunder. Did not send anything to market today. Harpers cleaned the cesspool out today. Turnips just getting out into rough leaf down the Common.

Oct. 15th It has been fine all day but rather cold and gloomy and drying. It was an extremely fine warm day yesterday. The sun shone all the day long and I painted the wheelbarrow on that day. John Druce finished digging his potatoes up on that day. Had the first meet with the beagles on Thursday last but it was bad sport, the hounds could not run at all but plenty of hares. A warm muggy dull day. Began wearing my new shoes on Tuesday last, the 13th Oct. The mangolds grow very fast down the Common. Have been down there tonight and had a look at my plants. It was dried a little on the top and I could not see any of them gone with the grubs. I pulled up some peasticks last week and if it is moonlight next I will pull them all up. Saw the first bird game shot this year on Friday last when A.C[linkard] shot two pheasants down in the Smiths Mead. Wrote to Ted tonight. It was so dark tonight when I got down the Common that I could hardly see the plants and most likely will be the last time this year.

Oct. 23rd I missed the swallows and martins on Tuesday last 20th. It has been a glorious day today bright warm and still – haven't been such a day for some time. We had a glorious days hunting on Wednesday last with the Old Berkshire hounds. They met at the Break and ran about sometime and then they brought a fox down to the Copse and ran about the grounds up in the village and back to the Break where they killed him – found another down in the brier Bed and ran him round Sandford back to Break and to Breach Copse and round to Baldon where he ran to ground and we came home. I saw the fox several times at the Copse and the other one come to the Break. Had a run with the Harriers on Monday last and on Tuesday the S[outh] O[xfordshire] hounds were at Shotover and killed a fox in Watson's Copse and another at Brasenose Wood. 2 badgers have been down the Common the last 3 nights – it has been moonlight. Pulling up peasticks and it is as light as day now. I am going tonight. Cooper busy taking his potatoes. Finished pulling sticks up on Upper Piece last night – has been nice weather all the week. Cut some Cauliflower in garden today for Market and finished pulling up peasticks in garden tonight and finished planting Cabbage plants today and watered them and hoed plants yesterday. Transplanted Lettuce yesterday.

25th Went to the Railway Bridge with A.H. and Lizzie – a glorious night – bright, still, moon nearly full – got home little past 9 o'clock. Harpers came up and we were not at home. Went to Church and weared Black Coat.

26th A.H. came up after the game. I shot it off down at the bottom of the garden. It did echo wonderfully. Very foggy morning now and cold for the last week or 10 days and no rain. Was hoeing today. Paid Winspurr today 12/- and he measured me for a new coat.

27th Very cold and foggy this morning.

29th It has been very cold and wet, drizzly and very high wind. Done the Lily bed up today and planted the Monthly Rose against the Garden House. Yesterday it threatened wet all the morning and turned out a very fine afternoon. Went down the Common and hoed the Cabbage plants and trimmed the paths. The Mangolds are growing very fast now. Most of the Mangolds are took up now and some of the Carrots about but the weather continues open and mild. Sent nothing to Market on Wednesday.

Nov. 7th   It has been raining a small drizzly rain nearly all day. It was fine yesterday and Wednesday and that is all the fine weather this week. The Harriers ran a hare from Watsons Field down to Gales field last Tuesday and lost her. The weather is very mild and the early part of the week it was very windy and blew a terrific gale damaging the shipping considerably etc.[14] Went down the Common and pulled up the Mangolds on Monday last and pulled the Carrots up on Wednesday and topped the Mangolds on Friday and some of the Carrots. We have had no frost up till now and the weather is very wet and mild and the leaves hang on the Elm and other trees wonderfully; some of the trees are quite (the Elm) thick and green and some of the Ash so too. I had a sack of Meal from Holly's and paid for it and cleaned the pigstyes out today. Stored the potatoes in the Cellar on Friday. The Cabbage plants are growing fast now. Had a short walk with A.H. last Sunday. Had London Journals on Monday.[15] Fetched all the onions down on Friday. Saw some Cauliflowers, good ones fit to eat, on Druces lot down the Common yesterday.

12th   It has been a sharp white frost every morning this week and it was quite bad this morning – not gone away by noon in the least. Been getting the Parsnips up down the Common all the week and today I and R.Q. have got them all together and covered them up with haulm and leaves. It appears like a frost tonight. Had a walk with A.H. on Monday. It was cold and frosty. Did not send anything to market this week; the leaves are falling rapidly now. I saw 2 herons on Tuesday last and quantity of Felps etc. The grubs do not hurt the plants since [I] hoed them. The turnips in – parsnips are good for nothing. I dug some up and the turnips on potatoes land will come to nought . . . A good deal of blasting going on at the Railway bridge, L[ower] R[oad] and Littlemore. Goes off like a cannon and can hear the rattle of trucks at Horspath and roar of the Engine at Wheatley. They are getting on well with it now. Gathered grapes on Tuesday they were ripish and sour.

16th   Proper cuddle on Monday night.

19th   It has been very warm and still for a week now and yesterday it was a beautiful day and today it has been a glorious day – warm and mild and still but no sun. Shooting at the Break today and we had a famous touch in the Copse last Friday. We killed 29 rabbits and 1 pheasant. I had 3 rabbits. Finished getting my Mangolds, Carrots and Parsnips together on Saturday last and banked them up and today I had Surmans cart and fetched the rough Parsnips and Carrots up and other Peasticks. All the Currant trees Peas haulm etc. home. I planted 6 Lettuce plants and 2 Cabbage plants on Wednesday. Yesterday poor old John Phipps was shot accidentally in Gales field through two boys playing with a gun. He was shot in the shoulder about 7 or 8 yards off. He is not thought so bad as was expected and most of the shots are extracted. Went to Coombe Wood sale on Tuesday last. There was a good many there and it went very dear. Harper and I bought one apiece for 27 and 31 shillings – most of the Garsington men bought. Saw the new road they have made down Ladder Hill. E.A[ldworth] was here on Tuesday. Paid 4/- Deposit on Tuesday for Wood sale. Holloways sheep eat their Wheat off on the Little Common today. Had walk with A.H. on Sunday last. Plants and everything growing up very fast. Mended door lock today. Had Dray in on Tuesday.

Dec. 5th The weather has been very mild and warm, about ten days ago it was frosty mornings and on Thursday last it was a tremendous rough, windy day and very cold indeed. I believe it has done much damage. It threatens rain now and we have not had about 10 frosty mornings this winter up to now and it is very mild now. The plants all grow fast. Put 2 Lettuce and 2 Cabbage plants in down Common yesterday and wheeled ash heap away down below the pump where I have cleaned the weeds off this week and today I have mended the pigstye gate and done the stye up and put my pig in: killed ours on Monday last 16 score.

10th Went to Oxford on Saturday last and bought woollen stuff for 2 shirts. Had a letter from T[ed] W[atson] today. Harper killed his pig on Tuesday last and weighed 13 score 9lb. Went to Nuneham on Nov. 24th and bought a plot of wood for Harrison at 1/1 per pole. It was wet in the morning. Got home about 5 o'clock. Went to Coombe wood on Sunday last and exchanged plots with Eli Harper I paying him the difference. Man killed on the railway on Tuesday last making the bridge on Lower Rd. (Railway) now. Hoed Cabbage plants in Garden today – went birding last night.

18th This morning we had the first frost of the season, in fact, this year. I saw ice half an inch thick. It was dry and the wind was rough yesterday and our pack was out. It was very cold rough – plenty of hunting but did not kill. It has been very warm and before all the year before yesterday. Took the fence down last Wednesday and finished digging it all up ready for planting today. It is cold and a splendid moonlight night. Lizzie began making my woollens today. Had the foxhounds at copse a week ago last Monday. Had a good run from Lower road to Denton and killed at Chiselhampton. Had hair cut on Wednesday. Had sack of meal home from J[ames] A[ldworth] today. Shot 2 small birds. Tidy good deal of blasting at the Iffley cutting and can hear the roar of the trucks and engine very plain today. Had a walk with A.H. Sunday Baldon.

Dec. 29th A beautiful day today, very mild but rather rough and it has been very mild since I wrote last. Went wood (Coombe) on Monday 21st and 3 following days. I was very tired and poorly. For the first day or two could not eat anything but was all right at last day or two. It froze wonderful sharp for a little while on the 22nd but mild the next morning. Harper went round with Bills on Wednesday and we finished the wood on Thursday and had a supper on Christmas Eve − 32 to dinner. Had a very pleasant supper and party. Planted the piece below the carthovel with fruit trees on the 19th and finished them today. A very mild day on Christmas. The sun shone very bright and warm all the morning and the bells rang so pleasantly. A glorious morning. A.H. came up to tea after church. Stayed till 10 o'clock and went home with her − moonlight glorious. Mended tools next morning and had a run with the Harriers in the afternoon. Had a famous run and killed on the Downs − no dancing − Boswell gone to Baldon. A.H. came up in the evening − brought mistletoe up. I had a bit and kissed under at night when I went home with her − Miss Belcher with her. Did not go to church on Christmas. Harper went to Oxford station with horse. Quiet that night. Went to church next morning − rather gloomy morning. Met A.H. at the trysting style at 6 and had a walk to Baldon and back to style. Did not meet anyone nor never have of any consequence. Got home about 9 o'clock vexed with myself for keeping her out so long. When we was walking down Baldon lane all at once a bright light shone around us and turning quickly round, startled, I saw a falling star coming apparently straight for us in an oblique direction with a bright train of fire behind emitting sparks, and fell about 20 yards on the other side of the hedge. Could not see it strike the ground for the hedge. The appearance was precisely like a Roman candle.

Monday Yesterday did not do much and in the afternoon a band came here from Hazeley etc. and played round the village and came here at night. Had a fire in the parlour and dancing afterwards. But not much.

Garsington bell-ringers with Harry Turrill (to the left of the back row)

Done a very good trade. The Ringers came round at night.[16] They went round to Stadhampton, Drayton, Dorchester and Baldons on Saturday and did not get here till 11 o'clock at night. The first time they ever missed coming round on Saturday after Christmas Day. A.H. and Belcher went to Littlemore, Cowley etc. in the afternoon and came up here about 9 o'clock and stopped outside till nearly 10. I ran down home with A.H. and Jack with Miss B[elcher]. Thinks we were noticed last night. Splendid walking now – dry. Went to Baldon Church the Sunday before. It was very moonlight last Sunday. Mother has never said a word yet about it. New arrangement with Morrells [tenants?] last Wednesday. Went down the Common last Saturday. It all appears all right. Weared my red woollen shirt and Bedford waistcoat collar on Christmas Day. Felt rather queer the first day but likes them well now. J. Aldworth had a party on Saturday night and R. Clinkard last night. Quite a strong job with Lizzy Aldworth and G. Holloway now. No fighting at all this Christmas. We have had no rain only . . . or so for a long time now. It just missled every morning at woods. New Years Day next Friday.

1864

Railway construction continues night and day – workers killed – 'panic' over smallpox epidemic – sees first mowing machine in Garsington – anxiety about mother's illness – visits local flower shows – long summer drought – railway opens.

Jan. 10th 1864 Sunday. It rains a little now and looks like it. Lizzy is gone down to A.H. for a parcel that is come there. It began freezing on New Years Day and it has froze ever since till yesterday morning when it began to thaw and it has been thawing ever since. It froze very sharp all the week and the ice was very thick. Inquest at S. Phipps on New Years Day . . . Paid my rent 8/- that day. Went to Nuneham wood on Tuesday. Stayed at home on Thursday, J. Aldworth promised to fetch my wood home but did not. Got it home on Saturday by T. Smith's team. One load got home about 1 o'clock. Went down and got his wood in and then stacked my own. Last week was the only frost we have had this year and it was very severe. Got my other woollen on today. Had Gin and water touch on Saturday week at Harpers. Had a walk with A.H. on Sunday last – it was bitterly cold. Disappointed on Wednesday last timber sale at Baldon. Birth of a son of the Prince of Wales on Friday night.[1] The Cabbage plants in garden look quite fresh today but the other things look very faded. Deal of skating in London etc. 7 o'clock. Just been home with A.H. It rained nearly all the way and very dark. Did not stop – got back in an hour. It looks very much like rain. Harpers just going to bed. Going to Wood tomorrow. Finished planting the piece below the Cart Hovel with fruit trees the day before the frost began. Another man killed on the railway, young Clarke of Wheatley on Friday night slipped and loaded truck ran over him.

Jan. 16th Went to Nuneham Monday and finished Harrison's wood up about 12 o'clock, then went and looked at the cottage.[2] The ice was thawing on the river and it all looked desolate and dreary. Then we started off to Abingdon, had dinner at the Waggon and Horses at Culham, got to Abingdon half past three o'clock. It is a nice little town but very narrow pavement. It was market day. Tried to buy some rabbits but could not. Went to the market and pig market and principal streets, had nothing to drink there and then started back. We had some beer in a bottle which we drank as we came home. It was getting dark when we went through Culham Lodge gate. Saw an immense number of Rooks on some trees just before roost time. Got home about half past seven o'clock, met A.H. in Baldon Lane. Joseph Turrill married to Miss Harvey on Thursday last by licence at our church. There were a couple looked very nice. Went and saw them married, an immense lot of people there. The Ringers rang a merry peal on their return and at night they illuminated the tower with candles. It was a foggy wretched day as it has been all the week. The tower looked very nice at night and the ringing and firing was first rate. Went to Mrs Druces and bought some dung and then hunting in the afternoon but it was so foggy we could see but very little of it. They killed one and had a first rate day. Heard them again today, ran one from Dorchester to Chiselhampton but did not see them. J.T.'s wedding was kept at her house. It rained on Wednesday night. Began doing the flower beds up yesterday. Went through A.H.'s yard on Thursday but did not see her. Heard that we have been seen together for the first time by the people last night. The fog has cleared off today and the wind is colder. Sent first parsnips to Market yesterday.

Jan. 18th Froze very sharp for an hour or two on Saturday night and then rained. The next morning it cleared off and has been foggy ever since and mild. Began making another part of Cricket Ground today. Did not go. Met A.H. down again her house, just walked about L[ower] G[round]. Got home 8.30. Shaved the lower part of my whiskers off yesterday.

Jan. 20th It has been a damp dirty day. I went down the Cricket Ground today and helped a bit. Mother went to Oxford. Went under the Railway Arch to Oxford . . . on Monday.

Jan. 30th It has been a good deal of foggy weather lately but it was a beautiful day yesterday, bright and sunny. Took my dung down the Common and brought Carrots and Parsnips up. Met A.H. last night. It froze very sharp last night and all day in the shade and is freezing very sharp now. Been down the Common and finished digging the rough piece at bottom of Lower piece. The Lettuce looks shocking bad, looks to be all dead now. Terrible rows up at Druce's now. Just six years ago today

The lock-keepers' cottage, Nuneham

that I had accident with gun. I shot a bullfinch and sparrow today. Met A.H. last Wednesday night at 9, stopped till nearly 10, very dark. Had a shooting touch at copse on Monday last, we killed 40 rabbits, 3 guns. A[lf] C[linkard], W. A[ldworth] and J. A[ldworth] kept on till dark. I had 2 and we are going to have a hen and them tomorrow. Killed my pig on Tuesday at Half past 3 o'clock, J. A[ldworth] did. I sold by Howard to Mrs Birt. He weighed 13 score, 8lb at 9/- per score and Howard took him down. The next day had the money £6. 0s. 6d. The Harriers were round here last Saturday, killed one. Finished flower beds on Thursday. Mrs H[arper] Sen. spoke about it for the first time last Sunday. Gooseberry buds just beginning to swell now. Rumours of war now.[3] Had ramble to Baldon last Sunday night, it was gloriously bright and moonlight. J. Hilsden fell ill with the Small Pox on Sunday last, he is lodging up at Will Yeats's and is very ill.[4] Cogan has made arrangements to Vaccinate anybody that wants to now, have not heard of its spreading.

Feb. 3rd   They are working night and day at the cutting and tunnel, they have large coal fires to work by. Mrs Elias Woodward and Lizzy Turrill of Great Milton both very ill. Met A.H. last Sunday below with

Men working on Wheatley tunnel (built 1864) in the 1880s

Tom Smith and Mark H[olloway]. Just walked round the road home, parted at 8 o'clock, seemed rather cool. The frost all went away on Monday morning and it has threatened wet ever since. Have not heard of the Small Pox spreading yet. Began digging my ground Upper Piece on Monday, it digs tidy. Tom Phipps planted some Large Peas today.

Feb. 7th   Sunday, the first Sunday that we have not met when the weather has been fine. A.H. told Lizzy that she should not come out tonight, rather queer, still it is a beautiful bright starlight night. It freezes very sharp now and looks like it. Finished digging the Upper Piece last Friday and began Lower on Saturday, it digs well. The first news of the war having begun reached me on Friday last but I do not think England will have anything to do with it. We can see the glow from the fires at the Railway at Horsepath on dark nights. Cut my toenails today, did not go to Church today, got a breaking out on my throat. It has been very cold and frosty since Monday.

Feb. 19th   It is a very sharp frost now and has been for some time, it snows and freezes now and it's a bitter North Wind. The Small Pox appears to be spreading. W. Yeats and his wife are both dangerously ill now and Nancy Robins Wife is took with [it]. Great excitement about it. There was a meeting about it last Tuesday night at our house which lasted till half past 11 o'clock. J.G. Wilgress and all the farmers were there. They are trying to get the Counting House over the Way and James Aldworth was empowered to do and give what orders he liked. They are having a great deal of Brandy and Beer here. Lady Slack is messenger, she stands outside and calls her orders out. Had a nurse from Wheatley yesterday morning and yesterday Cogan Vaccinated a number of Children and James Aldworth, T.H. was done. Cogan came up to Druce's and told Mrs Druce and Lizzy to be at the school at half past one next Thursday he would do them. I and a party went to Stadhampton to see the Doctor about Vaccination, he had got no matter, was to go in a weeks time. Went to Aunt Wixon's and stopped till 11.30. I have been teetotal for 3 weeks come next Tuesday, did not drink anything but water there. Left them on Osborne's Hill and came home by myself. Had a good deal of chaffing about A.H. all night – met her below last Sunday and walked round the road home, did not stop long, got home 9 o'clock. It is beautifully moonlight now. Went to Church last Wednesday [i.e. Ash Wednesday] with E[llen] S[tone], very good sermon. A.H. not there, good congregation. I have had a breaking out all round my neck but it's

The old Rectory, where the curate Revd Wilgress lived

getting better. The greens I planted down the Common look very bad, carrots not gone yet. The Farmers meeting adjourned till next Tuesday and Levi Godfrey's wife and children removed into the next house yesterday. Have not heard of anyone else being took with it but those four. The gooseberry trees are just swelling out now and the bullfinches are very busy at them now. I shot 2 cocks this week . . . Finished pruning all up to now on Monday last – Apricots and all. Sent a Valentine to A.H. and E[llen] S[tone] on Monday and Tuesday last, had one sent me. Cleaning bit below the Pump now.

Feb. 22nd It is a very sharp frost now and every likelihood of its continuing. It is gone in the Ground a goodish way now and it does not get out all day. It has snowed a little the last 2 or 3 days and the wind is a bitter north-easter. All the Lettuce are dead and the Cabbage plants cut a poor figure, the birds work the fruit trees a good deal. The weather is very cold and sharp for Feb. The Excitement about the Small Pox is got into a perfect Panic now and everybody is frightened to death about it.

Poor Will Yeats and his wife are both dead. The latter died on Saturday night about 6 and the former on Monday morning about 6 o'clock. The latter has been very ill all along but the former was considered to be recovering but on Sunday about half past 2 he was taken worse and he died next morning.

Feb. 24th   I was in the parlour last night writing the above when Mr Buswell came in and told me that Levi Godfrey had got the Small Pox and that J. Hilsden would be sure to die. Nancy there is not much the matter of at present and Eliza Clarke was ailing. There was not many at the meeting and there was not anything settled, it was adjourned till next Tuesday. Watson came and kept them there till 12 o'clock. There is some dissatisfaction about Cogan's having the windows open as in Levi's case it is all closed up and he states that he will have it very light. The expense is enormous something like £8 per week. There was a terrible bother about burying them and J. Aldworth went to Wheatley to Cullams and stopped whilst he made a coffin and brought it home at 1 o'clock and it was agreed to bury her at 6 o'clock next morning. Snowy and Wigs was sent off on Saturday night to dig the grave and when, the next morning, Willgress went to look at the grave it was only about 2 feet deep and the nurses could not get the coffin down the stairs and Snowy and Wigs carried her to Church. Wigs went upstairs and helped get the body down. I recollect seeing them when I stood again our door on Sunday morning about 10 o'clock with the Bier and coffin up again Godfrey's, they was resting, there was a white cloth just thrown over the coffin. It was snowing at the time. Lady Slack was at the door for beer and said that Bill Yeates was better. He was buried at 9 o'clock on Monday night. John Yeates (his father) took him down in his pony and cart and Wigs and Jim Goody helped with Taylor, Strong and Policeman as Guards on the road. I was up at Mother Jobs that night, met S.T. there. Taylor was just going up to see when the body was coming to let the parson know. The bells did *not* toll.[5] Jim Goody came in here the next morning but we ordered him out and people will not have Snowy about their premises. Mr Gale sent two suits of clothing up for the two men who carried him to the Grave. There was no service read at the Grave. Lady Slack has just been here (8 o'clock) for beer and says she is going to bury the sheets, clothes etc. in Holloways field tonight. Vaccination day tomorrow. Made some Brimstone and Treacle last night and took teaspoonfull this morning, my face is got well now. I have been to Church tonight, a goodish many there. First Nelly Stone with John Harper tonight. The whole management of the Small Pox Relief is left to James Aldworth and they nurses. Dr Cogan say that thousands is awfully bad. Mr Wilgress asked in church last Sunday. Mother been to Oxford today and I began cleaning the long grass out of the Gooseberry trees today. Finished thinning the apple trees out on Monday. The weather still continues extremely sharp and frosty. The Carrots went away yesterday. Wrote to Ted Watson on Sunday night – sent off on Tuesday. Lizzy and A.H. and I agreed to go to Cuddesdon Church that evening but she did not get here soon enough so we went the railway Arch and back home, got home 8.20. Bought 2½ peck of Midsummer's potatoes of old Richard Quartermain last Tuesday week. Jim Goody Sen. had order for the Workhouse last Monday. The gooseberry buds are swelling out. Old Druce had notice to quit his house on Tuesday. Jim Aldworth had his new cart about a fortnight ago. Nothing to be heard about now but the Small Pox. Great excitement and alarm about it. Five men hung at Newgate Monday and two reprieved.[6]

Feb. 29th The excitement about the Small Pox is subsiding now as all the patients are getting better now and Jim Hilsden and Levi Godfrey got up yesterday and no more cases has fell with it yet that I have heard of. Lady Slack was told to come here today for relief as J. A[ldworth] would have nothing to do with it. Some dissatisfaction felt about Cogan's having the window open and Levis shut. J. Godfrey and George Sturges went to Stadhampton last Friday to see the Doctor about the Medical Club. He proposes to take persons at 4/- per annum. 33 names down now and he is coming over on Thursday. The frost broke last Wednesday and on Thursday last we had a day with the harriers round here. J. Gales ran to Dorchester and to Milton Hills. Went round Harper's fields, some of it was in good order and some of it in bad. The wheat looked very well and the bean land fairish, we trampled it about very much. They killed a hare up again the Model Farm and ran another round the Smiths Hill. Went down round Buswell's grounds on Friday last and got some Briars and then at night to Willis's to take a hamper for some seed potatoes, one bushel. Met A.H. last Sunday on the Lower Road about 7 o'clock, she had got a new hat on and looked well. We came home with Lizzie and then down home, parted at half past 8 very well. Shaved myself and had my hair cut, Finger nails, toothcombed my head and had a good fire in the Bar, stripped and washed myself all over before dinner yesterday, shaved clean off. Did not go to Church yesterday. I am tee-totaller still. Foxhounds came to Baldon today, killed two foxes, tried Break and Copse, didn't find. Began digging garden for potatoes and planted

Cabbage plants out today. The weather has been raw cold lately but yesterday the wind shifted to South and it has been very foggy and now it rains. Mother and I settled up last Saturday night.

March 3rd   It is raining quite heavy now and it began to rain about 11 o'clock today. It has been a wet raw week. The Small Pox appears to be dying out now as I have not heard of anyone else falling with it and they all are getting better. There was a meeting last Tuesday night about it, they settled various things. I left about 11.30, not many there. I began planting Potatoes in Garden on Tuesday last and finished Willis's bushel today. Planted row of True Ward's nearest the flower beds on Wednesday. Bad seed Potatoes. Went to Old Townsend's and fetched Half bushel of Midsummer Seed Potatoes 2/6 today. Took Willis's Peas a Quart down tonight and he wants another pint all True Wards. Took a quart to Harper's for John Yeates. Hugall's day at Horseshoes today. Harper digging his Garden up today. Measured Peas up – the Mice has been working the Peas down Common. Went down today, the Lettuce all gone and the Cabbage are looking tidy. Very wet, the Gardening will be all behind this year. Wind North East.

Sunday, March 6th   It has rained all night very heavily and there is a flood out - the first for some years. It has rained on and off all the day and it is raining now, 7 o'clock. Did not go to the meet tonight as it rained and looked like it. A fire last night top of Ladder Hill and Joe Townsend had a fit and fell into the fire today. Mr Spearing has took the house over the way on Wednesday and is having it done up. The Small Pox is spreading now again. Heard on Friday afternoon that Vincent Godfrey and Joe Evans had both fell with it. Nancy and Eliza Clarke both discharged. 8 men killed altogether on the Railway. Terrible Murder at Buckingham last Saturday night and the murderer cut a young woman's throat and then his own – he is alive.[7] The mice work my peas very much down Common – put some poison down last night.

Monday, March 14th   8 o'clock. It rained on and off all the beginning of last week and a heavy flood is out. On Wednesday last it began snowing at 6 o'clock in the morning and it snowed incessantly till 6 o'clock at night. It partially thawed during the day but as it was a very sharp frost the ice was half an inch thick. The day before I fetched slabs from Malthouse the price was 2/- and on Wednesday I began making them into stools.[8] I have shaped 2. On Thursday a Steeplechase took place at Denton with College Guests, Lord Parker was Steward.[9] There was 4 steeplechases, a flat race and a hurdle race. There was a good wide brook to jump, 14 feet wide and thorn at the brook. It was capital sport but terrible cold, got home about 7 o'clock. The weather was drier since Friday and it is very drying today and Saturday planted onion seed, Lettuce seed, and Gooseberry and Currant cuttings. Put soot on Peas on Saturday. The roads etc. are beautifully dry today and I put 4 rows of Garden peas in on Upper Piece, 3 above the Plants and one at bottom. Harper put his Onion Seed in tonight and Tom Phipps and Jimmy Goody have been planting potatoes today. Harper finished planting potatoes. At home Saturday night. Planted remainder of Lettuce plants out today that was left. Another boy killed on Railway last week. The Small Pox appears to be over now as there is no fresh cases and the patients are getting better. Ben Hilsdens children have the Scarlatina but they are getting better now. Went to the last named meet last night and waited a good while. A.H. did not come, got home at 8 o'clock. Met her last Monday, Club night, short. Did not go to Club, went to Job Smith's, met S[ally] T[urrill] there. A.H. had been there. Confirmation next Sunday. Cricket Club and Parish meeting held here last Tuesday, the last Parish meeting. Made a roaring fire, closed at 12, total extra expense 8 odd. Baker paid our Bill. Shall begin planting seeds tomorrow. (Prince of Wales son christened on March 10th) Teetotal still, clean shaved yesterday. Wind very rough now. The Moon is shining now. Buckingham murderer alive.

March 22nd It threatens rain now and in fact it is raining slightly from the North with a cold wind. It was a beautiful week all last bright and drying with Moonlight nights. I was down the Common all the week and every night. I have finished planting everything but the Flukes and K. Beans and I want the Mangolds brought up and then I could finish planting the Lower Piece. The Quick Hedges are just sprouting now. Went up to T. Aldworths and bought a sack of Flukes today. The weather is sunny in the daytime and very cold frosty nights. Spreaded the dung at bottom of Lower Piece tonight. Saw J. Hilsden and Levi Godfrey down the Common today. J.H. looked fat and red in the face and pitted much, t'other looked very well. They all appear to be got quite well now and their relief is stopped. Terrible Calamity at Sheffield on Friday night week.[10] A reservoir of 95 acres of water burst in the middle of the night and destroyed everything in its path, about 250 lives and £500,000 lost. Subscriptions are being collected for them. There's also a subscription all over the Parish for the purpose of Presenting a Testimonial to

Mr Wilgress on his approaching marriage with Miss King of Cuddesdon.
Did not give anything. Heard of this Notice affair up at Druces today.
Last Sunday was a beautiful day. There was Confirmation here about 20
in the afternoon. The Church was densely crowded in every part, a great
number of strangers there. The Candidates looked very nice in their white
dresses and caps. Nelly Stone eclipsed them all. Had my first walk out on
Sunday after tea on Sunday March 13th. Went down Common up to
Harpers and home. Last Sunday went to the Common and saw A.H. with
Mary coming along the Lower Road. I caught them at Church Close
Stile and went back to Baldon Stile. Mary left and we went up to Baldon
and back through Gale's fields then home. It was a glorious bright, warm,
moonlight night. Enjoyed the walk much, had not seen her some time,
got home about 9 o'clock. Began Cricket down Aldworths Common on
Sunday March 13th. Began letting my beard grow on Sunday March
13th. It appears to be a late, cold Spring. Payday at Coombe Wood next
Tuesday.

March 25th   Good Friday. It has been Glorious weather since I wrote
last. The next [day] it was very bright and clear. It is a sharp frost every
morning now, the Apricot bloom does not appear hurt. I finished planting
my Flukes on Wednesday last and had Mangolds brought up that day. I
planted a bushel in 14 rows down the piece. Taylor's wife died last night
about 10 o'clock, the bell is tolling now. Just been to Church, there was a
good many there. A party at Cricket down the common this afternoon.
Lifted Mangolds in Garden. Lizzy Aldworth here last night. Hoed
Cabbage plants in Garden today. Some of Spearings goods came here
yesterday and a man and Woman here to live. Had the new bats come
home yesterday. Another man killed on Railway week ago tonight makes
10 or 11 altogether. Began Skittling on last Wednesday night, had 2 cocks
myself and then down common and to meet but did not come. Got home
about 9 o'clock.

April 1st   It has been stormy and cold with rough winds since I wrote
last and it is raining now, 2 o'clock. There was a steeplechase at Primrose
Hill on Wednesday but did not go, a cold cloudy day. J. Gales mare won
2 times. There was a burglary at Horspath on the 22nd March and the
Police have been searching about here this week but they have not found
anything out about it. Went to Wheatley payday at Crown Inn on
Tuesday, paid £1 7s. 10d. – did not stay long. Harper did not go and did
get home about 6 o'clock. Began drinking beer last night again. Joseph

Gale is churchwarden this year. Did not go to Primrose Hill, found of the dryness of my throat yesterday. Was up at Druces again now. W.H. nearly always there. Going to Oxford tomorrow. Met A.H. again at the Church last Sunday, had 2 or 3 short walks and then home. Met D[avid] S[tone] and J. A[ldworth], it was dry and cold, got home about 9 o'clock. The Stag Hounds, Her Majesty's, came across here from Stonor Park today.[11] They ran across Southend up to T. Aldworth's Farm, up Blenheim, down across Smith's Fields, along the road to Cowley and Rose Hill where he ran to cover.

April 10th   Sunday. It has [been] a remarkable dark gloomy day all day but very warm and muggy. Went to church this morning, strange parson there. Wilgress was married on Thursday last to Miss King at Cuddesdon Church. Lizzy went. Our Ringers rang a merry peal and illuminated the tower at night but they could not get the candles to burn. There was a Cheap John on the Hill last Monday night and a presentation of a silver salver by the parishioners and a Bread Plate and knife by the schoolchildren altogether of the value of £19 0s. 0d. A row up at the Plough last Tuesday and I think that he will have to Leave it and H. has been to see about it last Saturday. Will hear in a day or two I suppose. Elias Woodward's wife died on Thursday and was buried today. Robert Fortescue died on Friday night of inflammation. There was a summonsing job down at the County Hall with Druces.[12] They pulled the old man for damaging the flowers – case dismissed. Harper and I went there and bought a grate and Cloth for coat at 13/- per yard. Had a talk with Mrs Harper at Oxford, saw A.H. there several times. The weather is very warm now and the trees are just budding out now and Quick Hedges are just budding out now. I had a walk down the Common tonight with Harper and then home. A.H. did not come out tonight, I don't know the cause. I had a nice walk last Sunday along the Lower Road up home and then down home. We parted about 9 o'clock, not very well pleased though tonight. Began beer drinking last Friday. Harper up here tonight. Making stools – now finished one.

April 13th   It is beautiful weather now bright, warm and sunny. I have been stripped out all the week. Have been mending the railings L[ower] G[round]. Going to Wheatley directly about the Measures. The Cricket Club meeting here last night, paid for the Ground, agreed to buy the tent, kept it up till 1.10. The Apricot trees going out of bloom. Wrote J. Radford on Monday night, took to second best suit on Monday. The

Elm trees are just budding and the best time of year is just coming now. The violets in our garden smell delightful now, the Onions up in full drill. Harpers had a tremendous lot of violets on Saturday last.

April 16th　It began raining last night and has rained off and on all day and the plants etc. are growing very fast now. Dug the bit against the Privy yesterday and planted it with Flukes and a row of True Wards. All Gales men struck work yesterday.[13] Mrs Harper was brought down from London in a mourning coach yesterday and buried here. There was a terrible bother and fuss, a long procession. Had a touch of sparrow shooting yesterday and day before. Garibaldi[14] is in England and is made a great fuss with. Crystal Palace today and is expected in Oxford soon. The rhubarb is shooting up well now. A supper next Tuesday night at 7 for Cricketers. Have been carpentering today. Mend[ed] beer stand, bored stools etc. There appears to be no chance of x tomorrow night. The station at Wheatley nearly finished. First of Joseph Hatton and Emma Turrill.

April 19th　Tuesday evening. Tonight is Cricketing supper and I am sitting in the parlour just lighted the fire to write a little. The weather has been glorious since Saturday but cold night and morning. We have got a leg of mutton, a piece of Beef Salt weighing 16lb L.M. [leg of mutton?] weighs 13lb nearly, Potatoes, a good big pot full of Greens and some Turnips with 2 pieces of Cheese. We expect 20 to supper. Butcher went about the tent but G. Sheldon would not sell under 50/0. Left it. Met A.H. Lizzy went down and fetched her out and she and Mary and I went to Baldon and had a very pleasant walk round the Church and back down the road to Church Close Stile. There we left Mary and Lizzy and we went to the Gate leading out of Gales field to Spittal and stayed some time. It was gloriously bright moonlight and warm. She was in a good humour and we had a interesting conversation to ourselves. I told her a little of my mind but she is cautious especially about C.W. [Coombe Wood?] – would not promise to go to C.P. [Crystal Palace?] with me in May. Did not see anyone about. She promised to x at the Tryst Style tomorrow night 6.30. 1-1 at 10 minutes to 10, the latest out yet. h.k.[15] The Elm trees are just budding out and the Quick hedges are quite green and the Grass fields are looking so fresh and Green. Spearing and family came up here and stopped all day on Sunday and some of them are here now. He goes every morning and back at night. They were all at Church on Sunday, twice. First noticed that Mother was very unwell and her cough and breath was bad this last week – she complains of no appetite, weakness. Sent for some Keatings Cough Lozenges and tried Onion Porridge last night. Must take some of the work off her hands now or we shall lose her before we are aware of it, but I hope and trust that she will be spared to us longer yet. Wrote to Ted Watson on Sunday and sent it off last night. We have some skittling here a little now. First practice night C.C. [cricket club] I shall be paid. Harper is working at Baldon and two more of his men left yesterday morning so that he only got his cattle men now. Saw Cuckoo I thought down the Common Sunday night but was not sure.

April 22nd, Friday It has been glorious weather since I wrote last, bright, sunny days and cold nights. Everything now is looking beautiful and fresh and green. The trees are all coming out in leaf and the beautiful springtime is come at last. But how quick it seems to go, it is scarcely here and we seem just to be enjoying it and it is gone. The hot summer sun glares down for a few weeks and we are too busy to notice or enjoy the short summer months, when the autumn with its falling leaves and shortening days only too soon ushers in the cold, gloomy and cheerless winter which always seem *so* long but so it is with life. In our young or springtime of our life we are as happy as the day is long. No care or trouble about the future and all is spring with us then, in our prime, just when we suppose that we have got to the zenith of our wishes, there is trouble and anxiety, hard work etc. that causes that stage of our career to be dry, empty and soon over. Like summer we are too busy and there is too much to do to enjoy the summertime of our life and beyond that it is a sealed book to me. I was sitting today after dinner in front of the Garden House reading a paper in my dinner hour when I heard the cuckoo singing for the first time this year. He appeared to be over in Church Close and I heard several times in the day. Went down Common and finished sticking long row of peas.

April 25th It is about 10 minutes past 7, morning. Harper called me up for my hoe, it is a beautiful morning bright and still. It was gloomy yesterday morning and looked like rain but it cleared off and turned out a beautiful afternoon but rather cold. Went to church in the morning yesterday, down to Harper's and finished J. Radford's letter – must be sent off today. Had a walk with A.H. last night. Met at Lower Farm and went to by the Break and down the road towards Sandford and then back to Break Lane. Then we left Mary and Lizzie and she and I went along

The cricket team setting off for an away match

Break Lane and up to Baldon Road and down B.L. home. Met someone coming home, her would not stay out and went at half past 9. She said her mother wouldn't like her being so late as she had been lately. On Wednesday she met me at the T[rysting] S[tile] at 9 o'clock and stood behind the tree. It was moonlight till 10.30. She positively refuses to go to C.P. with me and so she did last night. It was a beautiful walk last night and the Lane bushes at Break was out in splendid bloom. We had three meetings running at our house last week. On Tuesday we had a cricketing supper when there was 20 to supper, covers laid for 28. We all sat comfortable and had a good supper. There was not much left and about 1 good dishfull of potatoes. The meat came to 19s. 8d. and we charged them £1 8s. 0d. which was 1s. 6d. per head. We then had a sixpenny whip and what they chose to give afterwards. 5 or 6 more joined them afterwards. They was very merry and kept it up till 2 o'clock in the morning and then they had a good deal of acting out in the road till nearly 3 o'clock. I caught J.H. in Clarkes garden stealing broccoli leaves at 2.30. There was a deal of cheering and singing and acting in parlour. They broke a table and could not spend all the money by 2/- which was spent the next night. On Wednesday night there was a meeting of Farmers for the purpose of presenting a purse and £4 11s. 0d. to Mr James Aldworth for his energetic and praiseworthy conduct during the late severe and alarming visitation of the Small pox when he, at considerable personal risk and inconvenience undertook the management; and in fact was a temporary relieving officer as he had to appoint nurses, grant immediate relief etc. and at all hours arrange the funerals and at a time too when most people was afraid to go anywhere near the infected portion of the village. And also for the straightforward and satisfactory manner in which he has discharged the duties of assistant overseer during the past twelve months. Mr J. Watson presented the purse and in a speech of some duration, passed a high eulogium on Mr Aldworth who he said had come forward at a very critical time and offered his services to the whole parish. And he, on behalf of the whole parish, begged to thank him for the satisfactory manner in which he had performed his duties, satisfactory alike to the poor patients and the ratepayer who, almost without being asked, subscribed a handsome sum of money which, together with a purse, he handed over to that gentleman. Mr Aldworth in short speech thanked them for the honour and assured them that [he] expressed his heartfelt thanks for such a handsome gift which he valued, not so much on account of its intrinsic value, as for the expression of confidence and esteem which accompanied it. There was some cheering and in fact it was the no[i]siest and merriest meeting of farmers here that ever I knew. I was very unwell – had such a headache. J. Aldworth paid for all they had to drink. Broke up at 1.30. The next night there was a meeting for farmers to raise the assessment of Mr Joseph Gale's farm. There were 7 farmers there, an adjourned meeting from the Church. They agreed to put the rateable value at 2/- per acre. Old Wells was there, kept it up till 11.30. A terrible touch with R. Druce and Watson Wednesday week.

May 2nd   It was a glorious week last week, fine and warm and sunny. I was busy all the week gardening and every night but one down the Common. We had the tent house on Tuesday night and A.H. came along the bottom to Townsend by mistake. I missed her and did not see her at all nor the next night when she came up here. E., A.H. and I went to Oxford on Wednesday to buy some clothes etc. I have stuck all my peas but one row down the Common. It was a beautiful day yesterday. I went to Church in morning and at night to Common and along the L[ower] R[oad] towards Chiselhampton and back up through Church Close. I nearly did not see her at all . . . Got home when the Cricketers did. A smartish party and kept it up till past 11. It began raining about 8 o'clock and rained all night very gently and today it is very gloomy and windy but mildish. Sent my cloth to Winspurr to be made up last Monday and expect it home today. Garibaldi has been visiting in England and has been made a terrible fuss with. More so than anybody who ever came to England, but he is going away again and people suppose that there has been some underhand work to induce him to leave these shores. He went away last Wednesday in the Duke of Sutherland's Yacht for Caprera. I enjoyed my walk very much last night, it was so beautiful and still and warm. I heard a landrail croaking away and some singing up at Baldon quite plain. The roads are very dusty and the crops, specially J. Gale's wheat, looked splendid. The trees are all green and the hedges and the Apple trees are looking splendid now, just ready to burst, and this shower makes everything look so fresh and green and the Nightingale and Cuckoo sing all day long and night too. Expected Ted Watson down here on Thursday last but he did not come. The Wars in Denmark and America still continue, a conference is sitting in London about Danish affairs.[16] Was disappointed last night because it was a fine night.

May 4th   It is raining fast now and has rained all day, we wanted rain. The Apple trees are looking glorious now, the buds are ready to burst.

Had new Alexandra Coat home on Monday last.[17] Began taking physic again today. Some skittling all day today. There has been an inquest today on poor Old Sarah Hilsden, wife of John Hilsden Senior, who fell down dead in her garden yesterday afternoon. Did not hear the verdict – the inquest was held down at the Cottages. The jury men just called in but did not stop.

May 12th It is a bright morning, 8 o'clock. Has been gloomy all this week with occasional showers. The Apple trees are blossoming wonderfully well this year and now they are out in all their glory. Mr Wilgress came home with his bride on Friday last. There was bell ringing, attempted illumination of the tower and then the ringers illuminated the front of Mr Wilgress's house but it soon began to rain and put it out. And last night there was a concert by the Cuddesdon Choir under the schoolmaster Mr Ashby who played the pianoforte and harmonium. It was delightful especially the solo singing of young Buswells. It began at 8 and finished at 10. All the principal inhabitants was there and 53 kept the door.[18] A.H. was there. I went home with her down the road as far as Giswell Spring and thro' the backway. She did not seem in a good humour, was disappointed about the . . . Made it up on Monday and Mary came up on Tuesday with Bills for patterns. I did not see her and it was C[ricket] Club night. There was not many there and altogether it was the dullest meeting we have had, broke up at 12. Sent 2 challenges off, one to Kidlington and 1 to Warborough last night. The weather is rather cold and gloomy now and we are looking forward to Whitsuntide now but it seems as if it will be a wet one. Made Ginger beer on Tuesday and bottled it last night. Weared new coat and straw hat last Sunday. Went to church and had a nice walk out with A.H. Went along the L[ower] R[oad] and up the lane to Downs and back part of way, along towards Shepherd's House and back home. We went to T[rysting] S[tile] it rained a little, we stood under the tree, good humour, stopped till nearly 10 o'clock. Agreed to meet again last night. Did come out on Sunday before but we missed one another. All gone to bed when I got home. No x next Sunday. Had touch clock mending on Monday last upstairs. Saw Wilgress' wife last night, rather small featured little woman.

May 20th It is glorious weather now, the sun shines all day and moon all night. It has been very sultry hot out. Today there is more air and pleasant. Just fetched the tent up out of the barn where it was took on Monday last and used on Tuesday. It has been fine all the week and very

Upper Farm (now Manor Farm), where the Holloways lived

hot and sticky. It thundered a bit and threatened to rain and in fact it did rain a little and at Toot Baldon it rained heavy. I went to Oxford on Saturday last to fetch some cups. Rode with [carrier?] there and back, very warm. Went up their Market to fetch a flat but did not see A.H. Whitsunday was a beautiful day but very warm and close. I went to church in morning and at night down the Common and along the road towards Chiselhampton with Mrs and Harper. Met A.H. at Baldon corner and she went with us to Gale's mead to see some flowers there. The May was just beginning to bloom. We gathered some and we came to Harpers and stopped there a little while and then went down the lane and across Church Close home with her. Got home 9.30 – not much doing and no strangers about. It was very close. Whit Monday was a glorious day. The band was very late coming and when they did come they came in a drag – 9 musicians. I went up to Club just behind them and had lunch. We started to church about half past 11 and got out before one. Mrs Harper was there and A.H. and Lizzie but not many strangers . . . The band played well – the bells rang a merry peal. We had to wait some time for dinner and I stood outside with A.H. and C. and Mary and several more till dinner. She would not stop to dinner as she had some work to do. She promised to come to tea but she got behind and did not see her till the band was gone, and then I saw her with the band again the Plough. Stopped outside Watsons and had a word with Harper about stopping at home. There was nothing to do at home and so I went out with the band. Went down to Harpers and had some tea and there got a blowing up from Mrs Harper about the same and last night too. I went round with the band and up to Holloways. When I went home I put the other coat on with straw brim. Saw Billy's colour, it was done up very well indeed and up to supper which was very late indeed. Had a talk outside and then she went down home to change her clothes. E. was very rackety, clucking about. We was very busy and I did not see her for some time when I took them something to drink. And there being no chance of her coming in, she stood outside till the dancing was over. And then we went inside and put the light out and sat very comfortable in the dark till nearly two o'clock, when I enjoyed myself more than I did all day. We had nearly cleared out and went and fetched some beer for Mother and then Lizzie and her slipped out and I off home with her. We went the back way . . . down to the gate leading into Spittle Green, where we stood and saw the moon set. And then to the Stile against her house where we stopped till the sun began to rise and the birds to sing. It was getting quite daylight when I started home. Got there – all gone to bed and house locked up. I knocked and Mother let me in and off to bed till 9. Next day made Ginger Beer, gathered apricots and down the Common till dusk and then washed, rigged and to work waiting and straining ginger beer. A.H. came up again and went to Harpers where she did not stop long. They never spoke and E. got a good blowing up about going on so the night before. She came and sat out in the Alley till the dancing was all over and then in Washouse and had supper and then home at 12 o'clock. We went very gently but did not stop long and got home at 1.30 and then had to take a flat full of cabbage to Harpers. Slipped the back way, did not see anyone and she got in all right without anyone knowing. Agreed to meet along the same road next Sunday. I had a little chaffing on Monday. Billy went home on Monday night. There was a good dansier and supper and I never sat so comfortable before. Tom Harper done the baking. Baldon Club yesterday, a great many people there, and from Garsington I heard the band playing beautifully up at Baldon and it thundered heavy behind me. The little girl was with her on Sunday. Cousin Turrill of Oxford. Very bad at Smith's. She was taken away at night and Jim Godfrey, who was fetched away on Monday to Her, has been with her ever since. The young Holloways Jim and Bill down here, they are looking well and say they are doing well. E. had letter from T[ed] W[atson] on Sunday. Have been making Ginger beer nearly all the week. Mother very middling still. The weather appears to be on the change now 3 o'clock. Not much cricketing this week, too hot. The candles in our large bedroom actually hung in drops and obliged to move them. The Cuckoo was singing and nightingale on Monday and Tuesday night, beautiful, and was so warm. The pleasantest time of my life then. This Whitsuntide passed off as I never knew it before, not a word carries and as quiet as could be. There was Wilgress and Gale and they was all beside T. Smith, Gov. Buswell etc. There was not much speech making nor cheering. Wilgress in the chair.

May 30th   Monday morning 8 o'clock. We are going to Warboro' to play a match at cricket today, starts at 9.30. The weather has been delightful since I wrote last, no rain but frosty mornings and now a sharp frost on the morning of Thursday last. It cut all the kidney beans down, topped all the potatoes off and it is even cold this morning and a frost. William Druce was brought home on Wednesday and he was very bad the next day and bit Mrs Druce's finger, obliged to have 2 men up with him all night. There was a terrific thunderstorm passed across the county last Friday week, and although it thundered here a little, it was not much. I have been cutting the grass down the garden all last week and adzing my potatoes up in Common. I met with A.H. last Sunday at the Lower Farm, and we went up to Break Lane and along up to top of Nineveh hill and back and along the Lower Road home. We thought it was 9 but it struck 10 and we parted in a hurry and she would not promise to come out at all. So last night I did not see her at all but fancied I did in their field. I went along the road up to Hill Gate and back up home. Harpers was up here and stayed till supper. Poor old Mr Quartermain died on Thursday morning at 4 o'clock. He had been ailing some time and on Saturday night in Whitsun week he was took very ill and gradually sank. Till he died he was sensible and his constitution was regularly broke up. He is going to be buried on Wednesday. There was not much doing up here on Whit Saturday night. A running Match between Ned Buswell and Mark Currill on Wednesday night, 1 mile straight for 5/- each. Ned won it easily. It was a beautiful night last night and she ought to have come out. Lizzie in a ugly humour and has been all the week. Wants rain.

June 5, Sunday   It has been beautiful weather since I wrote last except on Tuesday when it rained gently all day. We went to Warborough on

Monday last, we started at 20 minutes to 10 – 5 carts. I rode with
G. Holloway, we took 19 there. Stopped at Aunt Wixon's a little while
and then on to Warborough. It was a very pleasant ride and we got there
in good time. There was a lunch bread and cheese and no salad. We lost
the Match by 48 runs, the Aldworths did nothing, J. Humphis [James
Humphries] was last man on our side. Nothing but ale on the ground and
at 6.30 a cold dinner. There was a baked leg and shoulder of Mutton and
a bit of baked beef with 2 dishes of potatoes, Lettuce and onions, scraped
horseradish and a little pickled cabbage. We ate everything up with
cheese. I drank no beer but went up to a house on the Green and had
Ginger beer and brandy. It was a beautiful place to play. We started home
about 10 and stopped again at Wixon's a while. Thomas Smith and
Richard Clinkard were there and they brought the news home. They did
not fix the time of the return Match. We got home at 11.30. I scored.
Finished painting the front gates on Thursday last. Harpers took 28 doz of
Cabbages to Market last week. Did not go to Church this morning,
intend going to the Flower Show on Tuesday next. Young Whitmill died
on Friday last. News of terrible fighting in America from 40 to 60,000
killed and wounded. It is frosty mornings now, no alteration over the
way, going to have a sale.

June 9th, Thursday It has been beautiful weather since I wrote last,
warm and sunny, and now it rains a little and looks like it. We wanted
rain very much, very bad indeed, things were drying up. Smith's men
have Mowed Woodpiece and it is carried and today they are mowing
Shepherd's Hill. Duckland is cut. Went and saw Joey Gale's Mowing
Machine today the first I ever saw at work.[19] It is a very compact, simple
and effective concern and does its work well, but it wants to be drove
very true, pair of horses draws it – the first ever at work in Garsington.
R[obert] Wells has got one and they appear to be getting about a good
deal now. Wrote to Giffords on Monday and went to Flower Show on
Tuesday.[20] Lizzie and I walked there and back, was tired. It was a lovely
day and warm and bright. Saw a horse run away and George Cullam
clinging to it. And to Brewery about Quartermain's house, got the first
offer of it, and enjoyed myself so much at the Flower Show. The Garden
was delightful and music beautiful and the flowers especially one, a
Geranium, was extraordinary good, it was named 'The Cloth of Silver'.
There was a very fine show of fruits and flowers and a good many people
there. We went into the Botanical Gardens on coming home, it is a fine
place. We got home about between 9 and 10. We went to Brachers and

Hay-making on Shepherds Hill

had our portraits taken.[21] I had 6 for 6/6 and she 4 for 4/6 – expect them by post tomorrow. Received no receipt from London about the rum yet. Went down the Common on Sunday evening. Took a paper in my pocket and along the Lower Road to Wells Corner to look at Gale's Machine mowed clover, and back up Salters Lane over Church Close and home. Did not meet A.H. and waited at home a bit and was standing out at the gate when her and Mary and E. S[tone] came up the hill. They had been to Cowley to tea. I asked her to go the back way with me but she would not but passed on down home. I turned back. She said she had got some work to do at home and was coming up street – very cool indeed I thought. She refused to go to the flower show. Made some Ginger Beer yesterday and hoed the young trees and moulded flukes in Garden yesterday. Gathered Gooseberries on Monday. It is raining nicely now.

June 15th It has been threatening wet for a week or so, but it has not come any yet except a little drizzling rain. We want rain very bad now. I have been to Oxford today to the Brewers. I ordered and paid and went into the house and had a good mutton chop dinner and out up in the

market to Harpers. I met Mrs Harper Sen. and had a talk with her, she
went home early and we got home at 4. I had a photographic portrait
altered today. Mallam up here tonight at Quartermain's about the sale.
Put some straw in their stye this morning. Mr Taylor told me at the office
this day that he had had the notice from Quartermain and that it was to
take from Michaelmas next and we could choose our own tenant. E.
A[ldworth] was up here on Monday night. We sat in the Wash house
some time and at night I went down the grounds with her for a walk. She
appears to me to be very sweet upon her George and fully intends to
marry him. A bother about the Club doctor last Club night. Cricket Club
meeting last night, not many there and not much done. J. A[ldworth] not
there. I took 5/6 fine. Wrote to T[ed] W[atson] tonight and gave
E. A[ldworth] my portrait on Monday last. A bother with J. Goody and
J. Aldworth last Sunday. I went down the Common with E. and E. S[tone]
and then along the Lower Road to Wells' Farm reading a paper and back,
and then up Baldon Lane a little way and up Church Close and home.
Did not see or hear anything about A.H. and I suppose that she has given
it up all together now at last. I shall not trouble anything about it now if I
do not see her on the next fine Sunday, and I think it is too bad as it has
been beautiful weather and I intend going out wider on Sundays for the
future. Heard on Monday night from Mrs Q. 'that I had taken the house
and was going to have a wife and go and live there'. I whitewashed all the
upstairs but one room last Monday and Tuesday. No go at all with A.H.
Paid Old Winspurr for making coat last Monday, 10/0d, and agreed to
alter coat and trousers. Sent nothing at all to market today. Went to
Stadhampton last Thursday and stopped at Stadhampton at Wixons some
time with W. H[arper] and J. A[ldworth]. Haymaking is getting about
very general now and Joe Gale's machine is heard all day long. Harpers
have nearly carried all theirs. Wrote to Warboro' tonight. Plenty of
Potatoes at Market today and cheap. Deal of skittling going on now.
Harper bought a pig – I shall buy two tomorrow I think of J[ohn]
A[ldworth]. Had first bundle of straw of T[homas] A[ldworth] tonight.

June 22nd It has been very fine and dry since I wrote last with the
exception of Saturday morning when there was some tidy showers and
looked like rain. I was down the Common at quarter past five to get some
potatoes up but it rained so that I did not get many up. I saw A.H. and
her mother go along at 8.30. I pulled stems up etc. got rather wet. It soon
cleared up and have had none since. It rains a little now and looks cloudy;
bought pigs last Saturday and offal of J[ohn] A[ldworth]. Terrible works

up at Druces with Druce now. They want to get him back in an asylum again as he is no better, at times unmanageable. Whitewashed the cellar on Thursday last, it begins to look white now. Went down the Common and played at Cricket last night and our young boys went played Toot Baldon. Heard that Matilda was going away next week. Had private and confidential talk with Tom Smith last night. The Apple Grafts that I put in are just beginning to shoot now. Mended trousers and coat – today I hoed the Garden. Went to Church last Sunday morning and at night down the Common and along the Lower Road to Hillgate reading a paper. It was a beautiful day, did not see A.H. There was a terrible row down there last Saturday night with Janaway who hurt Mrs Harper's leg and threatened them. They sent for policeman who advised them to get a warrant, but they have not and I suppose will not. If I was in their place I should. A.H. came up here on Monday night nearly 10 o'clock. I happened to hear her call outside and went out and down the fields way home and along the Lower Road across to Church Close by the Grove, below which we sat on some hay for a long time, very happy and loving. I told her that I do not like her keeping away so long and she said that her mother made a row about her stopping out so late. Then she said that she could not go out for a month and she kept her word. Said she thought her mother suspected something by last Wednesday at market. Sent Mary out last Sunday but did not see me, forgive and forget, promised to x next Sunday at S.T. [trysting stile], if wet to come up here and bring some cherries. She seemed pleased to meet me again and of course I was. We kissed and parted at 12.50.

July 3rd, Sunday   It has been raining nearly all day. We wanted rain very bad and we have had no rain for month before, not so much at least as we have had last night and today – everything was drying up. We was very busy last week with the Cricket Match with Warborough, making Ginger Beer, bottling etc. It had been gloomy before but it cleared off on the morning of Thursday and was a beautiful day. We was up early and got the tent down but there was not strength enough to rear it and we could not and broke the scroll iron in two. We left the tent down there and came to get it mended. Whilst we went up, the horses tore the tent about awful and we had a rum job to get him up at all. We pinned a cloth over him and fixed him up well and then home to bring the beer down. It was very warm – had baker's horse and Spearing's Cart. I cleared and went down. They had all had lunch and was down there. Garsington went in first, got 152 runs. J. Aldworth got 5 and Warborough got in both innings 83, so Garsington beat in one innings and 69 runs to spare. We had a good day and sold a deal of Beer and Spirits. R. Quartermain and Taylor was waiters on the ground. Obliged to fetch some more beer down and at night we had 40 to supper and had a good touch. They was a very good side. They went away at 9.30, 10.30 and 11.30. Sold a deal of spirit. A. Harper was down here. I had a terrible headache at night. The butcher was tight and he and they had a deal of acting outside. Went to bed at 2.30. There was a good many people on the Ground and it was a beautiful day. Went to Oxford the next day and ordered Brewers in and had a good dinner. Met T. Smith, then I came home with R.Q. When I was at dinner Mr Scragg came in to me and told me that the firm had agreed as soon as we had reduced our balance to £5-0-0, they would make us a present of that, and as it was, he put Paid to the Book and we are out of Debt with our Brewers at last. I thanked him and came off very well pleased. I went down to Oxford on Saturday week to take out the Licence and I got it signed allright, but the Magistrates told me to get the person granting permission to sell on his ground to write it on the back of the notice. I met with A.H. and her mother there and I stood and talked with them some time. She promised to take me up but did not. We met on Sunday at S.T. [trysting stile], she was late all through C.W. She brought some cherries which we ate. I had been in Holloways and had some strawberries before and Tom Smith and E. Clinkard was there. We went up Break Lane and up to Baldon and on to the Avenue on Baldon Common. It was a very pleasant walk. E. was with us and back again. E. left us at Break lane and we came home together to the Tryst where we stopped till nearly 11. She was in a good humour and promised to x on the Wednesday night. I met her outside on the Tuesday night but did not stop. We met at 9 on Wednesday, her dog kicked up a good row. We went up to railway and stopped till nearly 10. She refused to go to Aldermaston on Tuesday next and did not seem in a good humour at all. She wanted to know about Sunday afternoon with F. I told her but I don't think she believed it but it was the truth. It's very vexing of her not to go as I fully thought and depended on going with her there. She talks of coming up here tonight. It rains now and looks like it. The Conference ended on Saturday last and the War began the next morning with Danes and Austrians and Prussians but England will not go to war, I think, with them. They are fighting again in America, a good one but with no decided Advantage on either side. Had Woollen Cord trousers let out last week, bought shoe brushes, knives and forks last Saturday, used new stools the first time on Thursday. Quartermain's Sale on Monday week.

Spearings are up here now and there was a Club Funeral at Cuddesdon on Thursday. Poor Will Young died the week before and Willie Stone was took ill last week with inflammation and today the doctor says there is no hope whatever for him. Very strong job with T. Smith and E. Clinkard. E. had letter and Portrait from Ted Watson. Most all the hay making over now about here and I saw some of the materials laid for the permanent way along the Cowley Sands.

July 18th Poor Will Stone died on the next day and was buried on the following Thursday. Harpers were up at Quartermain's and we had a jollification up there till 10 o'clock. A.H. came up here on Sunday, July 3rd she brought some cherries and it had been wet. We went down the Garden and then up home, she stayed till past 10 and then I went home with Her. We stopped till nearly 12, our folks was gone to bed and locked the door. She was in a proper ugly humour. Promised to meet at S.T. [trysting stile] the next Sunday but did not come at all, and I went home and had my supper when Willie came to the door and said that Lizzy was wanted. It was her wanted E. to go to Headington the next day and they went. She lost her purse coming home. I went and met them at Railway Arch. She came up here with 53 and stopped a little while. Mother was not well and I did not go home with her. It was Quartermain's sale day. The auction began at 2 o'clock and everything sold very well indeed. I bought all the Garden for £2 15s. 0d. and the coal. Mr Mallam asked me about taking to [on] the outbuildings etc but I told him that I would see him again. Have had several applications for the house [by] suitable persons. It appears to be cheap enough but there is no telling. Dick is left in the house but with nothing to eat or anything else but a bed. He is on [working?] for the baker. Was busy all the week gathering fruit. Met A.H. on Friday night at Harpers and went home with her. We went to the T.S. where we had a very interesting conversation to ourselves. She was in a good humour and pleased to be out, it was such a beautiful night and I was stripped out in my shirt but I was cold. Got home at 12 o'clock, but I am determined, and she is too, to keep better times for the future and not be out later than 10 o'clock – it looks so low. I was up next morning at 4 o'clock and down the Common gathering peas. Harpers had got a tremendous load. I was obliged to send 2 flats of peas and large basket of Walnuts by a donkey cart and brought 1½ pecks of peas home. Had a challenge from Headington Quarry and a good deal of talk about it and that's all, I think, that will come of it. Our Cricket Club is going down very fast now. There was a Match planned to come

Harper's Farm, Southend, where Ann Harper lived

off today between the Club and Mr Smith and Holloways farms but it all came to nothing. There was a vote of Censure proposed by the Conservatives and after a very spirited debate for a week, it ended in a Majority for Government of 18.[22] Horrible Murder in a Railway Carriage on the North London Railway on Saturday night last but it is not found out.[23] I and Jack [Godfrey?] and Tom Cooper went to Aldermaston R.W. and O. Fete on Tuesday, July 6th.[24] I started by myself at 8 o'clock and walked to Cooper's and got Tom off. I thought Jack did not mean to come but he was at the Station first. Went off at 10 o'clock. Was lovely weather, bright and sunny, and stopped at Didcot a long time for the Cheltenham train. We got to Aldermaston Park at 2 o'clock. We got up an Omnibus and off to the Park which is a beautiful place and the house is very striking. There was plenty of Amusements and we enjoyed ourselves to our hearts content, the weather, the music and the ladies was delightful. We strolled about the park looking at 'kiss in the Ring' etc. and I had a touch at Archery but did not hit the target. There was plenty of Refreshments and we went round the house and gardens and finally walked as hard as we could back to the station. Got in the Carriage and off towards home. There was a man killed at Wallingford Road Station whilst we was there. An Excursionist by the Express train ran over him. Tom Cooper saw the accident and the man lying on the rails dead. We stopped at Didcot long while rather sobered and got back to Oxford at half past 11 o'clock, tired. We stopped at Railway Tavern with J. Clinkard and on to Coopers. Had some more refreshment and home, we was terribly tired. I got home at 10 minutes to 2 o'clock. Elizzy Aldworth brought me her 'Carte de visite' on Friday night week.[25] Met her and George Holloway up against the Break on Sunday week. A.H. promised to meet me at S.T. yestereven. It was quarter past 6 when I started and I went along the road and up to the Sandford Road and back by myself without seeing her. And all the while I was going up there, she and E. [and] Nelly was sitting down by Holloways Gate and when I got back they two with M. Holloway went up the Kiln Lane and she and I went back up to B[aldon] L[ane] along to Nineveh Ground and back home. We parted at 10.20. A beautiful night, the moon shone splendid and it was so warm and still. Such an extraordinary long drought has scarcely ever been known. It is gloomy in the morning and then the sun shines out as bright and hot all day and this has been it for a long time. In fact, with the exception of one or two showers, it has been no rain for months and no sign of any. It thundered heavy yesterday and rained heavily at Milton but it went round us and we had none, nor we have had no thunder all the summer over us only at a distance. The bakers pig very bad over the way. I stripped and washed myself all over yesterday morning in the bar. R. Quartermain went to Church yesterday. First saw a Locomotive and train of trucks on the new Railway one day last week and Saturday I saw it up against the Railway Arch. Mother very middling again now. Harper bought a new pony on Wednesday, a good looking one but it turns out to be a kicker.

Sunday, July 24th It has been Glorious weather since I wrote last. One day it missled of rain a little, just laid the dust for a little time but we have had no rain for a long time. On Monday last Mother was washing all day and it was very hot. I suppose that she caught cold for the next day she complained of being poorly and in fact she has been very ill ever since. She seemed restless and feverish and had no sleep and on Friday we sent for the doctor. Abe went and caught him, Mr Cogan, on the Downs and he came back and saw her. He questioned her about how she felt etc. Said she was a very weakly subject and wanted a deal of care and good living. Abe brought a bottle of medicine and pill and he came up again the next day and today he has not been.

July 30th Sunday night. It has been no rain since I wrote last except a little missly rain yesterday at Oxford but it was not much. I was at Oxford going to the Brewer's to order another lot of beer. I was there on the Saturday before. I had a good dinner and then I asked Mrs Saunders to lend me her pen and ink to write to A.H. which I did and posted it. I waited for Mrs Harper Senr. and then came home with her and nearly got thrown out by the horse shying at a Wasps nest burnt out. I have been very busy all the last week preparing and doing the Ground. Cricket Match with Headington. We did not get anybody to help us and on Sunday night E. A[ldworth] was up here with George Holloway, and then she promised to come up and make the pastry the next day which she did and made it well. 4 fruit pies and 6 small puddings and then Little Mary came up and helped us the next day all day long and a good one she was. We had a Glorious day and sold a tremendous lot of Beer. We put the tent up in good time in the morning and I stopped up and put the Lunch on and waited at table, and then down the Field where I stuck till night – at all events till the game was over, when Garsington won with four wickets to go down. They was a very good side and stopped late. I never saw so many people at a match in Garsington in my life; and the weather was delightful. We sold 3 barrells of Beer. Mother has been getting better since the doctor has been attending her, although she is still very weak and poorly. I have been very dull and tired lately but its no more than I expected but not quite so soon as this. Harper has sold his horse to Dr Hurst for £3 15s. 0d and this morning Sellars ran away along the Lower Road and pitched them all out in Wells Common – he is a kicker too I am thinking. We have had plenty of help this last week; Taylor came up over the way last Friday week. The peas etc. are all dried up now and no sign of rain now. Harvest operations have begun in earnest this last week about here. Saw the first Wheat shocks this year on Saturday last, the summer's creeping away wonderfull fast now, Wednesday noon. It has been glorious weather since I wrote last, no rain and no sign of any and today it is sunny and clear and very warm all the farmers have begun harvest now and all the corn wants reaping at once now. I have been making up my accounts today and putting my marketing all straight, which had been sometime about. I looked over all my peas yesterday but could only get about 5 pecks alltogether. They are all over now, a very bad touch indeed this year with them. I was compelled to give out writing on Sunday night and go waiting. We was moderately busy and a little before 10 o'clock I was standing up at the gate as I rather expected A.H. would come up that way from Littlemore

where she had been on a visit, when up she came and out came the
Cricket players too. I told her to go in the Lane and I would come to her
there. There was only 2 or 3 in the house and as I had felt a pain in my
chest all the evening, I said to Lizzy that I had a pain in my inside – I
should go below for a little while intending to go for a walk with her as I
thought it would please as well as do me good too. I went, found her in
the Lane and we went gently down home to our old T.S. where we sat
down so comfortable and loving and had a homely talk interesting only to
ourselves. It began raining and we got up and stood behind a tree then till
it was over and then home. We kissed and parted at 12.15, shamefully late
I confess, but then it was sometime since we met and will be some time
before we do again as she told me she was going on a visit to some
relations beyond Wantage for a time. Today I came gently home and
when I got up against our gate there stood Taylor and R.Q. with a
lanthorn and they had been all over the place looking for me as Lizzy and
Mother was frightened to death about me. Thought I was took ill and
could not get home. They had been to Harper's and called them up and it
appears they was all terribly frightened about it and Lizzy and I have not
spoke scarcely since. Her had my handkerchief. I was vexed although I
could not help laughing at them. Mother appears to be about the same for
the last 2 or three days, very weak. We have had Sall Till up here helping
when we wanted her. Saw the ballast train[26] up against our gate today,
wrote to Ted Watson and O.C. yesterday. The beans are all blighted and
they are mowing them for the cattle. All the springs are very low, never
was such a drought. Stiffer took ill at Crowmarsh fair yesterday. Hear
Spearings playing on piano very often now. Did not go to Club last
Monday. A.H. had her new dress and hat on last Sunday and there was
somebody at the stile close to her house last Sunday night.

August 7th   Sunday night. It has been a beautiful day, sunny and hot
and no sign of any wet. Maria Humphries is going to be married
tomorrow to Paddy Cherry and they was all day on Saturday cooking and
getting ready for it. Taylor and Johnny got throwed out of Sellars cart
again last night and rather hurt Tom and Johnny. Milton Feast today.
There is a comet visible to the naked eye now[27] and I wrote to Ted
Watson today and sent Carte de visite to him. Have not heard or seen
anything of A.H. all the week and I suppose she is gone to her relations. I
expected a letter this morning but I did not have one. Dug Forward
potatoes yesterday. The dust is blowing much now and how I wish that I
could go out for a walk tonight. I never seemed to think so much of it as

I do now I can't go. We never know the value of a thing till its over but my sweethearting has ended so abrupt and sudden that I can hardly realise it, but what is must be. The bailies in Surman's house and fighting down there last week.[28] Burglary at Cuddesdon last week, plums getting ripe.

Tuesday, August 9th   It is raining now nicely, the first for months.

August 10th   It did not rain much yesterday and it got in the ground about 2 inches. I sowed Turnip seed in Common and was out the night before to see the comet at 1 o'clock in the morning but saw nothing of it. It was the wedding night. There was a terrible lot there to dinner and all day and at night too, the place was crammed full and a deal of singing going on. I was there to dinner and tea but did not go to supper that night. They had a good deal of Beer from here, and was on all the next day: rather quiet today. Cricket Club meeting last night, there was only about 12 there and Mother paid £1 5s. 0d. towards the tent. I done the fires all up etc. – did not send anything to market at all today.

August 11th   A beautiful day – dug my Forward potatoes up down the Common, a tidy lot, and sowed Cabbage and Lettuce seed. Sold Baker a peck of potatoes, small ones, yesterday.

August 14th   Sunday night. It has been a beautiful day again today and ever since I wrote last. It has been very hot and still today. Bright moonlight night last night. A terrible row up at Horseshoes last night and fighting. We was very quiet last night and our beer is getting stale now. Went to church this morning, not many there. A.H. was there, the first time I have seen her since that Sunday night. I suppose she has been visiting at her relations but she might have wrote. The harvest is getting on bravely now and a great deal of the Wheat is carried now. The farmers are all very busy and it is Baldon Feast today. A great want of water felt about now. Mother is getting better and Cogan is here today now. Wonderful plague of Wasps now and a terrible Murder at Reading a woman threw her 3 children into the river and jumped in herself.[29]

Tuesday, August 16th   It is rather dull and gloomy today although there is no rain and no sign of any. It is a very serious time now, an unusually long drought. Druce's well is very low indeed and all other springs are so too. It was very hot yesterday and there is a good deal of sickness and English Cholera about now. The gardens are all dried up and the grass fields are as brown as a berry. The harvest is getting on wonderfully fast now, most of the white corn will be carried this week. A terrible plague of Wasps about this year, a good many nests – the plums are just coming in now. Watered the seed beds this morning. Mother is better now and discharged the Doctor yesterday. We was very quiet here on Sunday night and I went down the garden to look out and see if I could see anybody about. I saw A.H. and Mary coming up Birdsbrook. I waited for them and then I asked them to come over in the Garden. They consented and got over the low wall at Q. Garden and down the garden. I fetched some Ginger beer and then Mary went home and left her there. Elizzy was gone out and I was obliged to mind house. I kept cutting up and down but she waited very patiently till they was nearly all gone when Lizzy minded the house and I went down to her. She said she was just thinking of starting home. We went down to the bottom of the Garden and sat down there some time and then over the wall down home . . . We went to the T.S. and there we stopped till half past one o'clock. We was excessively foolish to be out so late but we seemed reckless and talked rather wild too but No harm. I was almost ashamed to come home. Mother was awake and blowed up a bit. She came home from her visit last Saturday evening and she had her photograph took at Wantage which she brought up for me on Sunday night. The other [photo] her relation had. It is full length on glass and a very good likeness too. Mrs Quartermain of Littlemore came up here, at least down there, yesterday and they came up this way towards 5 o'clock to go home. They called to see Lizzy and I went out to them. M. and her came this way back about 9 and stopped indoors till nearly 10 o'clock and then I went the back way home with her. We had a talk about the night before and made it all up again. She would not promise to go to Banbury with me, nor to the Theatre either or to see me before Sunday week. Taylor taking up the drains at Aldworth's yard. I gave her my portrait last night and she promised to write to me on Saturday next.

Thursday, Aug. 18th　It is and has been very fine mild weather since I wrote last, no sign of rain.

Sunday, August 28th　It is raining now and has been all day, gentle nice rain but unless we have a great deal more it will do no good or at least very little, as it has only just about laid the dust. It looks very gloomy now 9 o'clock. I have been busy all the week gathering fruit and down the Common one day and I took the onions upstairs yesterday and cleaned the pig stye. The weather this last week has been fine but decidedly colder, more like Michaelmas weather now and the days are getting in alarmingly fast. Now it is dark by half past seven o'clock and there has been some very sharp frosts mornings now. Yesterday morning I was down the Common early gathering K.B. and it was a sharp white frost, the ground was quite white with a fog. The potatoes and K.B. was cut off quite black. The harvest is nearly over now. Nearly all the white corn is carried now and they cannot cut the beans, it is so dry. They are obliged to pull them and tye them up with wheat straw but there is very little worth reaping and the sheep was turned on them to eat them off. An entire failure the bean crop this year. Other crops about on average. The potatoes are small but sound and the meadows are all dried up, the ponds and wells are empty and all the farmers are obliged to go to Giswell and Phipp's well and other old strong springs. Our well stands it well though the grass grounds are all brown as a berry and no crop of turnip, swedes etc. at all this year and it will be a very trying winter for the cattle this year. All together it is a most extraordinary long and severe drought. I was down at Oxford on Saturday week to Brewers as we sent to 3 Horseshoes for 2 Gallons of Ale the next day. Sent young Dick Sturges to Oxford last Monday morning for some but they were coming that day. I saw A.H. several times but did not stop to speak as she did not seem in a good humour. I wrote to her [while] at Brewhouse and expected she would write last Saturday too, but she did not and I never saw her all the week. But last night I was coming from Harpers and I met her and went down home with her. She had been up to our house to take a pattern and a letter which she had written but forgot to take to Oxford for me. I read it this morning and it was a very good sensible letter. It is the first she ever wrote to a sweetheart. She refused to go to Banbury with me next Tuesday. She said she did not care to go there with me – her Mother would not like it. She don't mean to go anywhere with me by what I can see of it. We agreed to go for a walk today after dinner but it was wet and I have seen nothing of her. The return match with Headington comes off on Giles Fair Monday and I don't know whether I shall go or not. It all depends on the weather etc. I haven't been to the Theatre yet but I mean to go to Banbury next Tuesday if possible. George Woodwards is down here now, a full sergeant now and fully accoutred and looks well. The railway is nearly finished and will be opened next October I believe. Ned Boswell and Rhoda Humphis [Humphries] asked in church today. The war is going on in America as usual now. I wrote to Ted Watson and he wrote back the other day and said my C de V was like H.R.H. Prince of

Wales. I went to the County Hall and heard the Rape case at Denton.
Lizzie bought stockings and handkerchiefs, all the Mills are obliged to
work by steam now and George Fruin has had a Steam Ploughing
Machine at work at Baldon.[30] I saw the smoke in the field but did not go
to see it. It came through Garsington the other day but it is gone away
now, sold. A good deal of Cholera and diarrhoea about now. Mother
decidedly better now and gets about again and waits in the house a little.
Elias Woodward's baby died yesterday. Shall be glad to be rid of our
neighbours over the way. Trade very dull now. Bought corn of J[ames]
A[ldworth] this last week.

September 8th, Thursday   I have neglected my Diary lately but now
must make up for it. We have had it very dull and muggy warm this last
week. It began raining on Sunday night and it rained on Tuesday
morning, but it has not been enough to do the land any good although it
has helped the grass land a bit but it has not gone in the ground at all. I
went to the meet on the Monday following, the last, and stopped till
nearly 9 o'clock but she did not come at all and have not seen her, A.H.,
[since] last Monday night, when I met her up in Giles's Fair. I went to
Banbury Flower Show on the Tuesday.[31] I went in Quartermain's cart
with G. Woodward. We went to Morriss, the sergent at Oxford at the
Balloon, and George and I strolled about Oxford for some time and then
down to the Station where we stopped some time and started about 12.
We stopped at all the stations and arrived at Banbury a little past 1. The
Coldstreams went with us and marched playing up the street into the
Grounds. It was a delightful day and lovely music and if I had had a
companion with me I should have enjoyed myself first rate. As it was I
was very well satisfied but should have so liked to have had her with me.
A more lovely place than that, as I stood on the terrace in front of the
marquee listening to the exquisite music of the two bands and the flower
beds all gay with their beautiful flowers, I never was in. It threatened rain
when I started home so I went into a shop and bought an umbrella for 4s.
9d. and down to the station where I met one of the Stanleys of Wheatley,
a signal man at Banbury, and he and I had a long talk with one another.
He showed me how to turn the signals on and off. I sent for a Quart of
Beer and went into his room and stopped some time. I bought 2 Banbury
Cakes and off to Oxford. We was obliged to stop on the line in
consequence of the danger lights being against us but I got to Oxford all
right and then off to the Theatre at half price. It was the Hunchback, I
saw the finishing of that and the dream Belles.[32] It is fitted up very well

Banbury Market-place, *c.* 1878

and the acting was very good. I came out at 11 o'clock and walked home
by half past 12, very tired. It was a good show especially the fruit and a
good many people there. The singing of the Orpheus Glee Union was
first rate, the best I ever heard. One tent was blown down. On the
following Thursday and Friday I took my potatoes up down the
Common and got them home. Had letter from A.H. Sunday morning
2nd. I and Harper took a stroll to Nuneham after dinner. We went up the
Break Lane and right across the field to Baldon Common, down the
avenue of trees and into a field to look at a pony but there was not one
there. There was his old one looking all right. We called at all the publics
on the road and I saw Carie Jones. She don't look so blooming as she
used to. We looked at the new chancel of Baldon Church[33] and got home
about 8 o'clock and next morning off to Headington Cricket Match.[34]
We started in the Bishops dray about 9 o'clock and got all safe to
Headington. It was a beautiful day but rather rough. We had lunch and
then down on to the Ground where our side objected to their umpire and
a good deal of wrangling took place. However, they played and
Garsington won in one innings and thirty runs. Our Lizzy and Nelly

Stone came over there in the afternoon and I armed Nelly about all about
Headington and Mark [Holloway?] Lizzy. We left them up on a great
heap or hill whilst we went to dinner. But it was a long time about and
they came down to the house before I had done dinner and went inside
but could not drink. Then they and J[ack] G[odfrey] and M. and R.
Turrill started off in Holloways cart and then down to the Fair. We went
at a good pace and got into Oxford 8.30. We stopped at Jeffs and then up
to the Fair. We went into a Museum and on coming down we met A.H.
and party. I had had Nelly on my arm all the evening but then I took hers
and went into a show, and about the fair and then she and I started to
walk home. She seemed pleased to see me and so was I for I had not seen
her for some time. We came very pleasantly along to Cowley where G.
Holloway and our party passed us but we would not ride and kept on till
we turned along the Lower Road where we sat down by the side of the
road for a little while and rested, and then home up here. But our people
was all gone to bed and then we went and sat down under the trees side
of Phipps Close for some time till the Clock struck 2 o'clock. We sat
there very happy and tired and then down home. We stopped at the

St Giles' Fair, Oxford, *c.* 1868

Trysting Stile till 3 o'clock and then home and parted at 12.30 [3.30?], the latest out yet, and decidedly we must keep better hours than that for I was almost ashamed to come home at that time. I met Fan Trot under Watson Orchard with someone and saw someone lying down drunk. I got home and soon off to sleep and up the next morning and down to Oxford again to the Brewers. I ordered and paid and had my dinner, the family is there now and a great number of servants about. Had a good dinner and off up in the Fair, but it was nearly deserted and was nothing doing there. I met Tom Smith and he and I went down to the Cricketing on the Magdalen Ground where Stadhampton and C.S.C. [College Servants' Club?] was playing. We met the Horseshoes party and Emma Clinkard and promised to go back and bring them home. We saw Stadhampton beat the Club and then Charley Hedges and Tim Butcher and I went up to the Fair where we met our party and into the White Hart. I had Sally all the evening and when we started home I had them both arm in arm down the High Street to the Cape where Tom had got our cart ready for us and off we came. I was rather tired and sick of the Fair and glad when we got home. I went and had a bit of supper and then home to bed, tired I was too. They talk of going to London next Monday. Tom had Emma all the night and a proper rake she was too. The Brewers came here at tea time last night. I sent the Cricketing account off last night to the Chronicle office and last night [went] down the Common and sowed my lower piece with turnip seed, and she promised to come along but she did not. I went along to Baldon Stile and sat there a good while with our policeman and then up to Harpers and home. Sent nothing to Market this week. Accident on the Lower Road at the Swansea Brook. Paynes Cart with a load of butter pitched right over into the Brook, killed the horse dead and nearly the man. He was lying with a lot of flats on him on his face for 1 hour and a half and then R. Clinkard and Bob Yeates went and got him out and sent him on to the Infirmary. It was always a very dangerous place and now I suppose they will do something to it. Gales sale at Cuddesdon Tuesday and Wednesday. Serious illness of Old Norriss and Susan Hall.

Sept. 14th It is raining a little now and we had a few showers yesterday but not near enough to do any good as a few hours sunshine drys it all up again, and we have had no rain at all this year since early spring in fact. I should think that it is the most extraordinary long drought that ever was known. We have got no turnips or winter stuff of any sort whatever and there is no food for the cattle in winter nor no sign of any. I finished digging my potatoes up in Quartermain's garden on Monday last and picked them up yesterday morning. There was but a right little lot altogether about [number omitted] bushels of fair-sized potatoes which I have stored and about a sack of Riffraff which I sold to the Baker for 5/-. Began mending the railing side of skittle alley today only it rained. Sent another lot of corn off to mill yesterday. The apples etc. are blown down terribly this last few days, the wind has been so rough especially last Friday. We sent nothing to market today. I sowed some turnip seed down the Common last Wednesday. Some of the apples want gathering now. Our Cricket Club meeting last night and also about the Feast affair. They appointed a Committee of 10 to collect subscriptions and manage the concern on that day – we had a goodish touch and closed at 12 o'clock, Dick Belcher was there. I saw A.H. last Saturday night, she came up here to bring a basket for Lizzie as she had been to Oxford and rode home with her. I went as far as Giswell with her and then back home. We met next afternoon at Baldon Corner and had a pleasant walk up and down that road, got home at 4 o'clock and met again at night by Swansea Brook. Lizzie and Dick Belcher was with her, it was a lovely moonlight night and we had a very pleasant walk. We parted at 9 o'clock being determined to get in in better time now. She wanted to get home because Dick was gone home. He and Sally Turrill and Nelly was up here the next night and a fine spree we had too. I went down home with Dick. It was a lovely night and next night we had another lark with E. Clinkard and Nelly outside, a beautiful night too. News came over by last Friday's Mail that Muller the murderer was took and is expected home tomorrow.[35] No trade at all for apples or fruit now. Cabbage plants look well, not many lettuce plants.

Oct. 9th   It is a long time since I wrote and I have got behind with it. Dick went away on the following Wednesday, he was up here every night. I met A.H. on the next Sunday outside and went down home with her. It was Feast Sunday and a great many strangers about, we was rather busy but soon over. On the Monday morning I was up by daylight and up in Blenheim getting horse dung down and then home and got the tent out and up and then dressed myself and went down. We sold beer etc. I took the License out the Saturday before, we sold nearly 20 gallons and some spirits. Harper came and helped to get the tent down and I went home. It was a most lovely day, it was quite hot and there was a Cricket Match and about 60 races and a pony race. The sports commenced at 11 and finished by dark. There was a terrible lot of Beer drunk on the ground and a great many drunk. There were a great number of strangers there owing, no doubt, to my having put a report of the programme of the affair in the Paper and also an account of it the next week – both put in with scarcely a word altered.[36] There was a goodish meeting over the way there but not so good as last year, they was too drunk. They had a threepenny whip and it caused some grumbling, they left some Beer which they could not drink. I cleared the slaughterhouse out the next day. Barnes was tight and a fine spree we had over there. The door was open all night. A.H. was up here in the Bar a good while with Mark [Holloway?] and G[eorge] Wells. She went home about 1.30 without seeing me or saying goodnight. On the following night she and Mary came up and they stopped awhile outside, and then A.H. and I went down the garden and sat under the Blenheim tree and talked till past 11 and then I went down home with her. We had a out and out touch on the Wednesday night, the finish up of the Barrell money. There was a tremendous lot there and they had as much Beer as they could drink, they had a bucketful and handed it round and drunk out of it. We had a deal of wrangling on the Monday night but no fighting and quiet all the rest of the week. Boswell was up here tonight [about?] the tent and Taylor went to Baldon on the Thursday, New Michaelmas day, the day Taylor had to come out. John Quarterman came up about 10 o'clock but there was nobody at home and no preparation made for leaving home. They sent for Taylor from Baldon and he asked me about the house whether I meant to let it to him or not. I said no, I should not let it as a cottage at all and not now at all events as I wanted it myself for a time. He seemed put out and in a ugly humour. I came away rather upset too and he soon got his things all out; he took them up to Jim Godfrey's and had his horse and cart. About 2 John Q. brought me the keys and I went over and locked everything up and began putting the apples over there and have done so since. On the following Saturday I went to Oxford to the Brewer's. I met Taylor and he asked me whether I had got that party out. I said 'yes'. 'All right', he said 'and you had better send me an estimate of the repairs to the cottage'. I did and J. Goody sent his estimate at £2 15. 30/- for straw and 25s. for labour and he began it on Wednesday and has nearly finished it tonight. He will make a tidy job of it but it wanted a good coat all over. I put my lot of straw in the hovel and the riffraff will do for the pig stye. I have had several applications for it but none suitable yet. Tawney asked me about it and I told him that John Q. had brought me the keys and he said 'that's all right then'. I went into Mallam's office and agreed to take the fixtures etc. for £3 and gave John Q. my I.O.U. for the amount and have not paid him yet. I went to church on the following Sunday but she

was not there and I went up towards home and met E. S[tone] and
S. S[ellars?] and went down home arm in arm with them. And on coming
home I met A.H. coming up Church Lane and we went down across
Church Close and along the Lower Road and back home by 9.20. I met
her last Wednesday night and she promised to stop for me but she went
off home and I never saw her at all. I went and backed Giles's walnuts
today. The Railway is not passed yet and no sign of its opening. I had a
letter brought up by Willie a week ago tonight, Saturday night (October
1st) saying she would not come out last Sunday, her Mother made such a
row about her being out late. Last Monday Mother and I went to Oxford.
I bought some woollen stuff for 3 shirts at 4/- per yard double widths. I
stopped to the Theatre, it was the play of Don Caesar de Bazan and
Clockmaker's Hat – the latter was very good indeed.[37] I had Tom Cooper
with me and there was not many there. I went to Cooper's to tea and had
some bread and cheese and beer when I came out. I got home about
twenty minutes to two o'clock not much tired. A deal of throwing at the
walnuts outside last night and tonight. Lizzy and I went down to the
theatre about three weeks ago, it was a lovely moonlight night and we
enjoyed ourselves much. It was Grimaldi or the life of an actress, it was
very good.[38] A.H. promised to come up to tea and go but as usual she did
not come and Lizzy and I walked home by ourselves. Taylor and I are
very good friends now. It was Club meeting up here last Tuesday night,
there was not much done and 4 crossed out. Butcher is very ill tonight, he
was took middling last night and is worse today and Dr Giles has been up,
he spits blood so. Betsy Surman was married on the Thursday in Feast
Week. A.H. was asked to go as bridesmaid but declined and Sophy
[Fortescue?] went. They had a good touch at night and off the next
morning to their public at Chadlington where they are now. The weather
since I wrote last has been very dry and sometimes hot and muggy and
sometimes cloudy and dull but no signs of any rain, and the ground and
everything is as dry as ever and the water cart is always going. Norris had
a touch at our pump on Monday last, he throws it up better but goes
away as usual. Walnuts today 5/- per thousand, had some Cabbage plants
stole a fortnight tomorrow. Richard is away from the Bakers again. Had
my shoes mended Feast Tuesday and oiled them last week and sent my
boots t'other night to be mended. The Horseshoes went to London the
Monday after Feast and came back last Wednesday. Today was a most
brilliant day, hot and still and sunny. Lizzy and I had a walk last night it
was bonny still moonlight and so tis tonight. I wrote to Ted and
G. Woodward last Sunday, moved the pigs over to Q.'s pigstye last Friday

week, got rabbit for dinner tomorrow. A terrible explosion at Erith on Saturday fortnight, 2000 barrels, nearly killed 9 or 10 and alarmed people for miles.[39]

Oct. 27th It began raining on Thursday last a little and on Friday and Saturday it rained. I planted the Cabbage plants that day and the hounds were out and had a very good day. I did not go and finished the plants, it was wonderfully dry before it rained. The Butcher is much better now and is about again now, he is looking rather pale. The hounds (ours) were out yesterday, they met at the kennels but did not find till they went to Gales field and then they went right away to Drayton Field and we saw nothing of them afterwards. Sally and Emma Turrill was up here last Tuesday night, they went to Giffords the day they went away from London. Aunt and Lizzy was middling and living at Ealing, we have heard nothing of them since. I had promised a meet that night but was too late. We was cleaning Walnuts all the week last week and this too. I had letter by post from A.H. on Sunday morning; it was wet and A.H. was at church and told Lizzy she would come up at night. I did not go but in the

Wheatley Station, *c.* 1870

afternoon I went there. There was a good many there and I had not been to church for some time, finished gathering the Blenheims next day, Monday 24th. James Currell met with an accident that day, he was carrying corn out of a cart and the horse moved on unexpectedly and it fell on his back crushing him. He was taken to the Infirmary next day and the day after a letter came to Mr Wilgress to say that the case was hopeless and his wife has been down every day since. He lies in a quiet painless way with no feeling at all and no hopes of him; he was not dead yesterday. The Railway was opened to Oxford that day. I saw the first train go down about 30 past 10 and I came along the line from Oxford on Thursday last to Wheatley. It was licence day and I went and paid ours and the Horseshoes too. Saw a wedding party come out of church. Went to Maltby's to dinner, had sausages and then to the Station and home.[40] It was pleasant riding and the tunnel was gloomy. I believe I am the first Garsington person who travelled on the Line yet. I planted 9 rows of lettuce plants that night and 2 more the next day and 2 rows of Cabbage plants the next day, finishing planting down there. The plants appear set all right and no grubs that I could see. Taylor gathered the Bracknel Pippins on Saturday. Finished backing Walnut trees on Wednesday.

Oct. 31st   A beautiful day today with a fresh wind, it was gloomy all last week. Planted plants in Garden on Friday. Did not go to church yesterday nor cleaned myself at all all day for the smallest of my pigs was very middling and I blooded it and had to part them and sat up all night with him.[41] I had a good fire over the way and M. and E. was there. I left them and went to the meet although behind time. She was there waiting, we went down to T.S. and sat down till nearly 9 and then home, no x till Sunday. I saw her on the Saturday night and we arranged the x. She came up last Sunday and stayed till suppertime, started home at 10 and got home at 11.20. We went to T.S. and talked all manner of foolishness, and for the future I've determined never to stay out till such a disgraceful time no more. I was thoroughly ashamed of myself that night, it looked so awfully low. I was in and out all night last night but I don't think the pig is any better or worse. Muller's trial commenced last Thursday and we heard news came into Oxford by Telegraph on Saturday night that he was condemned to death. Been planting over the way today, feels sleepy now, looks like a frost tonight. I slept awhile last night in my clothes, it was bonny warm in there. First noticed my cough about a fortnight ago. Farmers busy wheat planting. Bought a sack of Barley and Beans Saturday.

Nov. 6th, Sunday   It was a beautiful morning, a sharp white frost but bright and warm in the sun; it has been cold and gloomy all the week and on Friday morning we had the first frost of the season. It was white and very sharp for overnight there was ice in Holloway's sheep trough an inch and half thick. Poor Jim Cur[rell] died last Friday morning and is to be buried this afternoon. It was a frost this morning, sat up last night, Gunpowder Plot night, till nearly 2 o'clock but nothing amiss.

Nov. 15th   I was taking the parsnips up last week and boiling the culls for the pigs, there was a tidy lot. I went down almost every moonlight night last week and finished pulling my peasticks all up and on Saturday I began trenching my ground. It was a lovely night, bright and still. H[arper] and I was at it till 10 o'clock. I brought my haulm up and put it in the stye today. It digs rather hard and very dry on the seed bed. Last night I went down and trenched till nearly 11 o'clock and done a good piece. H[arper] was not down there, his wife is bad. The baker was took ill last Wednesday and has had an attack of Scarlatina but is recovering now. I went and saw him today. We had a tidy meet last Club night, all paid but one and we commenced a subscription for Mrs Currell. We gathered 13. 6d. that night and 6s. 6d. since. The foxhounds was here last Friday. Ran a fox round Smiths Hill to Blackbird Leys Farm and killed him, we had a good sight of them that day. I pitted my last years Mangolds last week, and today I built the wall up against the Lane Stile and yesterday put the pane of Glass in the little bar window. We are out of coal now, a considerable deal of illness about the village now. Had my new woollen shirt on for the first time on Sunday. It rained all day that day. Went to Church in afternoon and saw A.H. there, have not seen her since Sunday week. We had a nice walk that evening up all round about the Break, it was a beautiful night and we enjoyed walk much. Got home before 9 o'clock. The Cricket windup supper next Tuesday night but expect it will be rather tame as the Baker and Butcher will be invalids. Going to Oxford tomorrow to Brewers, have not been for a long time. Coombe Wood sale and Railway sale next Monday. If it is light enough I shall go down the Common tonight, some topping going on down there now. Best Blenheims 1s. 6d. per bushel. The weather is dull, damp and gloomy but very little rain. Jim Godfrey is helping at the Bakehouse now. I've not heard from Ted Watson for some time now. Nothing for Market tonight, some talk about this ball at Christmas now. Got 2½ sacks of Good picked potatoes and nearly 2 sacks of seed besides, forward ones. Began giving my pigs thick stuff a week ago. We are still in the Washhouse.

The Bakery. The sign of the Red Lion can be seen at the top of the hill

Nov. 24th It has been dull damp weather since I wrote last. The next day I went to Oxford to the Brewers. I got the money for the thatching £1. 5s. but [will] take the other bill for straw down next time. Harper was there at Market as his wife was ill. I did not see him there though and he caught me coming home on the Marsh, I rode home with him. She is better now all right. Took some apricot trees up yesterday and planted them over the way and I wrote to A.H. the day I was at Oxford and sent a B[illet] D[oux] too. I had a letter on Sunday morning saying she would if wet be at the AH [T.S.?]. I went but saw nothing of her, and as I had left a good fire over the way I did not stop, but came on home where I was all night till past 10 o'clock – had roasted apples. I went with Harper and valued Coombe Wood and to the Railway sale, we got back about 12.30. I went and bought 2 plots the next day, very dear though. Harper made the Deposit money right that night. J. and R. Druce built 4 cottages on the tunnell but they had sold them again I think, at something under cost price. Next day we had the windup dinner with the Cricketers. We got a leg of mutton and a piece of Beef about 25lb, and 5 quarters of potatoes and 2 dishes of Greens with cheese. There were 19 to dinner, we charged £1.7s. The mutton was all eat and about half of the Beef. We had a good party and finished off with two bottles of Gin. Tom Smith was the chairman and stopped it out till past 12, we shut up a little before 2 o'clock. Heard that Richard Quarterman was dead that night and it is quite true for the bell tolled for him yesterday. He died at Lizzy Harper's in London, I have heard, on Monday. Bought some paper for papering the Bar and over the way on Saturday. Had both lots of Meal home that day. Very sorry for poor Dick. Killed the pig today, a nice pig about 11 score, trimmed my whiskers up tonight. George Woodward down here now again for 2 months. He is going down to his wife in North of England, he is quite well. Did not go to Church last Sunday. A Missionary meeting held last Thursday at school. I went, a tidy meet. Mr Jenkins, Macfarlane, King, Bolton etc. was there but not many nobs; gave a ½d. Jenkins went to see Mrs G. Woodward. A.H. was not there and I suppose she thinks that we have forgotten one another. We are going to have some liver and fat for supper tonight. Subscription list closed for Mrs Currell, gathered a sovereign for her. The weather is cold today and I wear my Knickerbockers all ways now, 10 o'clock.

Dec. 1st Thursday. It has been very wet since I wrote last and the weather has been very various, wet and frost, and last Sunday was a middling day rather wet and cold. Did not go to church at all and did not go out at all at night, I thought it was a most miserable day though. On Tuesday the harriers was round here and killed 2 hares. We had firstrate sport, we ran round the Hills and on to Joe's and into the Copse. Poor Dick Quarterman was buried last Friday; not many mourners there. He was at Ashenden [Ashendon near Thame?] till Friday and then went to London and died the following Monday. He was brought down in a hearse. Mrs Joseph Turrill and Mrs Jim Clinkard confined last Friday, one of a daughter and the other of a son. I have been planting Damson trees and plums about the garden this week . . . A.H. is up here now, 7 o'clock, have not seen her for a month before. Having my new shirt made. Sergeant Woodwards is gone with his wife to Newcastle yesterday. Cut some greens last week, a nice lot but cheap. Sent to market nothing this week. My cough is better now, see the trains go down every day.

Dec. 2nd It has been dull and damp and frosty white on mornings since and now it rains a little. Been planting damson etc. trees out and cleaned the pigstye out. Heard that my old chum William Cooper was going to be married to his mother's daughter today, I heard, on Monday next.[42] I wish him joy. A.H. stopped up here on Thursday evening till past 9 o'clock and went down to T.S. and stopped till nearly 11.15. We was very happy and did not mind the cold but it was fearfully cold and I thought so when I got home. Had a talk about her family affairs and wrote to her tonight about this will job. Meet next Sunday over the way. Planted the avenue of Damson trees there today. Had a headache last night and took walk and was better, owes J. Aldworth £11 12s. 1d. up till now. The Wooden Houses are going up in Blenheim on Old Druces ground.[43] First cheap excursions to London from Wheatley Station on Tuesday next. Think that Baker is going to have Coopers Close. He has bought his potatoes.

8 o'clock Sunday, Dec. 11th   It has been fine, cloudy sometimes foggy but very mild indeed, more like Spring. I have been stripped out all the week, nice moonlight nights now and finished digging down the Common by moonlight last Tuesday. Began doing the garden up on Friday, done the hedge and bank up, and dug old Gooseberry trees up.

Littlemore Station in the early 1900s

Last Sunday A.H. came up to my house and I had a fire over there and
we sat there all snug and cosy by ourselves till past 10 o'clock. It was later
than we thought but we was so happy and comfortable that we was loth
to part. However we went straight down home when we did start and
tonight I am going to the Littlemore Station to meet her [Lizzy] and A.H.
who are gone there this afternoon and from there to Wheatley and home,
if it is fine at least. It looks like wet now, 4 o'clock. Finished planting trees
in Garden, Damson etc. Killed Harper's pig last Tuesday – Harper and I –
weight 20st 10lb. Half past seven. I started down to Littlemore at 10
minutes to 5 and got there at 20 minutes to 6. I walked and ran all the
way. I waited and walked up and down some time and then took my
ticket. The train came at the right time 6 o'clock. I got in the carriage and
just as the train started, they came running down to the platform. The
train was in motion and I did not dare to get out, and besides I was not
very well pleased with them for getting behind time when they was so
close to the station and I had to walk so far. I went along properly vexed
and in fact am so now about it. Lizzy is just come home and don't look in
a good humour and no doubt it will be a huffing job altogether, however
it was entirely their fault and they will never get me on such a fool's
errand again. It was a longish train and the second class fare is 8d. to
Wheatley. It is a terrible disappointment altogether. The weather is
cloudy still but no rain and light 8 o'clock. Christmas Monday night in
the Parlour with Boswell playing the fiddle but nobody else here. It has
been a dull day, nothing at all doing, have not seen anyone or anything of
the ringers. Have been up at the Wood 2 days this year and on and off in
the Garden doing the scutching[?] but it is awful slow work. On Saturday
Tom Taylor and I done the Carthouse up a bit and shifted the Cider
barrells in the hovel, and at night I went down to Harpers and had some
elder wine etc. and on coming home I heard such delightful music at
Dick Newells, a young man was playing a concertina there delightfully. I
stopped some time and came when I saw a large fire at Great Milton.[44]
Stevens farm was burnt down, it did show very bright and looked much
further off than it proved to be. Bill Cooper's wedding in the paper the
last week[45] and Caroline Shepherd died last Saturday night and Old
Currell last Saturday night. Holds 1/0 for Ann Castle for laying out the
body of James Currell. Gales has been swinging the farms about. That
appeal case and the trial came off on Saturday but was dismissed till the
Assizes. The Duck job was settled too, 21 days.[46] Crawford set up Public
House on Saturday last, had 5 kilderkins of Beer in a very sly job
altogether. The Tuesday in Christmas week after I wrote last, we had a

tidy party of dancers but altogether it has been a dull Christmas. There was a row with Teddy and Jim Townsend and very nearly a fight but all passed off at last very well. Albert Godfrey was here with his lady and Jack and his lady. Albert's is a tidy, quiet, nice girl – they stopped till nearly 12. I saw Netta on Sunday week. She and Lizzy and I was over at the old house and stopped there till 10 o'clock and then I went down home and we stopped till nearly 12 o'clock. Mother kicked up about it smartish to Lizzy but did not say much to me and last Sunday her was up there again. We was all on the quiet and unknown to anyone, I believe, we was very happy and loving and loth to part but we did and I got [home] by 11 o'clock. By far the pleasantest evening we ever had together and no nonsense. We agreed not to meet again till Sunday but I heard that she had been up here on the Monday night, I did not see her. I sold my pigs to Sutton alive and sent them to Thame by J. Yeates' cart last Thursday morning and had the weight back last Sunday morning, 23st 5lb. We caught them in a string and put them up in the cart easily enough with plenty of strength. They will not hurt much I think. Jim Yeates charged 4s. 4½d. for carriage and 10d. for peasticks, 5s. 2d. Had a cricketing supper up here last night but in consequence of parties otherwise etc. there was but 9 to supper and we got food enough for twenty but it was Mother's fault and some that promised would not come. However we had a good touch afterwards – a gin hot touch and kept it up till after 12 o'clock. We cooked a leg of mutton and piece of salt beef and the pieces of beef ought not to have been cooked. There was bonny lot of potatoes left. I have had good deal of chaffing about Littlemore Railway Riding. Was at Wood yesterday, had a good deal of laughing and joking and fun all day. Ringers went to Warborough yesterday. Crawford sells in the wash house and gives beer away. Butcher is middling again, does not get out. It has been frosty cold weather lately but no snow and it thaws today. Busy fitting the Railway Row up now. Kissed Nora under the mistletoe last night. Spoke to J. Clarke's wife about house.

1865

Shoots larks for Oxford market – lovers quarrel – mother ill again – lets cottage –
goes to concerts in Oxford, to Malvern by train and to London for the cattle show –
hears of his 'bad reputation' re girls – A.H. upset.

Jany. 5th Paid John Quarterman his I.O.U. today for £3 0s. 0d. for the
fixtures, fruit trees, Copper, etc. borrowed £1 0s. 0d. of Mother. Put the
Bank Account right tonight. Paid rent last Monday, has been open but
wet yesterday fine Windy and cold today we have been in the garden
today and yesterday. Baker and I settled up on Saturday last. I had to draw
11s. 0d. and paid for Income Tax for Quarterman's for the landlord to pay
4s. 9d. Sent the 7lb Carrots to J. A[ldworth] today unpaid for. Had fire in
the Bar for the first time this Winter on Monday and Tuesday last.
Harpers was up here on Monday. Cooper has done with the Close today.
He and R. Wells and Baker up here tonight drunk. I think Clarke will
have it now – the Harriers out round here last Wednesday but not much
sport. It clung so. Johnny's sister and Mrs Powis with them on Joey's most
of the time. Met A.H. on Sunday as I was coming home below and we
went along the L[ower] R[oad] and up Baldon Road a little way and
home soon after 9. Quite late enough and I had my supper and off to bed.
It was a stinging frost and next night some snow. It thawed on
Wednesday morning though. Mrs Harper never spoke tonight took some
greens down. Got Harpers rifle up here but have shot nothing yet.
9 o'clock took to Cravat today.

Feb. 3rd I have been sadly neglectful lately in my Diary and must now
put things as short as possible. During most of the time since I wrote I
have been doing the Garden up with one day to Oxford to brewers and
walked home and wrote to A.H. The weather during that time was open.
More or less cold with frosty mornings now and then. We done the
garden up and trimmed the Walnut tree out in the road and done the
carthovels and shifted cider casks until Saturday week when we finished
all but planting. We had a good Bonfire at the bottom of the garden
where we roasted the apples and potatoes. J. and A.H. was up at the

House one evening very cosy over there till nearly 11 o'clock. We were very happy and nothing amiss. I have been walking out with her every Sunday evening I think. At the last Cricket Club night there was only 5 there and I hold the money still. Mother has had another sack of Potatoes of me and I have done 2 bushel of onions ready for market. I have been pretty well since. On Saturday week it began freezing and it froze till Monday last when it began to thaw and has thawed since but the snow lies about the hills now. On Friday it snowed and Froze all day long from the North. I had shot 10 big birds before so the night before we cleaned the rifle and next morning he and I started off in the snow. It was over our shoes. We went below and had a shoot or two and then up the lane where we got nearly stuck to Long Furlong and there we shot all day and killed 92 larks. We sent 8 doz. the next day and made 6/- of them. We laid 2/- out in ammunition and had 2/- each. I went up there and down the Common Garden and shot, up till Tuesday, 5 dozen larks and 1 doz. big birds. There was a tremendous fall of snow in some places on the Downs. It was up round your middle and the poor larks was starved to death nearly. I was shooting every day till Tuesday, saw some poaching. I fetched my wood home on Thursday (today week). Mr Smith's team brought it. I went the day before and got it all up on the top of the Hill ready. It snowed the next day and we started at 12 o'clock and got home before 2 o'clock all right. I sent in the waggon ½ 100 Withs 1 bundle R[ose?] Pegs and some Ash poles Props etc. We have continued sending the Blenheims off and yesterday Alfred Q. and I tried to get the wardrobe down but could not. On Wednesday Mother was took ill again, she had a bad night Coughing so and it made her chest so sore and bad and she has no appetite and is consequently very weak and low with her breath so bad. I hardly know what to make of it whether she will get about again or no but I hope so. She is no better today. We had a goodish party here last night. Taylor was drunk and has been all the week. We bought a waggon load of split blocks and roots and chips for 8s. 10d. of him. Brought home and had ton of coal from Watson yesterday. Heard from Gifford last week – aunt sent box of Lozinges. Had letter from Ted Watson from France a while ago, could make nothing of the address. J. Turrill's daughter christened last Sunday, Catherine Harriet. Looked a nice child – good many lately. Heard that George and Lizzy A[ldworth] were going to be married in the Spring. Netta was up here last Sunday, and Nora, and I talked to Nora a bit foolish and Netta I suppose did not like. I went down street with her – she said nothing then but on Tuesday morning I had a letter in which she said that I liked Nora better than her. I don't much

Ready for tennis? One of Joseph Turrill's
daughters   Joseph Turrill's son, Harry

like that and appointed a meet but it rained and could not go. I have a
proper mind to part now and I will if she is anyways crusty about it
because I told her all about that affair some time ago and she ought to
know that I care nothing for Nora. However it shall be as she deserves for
I hate jealousy. Tom Smith's lady is jealous of Lizzy and we had them all
up here on Wednesday night 8 o'clock.

Feb. 12th   Sunday night. It has been frosty very sharp lately and today it
has froze all day long. I have caught cold and don't seem quite the thing
now. Mark Holloway, George Clarke and Tom Smith have all been here
tonight and all in the sweethearting suit and I expect the two first after E.
Last Sunday night it rained and Netta came up here and brought some
milk. I wrote to say we had better part on the previous night. I was not
very well pleased with her about that letter. I would not see her or speak
to her scarcely but she left a letter explaining everything to my satisfaction
and I was pleased and satisfied. I answered it and she came up here over
the way on the Wednesday night where we was very happy and loving
but we stayed too long by ever so much. I really must keep better time
for the future. It was 12 o'clock when I got home. Had B[illet] d[oux]

this morning, no meet tonight at all. It is beautiful night moonlight and still and the bells are ringing merrily. The harriers appear to be a very dull go this year, they scarcely hunt at all now. Old Mrs Clinkard is very ill now again and mother is much better, gets about again. George Holloway comes to church with Lizzie Aldworth now. Gang of drainers gone to Worcestershire but not much good to be done. J. Aldworth has got his half of the Close dug up and Clarke has ploughed the other half. Harry has just brought a bat up here for the Club to buy or not for 3/6. Club night next Tuesday night. Began letting my moustache grow, this is the third Sunday I missed shaving. Have been shooting in the Garden lately. Steeplechase next Wednesday at Denton. The Railway Terrace is finished and lodgers in it. Farmers have begun to plant beans now. Greens sell tidy. Went to church this afternoon. Am in the washouse by myself. Our pig is bad and does not get any better. I don't know what is the matter with him. Sold nearly all the Blenheims. The Lettuce look very middling now.

Feb. 19th   Sunday night. The weather since I wrote last has been very severe and on Thursday afternoon it began snowing and snowed all night and next morning. It was deep snow a foot thick and drifted in places up round your middle. It has froze and thawed ever since but with a very rough wind. It is freezing now. Has been quite a gale today but has subsided now a bit. I was froze out all the week and was shooting nearly all the week. I killed 2 dozen up till Wednesday and Abe and I had a day on Friday and killed 2½ dozen and a pigeon and a rook. I had a walk up yesterday but no larks and a lot of guns. The larks all went away down south so that we had but very little shooting. I killed 6 at a shoot that day. We started a hare in Gales fields and Jack followed her about Harpers fields. I and Abe had a shoot at a quack and killed 2 larks in Harpers garden. I had a fire over the way yesterday afternoon and this afternoon and last night I sat there and trimmed cuttings and Lizette [Lizzy] played the Concertina which she bought of A. Woodward the day before for 4/6. It is a tidy one – 25 keys with 3 stops. Mother gets about again but in a ugly humour about something or other. Netta came up over the way on Thursday night and we stopped and had a very interesting talk all to ourselves till nearly 10 o'clock and when we went home it blowed and snowed and the snow was deep and it was proper rough journey. No meet tonight not till Thursday night. Mrs Clinkard Snr. much the same now. Sent a Val[entine] to Netta, one to R.T.B. Club night last Tuesday night there was not many there but we had hotpot and had a merry party till past 11 o'clock. Sold all the big onions and have done some of the picklers. Did not go to Church this day at all and did not clean myself till teatime. The pig is about the same. Took my boots to be mended last Tuesday. A wonderful lot of gunners out after the larks. This last snow and we have had a sharpish winter and a wonderful deal of snow. The first snow lies about the hills now and appears likely to be a late Spring. Mrs Wilgress was confined last night with a dead child and he and she too are very middling over it. Taylor and gang sinking a well up in Harwell. A great many pairs of birds about this year – very rough wind. J. and I wrote to Giffords last Friday. Big un spoke to me last week. Letting my moustache grow . . .

Feb. 26th It has been damp dull weather with frosty weather and on Sunday and Monday it froze very sharp wind sharper than all the Winter for a little while and on Tuesday it began to thaw and tonight it is very warm and muggy. I went to church this afternoon and has just been to the meet but she was not there. I suppose I was too late. I saw her over the way on Monday night unexpectedly and on Thursday by appointment. We was very happy and loving both times and stopped too late past 10. I have been over there. I had a fire every night but last night doing shalots and cuttings etc. and Lizzy has been over there playing her Concertina. Plays it tidy too. Put damp sack on Forward seed potatoes today. All the Blenheims gone. Letting my moustache grow. Nora here.

March 13th, Monday I have neglected my diary lately but must now make up. The weather since I wrote last has been on the whole favourable some snow and rain but little and frosty mornings and some days very cold indeed. It has been sunny today but a cold east wind and drying. I have finished the bit behind Q's house today and the papering over there tonight. L[izzy] and I papered the Bar last Monday night. Was at it till one o'clock and done it well and last week I was doing the house over the way, whitewashing etc, and last Saturday night I papered (repaired) the parlour over there. Had a fire all day and finished 12/30. Was planting potatoes all last week. Pruned Apricot trees on Wednesday and planted some Lettuce and Cabbage plants the week before but they look very bad now. The gooseberries are very late this year only just swelling out now and the birds work them. I have shot about a good deal lately and on Saturday I saw a pair of Bullfinches in the Garden. I shot 4 times at them with Jack's gun and only killed a cock – the record I have seen. There was a steeplechase at Denton last Monday week with Trinity College men. I did not go but the foxhounds ran a fox from the Break into the Copse and up to Watson's copse and there killed him. I planted some peas down the Common that day. The only foxhunt I have seen this year the foxhounds have been round here today but could not find at all. Nelly and her sister was up here last night and on the Thursday week Netta came over the way. I had a fire over there. E. Phipp was married that day and Charley Hedges came up here at night and saw and walked with L[izzy?]. Last Sunday we met later at the Oaks and walked down on the Cricket Ground and round Aldworths Common and back home by 9. The Sunday before we walked to Baldon and back and last Wednesday we stopped in Iffley till nine and meet next Thursday there again. Had a letter from Ted [Watson] last week from France and Lottery Tickets from Glasgow today. Mrs Druce moved down to Holloway's house last Friday in Pettywell and I suppose will leave the Malthouse.[1] Did not send anything to market last week. Have dumped seed Potatoes lately. Lizzy begins to play the Concertina tidy now. Another extra train put in The Railway again. Have Tom Smith up here a good deal lately of an evening. I had a days hunting with our pack on Tuesday week. We went from Joey Gale's field straight into Drayton fields and back to Chiselhampton and then into Dorchester field once or twice and gave out at dark. We went up to Sukey Harper's and had some beer and I was proper tired and stiff for a day or two. Mrs Harper just fell in the Brook about 3 weeks ago and Lizzie Aldworth is unwell now. A bad mouth. I suppose will be married after Lent they have been buying furniture lately at sales. We have been living on Rabbits lately. The Pig is bad, kicking still, and asked the Butcher to buy him today; no satisfactory answer though. Letting my new moustache grow.

March 27th I went to the Brewers about a fortnight ago and on Sunday week I went down to Joe Clark and told them that the house was to be let and that they could have it.[2] The previous week I had papered it and I was whitewashing it last week. The next Monday Mrs Clark came up and said they had agreed to take it. The terms were that he was to take the kitchen, parlour, scullery, 2 bedrooms and the washhouse with permission to share potatoes in the winter if they wanted it. The rent to be 4 pounds per annum to be paid quarterly with three months notice on either side and no lodgers to be allowed at all. To fetch their water from Phipps well and the flower beds in front of the house and those nearest to the Lane. I finished whitewashing on Saturday night and have cleared the house out today and been plastering. Mended the scullery and open the copper ready for cleaning out. She is coming to clean it up tomorrow. I bought a

heap of dung of G. Boswell for 3/0 on Saturday. Was down at A.H.'s last
night and heard what a beautiful character we had got in relation to
letting the house over the way of the market people. Went to church the
last 2 Sundays in afternoon. Walked out with A.H. last Sunday week got
home by 9. Agreed for Netta, L. and I to go on trip to Oxford by
Railway last Thursday. Netta, L. and I went, we started from here about 6
got there in good time, started at 7.10 second class 1/0 got there, went to
the Refreshment Room and had something short, back up to Carfax by
bus 1/6 to S & B's, brought some beef for Mother, heard a band, had my
hair cut and got home about 10/15. Netta stopped to supper and I went
home with her. Got back by 12/30. Got stopped on the road and I have
made a solemn promise to myself not to be out on ordinary occasions
later than 9 o'clock and never later than 12 o'clock. Leo and L. was over
there last night when I came home, with a good fire and we had quite a
serious and interesting talk to ourselves till 10 o'clock and that ended the
Chapter over there – many pleasant hours I have spent over there which I
never shall see again, such music and singing but its over now. Bought a

The Three Horseshoes, where Joseph's cousins lived

peck of Myatts Ashleaf kidneys of Harper for 1/6 and 3 pints of K.B. off of W. Weaving for 1/6 tonight. Barnes and his wife are going away next week they say. A young man and elderly female is up here now. Ester Pim had a son last Saturday. Butcher middling again. Taylor and Tom doing the Cricket ground up last Saturday. Excited Parish meeting last Thursday morning at Church and at night at 3 Horseshoes. Goodish walk to Cowley last Sunday week. Thrown my trenching down the Common last night. Killed our pig a short time ago and I sold it to Butcher for 15/6 per score weighed 8st 10lb. Mother owes me for a property tax. The weather was fearfully sharp and cold all last week, a sharp frost every morning and sunny days. It is an extraordinary late cold spring. I have planted Potatoes in Common and the gooseberries are only in bud and nothing in fact is moved or will this weather. It snowed proper on Saturday and we have had a deal of snow lately. J. Aldworths new pigstyes put up last week. This last frost has killed the lettuce in Q.'s garden and the plants look but middling. I hoed all our Cabbage plants and trod the Lettuce down the Common. Pigs very dear. They began chanting the Amens and intoning some portions of the service last Sunday. I didn't much like it though. Roger's pack was here again last Friday. Ran across Clinkard's field and to Sandford, a good day's sport.

April 2nd   It has been a beautiful day today. Went to church this morning and made a written agreement with Joseph Clark about letting him the house last night but I must get him to sign an agreement not to underlet or take in lodgers. Did not go to meet last Monday and have not seen A.H. all week so I had a B[illet] D[oux] this morning asking me to meet her tonight at 6 o'clock. J. Clark came up here on Thursday last and took possession and appears to like it well. He is a ganger on the Railway at Wallingford and is gone back to work today. He agreed not to underlet or take in lodgers last week but I think I had better have it in writing. Mrs Clarke done her flower beds up on Friday, Baker sacked Tom Harper last Tuesday and Gibbons is there now and heard that Jack had taken Druces House.

April 10th   It has been beautiful weather since I wrote last and last Saturday was quite hot, too hot, and today is very bright and hot. Netta came up here to tea. Did not go to Church. Was disappointed about Cricketing got no ball and there was none. Leo and Lizzy and I and Netta went to Coombe Wood for a walk. Netta and I went into CW and on to Wheatley and met them and back home first and off home with her. It was a beautiful night and enjoyed the walk much. Got home at 9 o'clock. Bright moonlight. She was up here on the Saturday night and I had the agreement done out and signed with Joseph Clarke and me about the house. Rogers, Painter and W. Currill fighting that night and row at the Plough. Had walk last Sunday week along the Lower Road with Netta arm in arm – met some Garsington People. Had a talk with G. Holloway last week about his wedding. He is to be married shortly after Easter. Harper went to Oxford for Constable on Saturday. Barnes went away week today. Beautifully warm now. Emily Cresswell died last Wednesday and Jane Phipps died the week before last. Butcher is but middling now.

April 16th   Sunday. It began raining on Good Friday about noon and rained all the next part of the day a nice gentle rain and things have shot up a bit since. Did not go to church. Planted Lettuce out and filled peas up and yesterday planted flukes and Peas and dug up side of the paths and planted Kidney Beans. The apricot bloom is nearly over now and forward bloom on plum trees just bursting. Onion seeds up and Cabbage running away. Have been busy stripped out all the week. Very warm for the time of year. Netta and I had a long confab about the future last Thursday night. Did not get home till after 10. Jem Pym took off last night for an unnatural offence at Gales Cricket night last Tuesday. Good attendance. Broke up at 1/30. Moonlight and warm. T. Smith President. A good many here last night singing etc. Have not been to Church for 2 Sundays. Sent a Challenge to Dorchester C.C. last Wednesday. The most beautiful time of year coming on now the Quick hedges and Elm trees are coming out beautifully now and the violets smell delightfully now. An immense quantity of violets and greens at market now. Mrs Fox over the way now. Harper bought for Gales B. Radford's House in Blenheim on Tuesday for £100.[3] Leo's John is come home for Easter Holidays. Harpers bought new clothes – call for eating potatoes, going to cricket tonight.

April 20th   4 o'clock, Sunday. Went to cricket for the first time on Sunday night played 2 games – a tidy party came up and stopped a while. Had answer that Dorchester could not play us yesterday and Primrose Hill Steeplechases too. E. Gales mare hurt. Went to Oxford that day and had Brewers in today. They made a mistake about the beer. Cleared the yard up and stacked the chips and mended the entrance court and played D.S. [David Stone?] at skittles that day. I could play very tidy too – on Sunday night I heard for the first time that Jack and Albert Godfrey was going to be married the next day, Monday, and so the next morning Jack took his clock, Clothes etc. off up to his house and wished them goodbye and off to Oxford and Albert and he was married. Jack came home on the Tuesday night with his wife. It was a very sly quiet job, no one knew anything about it. I have not said anything to Jack about it and don't mean to. I met A.H. last night at s[tile] in G[ale's] F[ield] and stopped and chatted till 10. Have been hoeing and planting peas, Shetfords Lettuce seed etc. today and tonight I went down the Common and moved dung on shalots etc. and 3 rows of Shetfords. The Cabbage, Lettuce, Shalots, are growing nicely now. Bought a new shirt and 2 collars and Braces yesterday.

May 8th The weather has been beautiful since I wrote last, warm and on Friday it began raining and has rained off and on ever since. Went to Church yesterday. Was cleaning bottles and bottling ginger Beer last Sunday and then to cricket. No cricket last night. Had a match last Tuesday but it was a very rough bad day and we done no good at it – the tent was blown to pieces and there was scarcely anybody there. Had a good touch at night, Jem Tromp was here. Shut up at 2 o'clock on Friday. I heard that the Savings Bank was broke.[4] There is a deal of alarm felt about it and a great number of people went to Oxford on Saturday about it. There is something wrong but what nobody knows and I don't think it is broken. George Holloway was married at our church on Thursday week to Cousin Lizzie. There was four couples T[om] S[mith] and S.C., M. and E.E., G.H. and H.H. and J.A. and E.A.[5] I did not see anything of it but I heard that Lizzy was very choked and cried much. There was Breakfast about 12 and the happy pair started off in a fly by hire down into Staffordshire to a relation there. We and Netta had some bride cake sent. I understand they are going to live at the Upper Farm but there is nothing settled yet. The Lower Farm House is done up well. Murder of the American President week before last.[6] I have met A.H. every Thursday night and had a long conversation and walk and stopped out too late. Been at Cricket on Sunday. Lizzy and I have broke the contract about D[avid] S[tone] and I will take no notice of her whatever if she persists in it. Went to Oxford on Saturday week to County Hall to ˙ get the certificate signed and bought New Bedfords [Bedford cord trousers]. Borrowed £1-0-0 of Mother. Went to Coombe pay day on the Thursday April 25th was behind. Had dinner and back at 6 o'clock. Dad gone down the Witney Country today bill posting. T. Smith told me about the Lizzie Edwards affair last week but he is so fickleminded that I don't believe him but if so I am sorry for poor Emma C[linkard] just as I thought her mother had been ill. Mrs Howard Rymel very ill.

May 17th   I am at home by myself, Mother and L. is gone to Oxford today. The weather is cold and gloomy but not much rain. Lizzy and George, bride and bridegroom, was at Church on Sunday morning, sat just behind me.[7] I could not see them though I noticed the orange wreath. Ted Watson came down here on Saturday afternoon on a visit. He looks very well and stopped at J. Castle's and is just gone back again in a fly which he drove up in. He was here all day on Sunday and had dinner etc. and off to Cricket at night. Had a bit of a jollification on Saturday, Monday and Tuesday night. Last night we had mixed dancing till midnight. Met A.H. last Friday night at Harpers. Had a short walk and meet tonight, if I can. All over with Emma C[linkard] and T[om] S[mith] now. L. and I are still at odds about D[avid?]. I have been very busy lately. Went to Oxford on Monday to Brewers. Sent Bedford Cords to tailor last Monday week. Match at Wheatley next Monday. Just heard that Butcher would not get over it. Baker said so himself today. He is not so well today. Practise Cricket every night now. The Savings Bank Panic is over now and it appears to be safe. Booth shot.[8] I am got behind gardening very much this year. The may is coming out and apple bloom is all over now. Half past 4 o'clock Sunday afternoon.

May 21st   I am just come back from a walk with A.H. along the Lower Road up to Break and back. It is beautiful weather Sunny and warm. I enjoyed the walk much. The may is out in bloom lovely now and the Cuckoo, Nightingales and all birds sing delightfully. I am going to cricket directly after tea and tomorrow off to Wheatley to play them. I think we shall beat them. Met A.H. last Wednesday night and had a walk and then to our favourite till 10 o'clock . . . Butcher no better. Going to seaside next Monday week. Mr Fox over here. Spearings going to leave. Cousin Lizzy sits behind me at Church . . .

May 28th   This beautiful month, how rapidly it seems to have passed away a few more days and the pride of the year is over and gone. The May is out now and weather has been beautiful. It Thundered last Monday morning the day we went to Wheatley to Cricket.[9] We had 3 carts. I went with Alfred Clinkard. We went off in style. I got out at Ladder Hill and went and posted Lottery letter and paid Cogan his bill, £2 6s. 0d. and then to the Crown to Lunch. They had done and I had mine by myself. Off to the Grounds. No tent up and nothing ready. Began to play about 12.40. Ours in and they stayed till 4. They all played well and beat in one innings and 44 runs. They put a sheet up and sold a fairish lot of beer. We had a capital supper and evening. Home by 12 o'clock. They agreed to come next Thursday but sent word up yesterday morning they could not come. Taylor and C.Q. mending the tent yesterday. Hoed the garden over this week. Met A.H. Thursday night in Gales Field. Walked to Baldon to see a fire there and back. Stopped till past 11 o'clock. Bob Surman out and D. Crawford in on that day and Holloways moved down to Lower Farm that day and Garsington Choir played Cuddesdon and got beat by 2 wickets . . . Sent account of Cricket Match to Chronicle. Inserted word for word. Appears to be a good stone fruit year but not Apple. Had New Bedford trousers last night.

June 10th Sunday. Went to Church this morning – have not been for some time. The weather is and has been beautiful all the last week – very hot. Rather gloomy today – last Monday, Whit Monday, was a beautiful day – I was on the Committee but did not do anything. Had my lunch and to Church in good time. I went and sat with, or rather in, the next seat with A.H. I spoke to her about coming up to tea. She came up and stopped all night with Lizzy and got up and helped next morning and gathered some gooseberries till after dinner, when Janaway came up to fetch her home. Her Mother was in a way – Mary had not been home all night and Janaway was drunk. However, they was soon all right. Mother was neutral. Mrs Harper was up here and we had a tidy day but it was a dull day alltogether. There was the usual speeches etc. after dinner, which was a good one. Baker and Hugall was there, did not go to supper, a terrible bother with Bruiser, Jack Cherry, J. Smith, etc. on Monday night and on the Thursday before with J. Townsend and on Wednesday morning that party broke Crawfords window and threw Gates etc. off they will be summoned I suppose. Met A.H. on Thursday. Had a short walk for an hour and home. Baldon club night. Harper had a maiden swarm of bees go away that day and Mrs Harper is very middling today, bed all day. New County Policeman came on Thursday last. Went to Oxford on Wednesday and wrote to A.H. and to Dr Mark's concert – very good too.[10] A deal of Drunkenness this last week. Mother is very middling and weak indeed. Mended and done Q.'s Pig stye up yesterday. Put tent up in Garden Tuesday last. Appears to be a good plum and Walnut year.

Sunday, June 18th It has been beautiful weather since I wrote last very warm and hot but cold nights. I go stripped out all the week. I have gathered gooseberries, taking potatoes up this week and picked the path to the pig stye up. Met A.H. last Sunday and walked with her and Leo and Lizzy to the church at Baldon and home by 9 o'clock. It was a beautiful day. Netta's sister, Mrs Howard Rymel, died that evening and was buried last Thursday. On the following evening I chanced to meet her outside and I went down home with her. We stopped till 12 o'clock I was up again by 5 and this morning I and Harper went down the Common and dug 2 bushels of potatoes up and I dug one up at home in Q.'s Garden. I saw some spots of the complaint there for the first time. Mr G. Holloway senr at church today. Have been for a walk by the lane and home. S[ally] and E[mma] Turrill have been up here but I have been dull all day and tired.

Tuesday, June 20th   I got up the next morning 3.30 and this morning at 4 o'clock sent 4 bushel potatoes off today. Shot a starling flying yester morning. A awful and fatal accident occurred last Saturday night opposite the Industrial School Cowley by which Tom Johnson lost his life.[11] It appears that he, in company with several other persons, were riding along towards home when he suddenly fell off the front board on his head in the road. He never spoke and when picked up by Ben Hilsdon he was nearly dead and died in 15 minutes the doctor was fetched but of course

Members of the Townsend family outside their cottage on Wheatley Road

he could do nothing he was brought home and last evening the inquest was held on the body at Townsends house. The body presented a sickening spectacle covered with blood. Verdict accidental death. Had paper from Ted Watson, Sunday. Flower Show today but I don't think I shall go. It was a white frost this morning but a beautiful day it will be, I think, hot. Harpers went to Market yesterday, today, and their rounds yesterday. Got home at 11 o'clock Southend. Not summoned yet. Butcher gets no better, rather worse I think. Heard about R[ichard] C[linkard] and Mrs C[linkard]. Beautiful hot weather. Mowing Bettycraft.

Sunday, July 2nd   The weather up to Thursday last has been very hot and scorching. No rain or dew and everything wanted rain the peas especially. The early ones were all dried up but on Thursday morning it rained beautifully and I was planting all day. I planted the Broccoli, Savoy and Cauliflowers out in Q.G. and C[ommon] G[arden] and Mangolds too. It rained next day and dull yesterday and today has been bright and sunny. I met A.H. on Tuesday week and had a long walk and last Monday night I walked to Baldon and back with her and home by 10/30. Grubbed the bit up against the pigstye in Q.G. last week and cleaned the stye out . . . yesterday. Wrote to Ted Watson and Art Union last Sunday and to cricket. Wrote to Wheatley CC last night.

July 4th   Wheatley went to Handboro yesterday and I went for a walk with A.H. along the L[ower] R[oad] to the Hawling Post and back through Thin Hay, parted and down Common. Dad and cousins up here I believe not much cricketing now. Ripe fruit coming in fast now and weather very hot. Visited Lizzy Holloway yesterday and had some beer. Rent day. Dad singing last night at Club – out of sorts with all at home.

July 6th   It has thundered heavy and rained this morning we wanted rain. I went to Oxford to Brewers paid, ordered and then saw the people come out of the C[hrist Church] Cathedral and then E[mma] T[urrill] and E[mma] C[linkard] went to the Museum and walked about that a bit. It is a magnificent place and a splendid collection of everything but we did not see half of it and then we went to the Cathedral and heard the Parish Choirs, 400 in number.[12] It is a beautiful place full of rich marble monuments and the singing was grand and beautiful, especially the Anthem. It was crowded. Netta was at Oxford and Liz but I only saw Netta as she was going home and I was with E.T. and E.C. I suppose she was offended for she would not look. I bought a R.C. coat for 10/- and 3

Pairs stockings and 2 handkerchiefs.[13] I came home with Harpers about 9, enjoyed myself much. Liz had her photo took. Saw Mrs Holloways photo Album last week.

July 19th   Went to Baldons for walk Sunday week and budded at Harpers. Monday at home and Holloways next night and next night I met A.H. with Alice Sellar. Walked home with them and back way with her, stopped later. Met her last Sunday had walk to Baldon up Break Lane, saw T[om] S[mith] and L. sitting in Hay greens. Went and played Marston at Cricket last Tuesday. Miserable day. Beat them and our J.C.C. played Baldon yesterday and beat them. I scored both times. A match next Monday, Thursday and following Monday here. Fine weather.

July 28th   The weather is beautiful now, plenty of sun but on Monday last it was very hot and oppressive . . . I went to Oxford on Saturday last to C. Halls for Licence. Met A.H. there and we went to Parks and had something to drink. She told me she had heard about Alice Sellar and men. After I got home on the Sunday night I was standing outside with T. Smith when she and Sue and mother came up the road. I had seen her but once before and we all walked down home and then for a lark I proposed that we should walk back part of the way home with Sue. We started. I had Alice, Bruiser Sue and I told Bruiser I would not have them with me. He was to go round through the Churchyard and we by Gizzel. Instead we darted down Church Close by the Oaks and as it was 11 o'clock we stopped, sitting on the stile a little while, looking at the lightning and she told me all about Will's wedding. We was home by half past 11. However, it appears she is properly offended about it and that night would not promise to meet again and so I suppose she must take her chance. Met Alice and walked down home with her last Wednesday night and took Sue Clarke home. Wheatley came up here on Monday and played the return match. It was very hot, we won with 9 wickets to go down. Did not sell a barrell of beer on the ground but lots of Ginger beer. Had a good touch at night and good singing especially Joe Coopers. They did not go till past 12 o'clock. 25 to dinner. A.H. was up here that night and I went outside and stopped with her some time then down as far as Gizzell and had some fighting at night, broke the little round table to pieces. She was very cool and in an ugly humour all night. R. Clinkard's house was sold by auction here on Wednesday to Wm. Galpin for £220 and afterwards Richard sold it to John Druce for £222 10s. 0d. but he came up next morning and backed out for fear of offending Galpin.[14]

Baldon was to have come yesterday but did not. Had a talk with Mr and Mrs G. Holloway last Sunday evening. Played Cousin Fred Turrill at Skittles yesterday and had Joe Hatto out playing last evening. David Stone went away last Wednesday. We had a meeting last Friday week up here and presented him with a bat, ball and purse of money. He played with us at Marston on the Tuesday and a party of Cricketers met him outside and went up in Blenheim with him and saw him go off. I sent an account of presentation and Match to Chronicle last week but it was not put into paper.[15] Heard a bad account of T.C. [Tom or Ted Cooper] this week. Liz had letter from D[avid] S[tone].

Monday, July 31st   It is raining now, it began about 11 o'clock and has rained steadily all day. I went down to Holloways last evening to see the rose buds. It was a beautiful evening and Mary and I walked and chatted about and then we sat down on the seat in the clump of trees at the end of the garden for some time and she went and fetched some wine and we drank one another's health and Mark brought his gun and we went off to the Butts to shoot a pigeon but could not see one. Mary went with us and I shot at some sparrows. Then Mark took the gun in and he and Mary and I went off up in the Motterells to look at the corn. We left Mary up in the Motterells and she promised to stop till we came back. Mark and I wandered about up there till nearly dark and then straight down home. When she and Harriet came in she had been standing at the gate all the while. I was sorry I did not go to meet her. She seemed pleased to have some one to talk to her after her shyness wore off. The Old Folks went off up to the Upper Farm. The buds are nearly all growing. Mrs Harper told me she had heard a pretty character of me at Oxford that day (Saturday) about me and the girls said I was a bad lot and one thing and another. A.H. came down there but she would not speak or come in and I believe I met her at night with some one but she nor I did not speak. Had Cabbage seed Ascot last night and going to fetch Sellars now.

August 9th   Sowed Cabbage seed on Crowmarsh Fair day and some more and Pickling last Saturday. It rained well on Monday. Bruiser and I went to Baldon Sunday evening only a few boys at Cricket and no meeting on Tuesday night. The Wheatley Cricket Match in the Paper this week. Butcher very ill indeed. Netta and I are still cool. Plum trees break about awful. Farmers are reaping and carrying in all directions now.

Sunday, August 13th Poor Butcher died on Saturday morning at 1 o'clock. They thought he was dying on the Thursday evening but rallied till the Saturday morning. He was quite sensible and calm to the last. It is about a twelvemonth ago he began to fail and he has been gradually fading ever since. He is to be buried next Thursday. I went to Church this morning have not been for some time before, very few there, a good sermon. A.H. was there I meet her now and then but we scarcely speak and so I suppose after all she means it to end. Well she may if she thinks it proper. The plum trees break about awful and I have propped them all now. I have thought about going to C[rystal] P[alace] on Tuesday but I don't know. Clarkes over the way have been away now for some time. Joe is over here now. Put the Myatts over in Cellar. Friday night. Gardens want hoeing again. Failure of the Atlantic Telegraph.[16] Cattle plague [17] and the high price of Butchers meat, some as high as 9d., 10d., 12d. per lb and the weather is very showery for harvest operations and Holloways was carrying 2 days whilst it was showery. Smiths have carried all their corn wheat and most all the White corn is cut now. Baker has just sent word up not to let the Cricketing tackle go tonight on account of the poor Butcher lying dead on Sunday.

Posing for the photographer during hay-making at the turn of the century

Sept. 3rd   It has been beautiful weather for the last week and today it has been very hot and close. Went to Church this morning. Have not been for sometime before. Went to Marston last Sunday, Jack and I, about the Cricketing but could get no answer. We went down the New Road from Marston Lane to the Museum and onto Albert Godfrey where we had supper and home by 11:30. Poor Butcher was buried on the following Wednesday I and W. R[yman], E. H[arper], J. G[odfrey], R.Q., T. H[arper] carried him to the grave. Mother followed. Sent his death to the papers and went to Brewers and C[ounty] H[all]. Had Certificate and Occasional License too. Tom Sellars broke his leg last Friday night. Their pony threw him in the ditch in Spittle Green. Took to the Infirmary. J. Hedges and W. Surman asked in church today – out-asked. Joe Turrill's daughter died last Sunday night and was buried last Thursday afternoon. L., Leo, S[?].W., F.W. carried in white dresses, Black Mantles and white cloaks, a sight.[18] Sue down here and F.C. and S. Cooper. Young Spearings rattling about here now. Plums [on] nearly all over now. Potatoes getting ripe. Gardens awful weedy and sowed turnip seed on onion bed in Q.'s G. yesterday. Finished Red Plums [on] 4th flowerbeds in their glory and Convolvulus too. Clarkes not come home yet. Not much cricketing about here now. Took lot of Flukes down the Cellar yesterday. Potatoes going off badly now. Bacon 10d. lb, Bread 5½d. Baker got the Contract for the roads here at £3 0s. 0d. per annum. Holloways and Clinkards and several others got Harvest home. Cattle Plague and Cholera still continue. Latter not here. Uncle John Turrill of Stadhampton died last Saturday week and buried last Thursday. T. and J. Aldworth went from here, a grand Funeral. Wixons wife but very middling. Sue, Cousin, just called in – looks well not proud. Netta and I are still on the quiet and do not speak. Well I do just as well without her. The Plough is roofed in again and they and Crawford got an indoor Licence.[19] Lizzy went over to Milton about 2 weeks ago to Rowlands [Turrill] and stopped a day or two have been gathering plums and getting potatoes, Onions up all my time since I wrote last. Sowed the potato Ground down the Common -Turnips in.

Sept. 10th   Sunday. Had a letter this morning from Oxford and on opening it I found that it contained the Carte de Visite of Miss M. Phipp of Oxford who I had the pleasure of escorting to and up the Malvern Hills on Tuesday last. She appears to be a rollicking merry girl and tolerably good looking too. We were jolly good friends that day and I suppose I must send her my C de V in return. She never said she was going to send it, neither did I ask her – we shall see what comes of it by and by. Netta and I are merely distant friends now and I have hard matter to preserve even that. I saw and spoke to her in Oxford Market yesterday and she seemed offended at it. She was up here last night but she never spoke to me. I went to Malvern Hills last Tuesday and had a lovely day. It was a beautiful journey going and coming back. We did have a job climbing they Hills and no mistake. I thought we never should have got to the top. We went up the highest of them. I had M[atilda] Q. and M[artha] P[hipp] and when we got to the top the view more than enough repaid us the trouble of climbing. It was a magnificent view, one I shall never forget. We went back up the Witch, a natural road out through the Hills at a low point.[20] The Hills are very steep on both sides, we sat on the top of the Hill and had refreshments and enjoyed the refreshing breeze, then down and up to the Links and on going I bought 2 views of Malvern Hills and I brought away some bits of Rock, and furze and flowers from the top. The Link Hotel and Gardens is a delightful place with Terrace rising above Terrace adorned with flowers, ornamental rock-work summer houses and there was 4 bands and dancing on the circular platform and a balloon went off just as we got to the station.[21] We got home allright at 2:15 but terrible tired. I had M. all the way home and the moon shone delightful. We sang and whistled and laughed all the way by rail. Was at Oxford too soon by an hour or two. Went to A. Godfrey's to Breakfast and supper. Was at Oxford Friday and Saturday to Brewers and next day to Supervisors for Licence. I asked him if he could grant me a Licence on the certificate I had before and did not use. He said yes but I was to put the new date on. I did so and he crossed the old date out. Called at Coopers both times. Bill [Cooper?] coming down today. The weather has been hot and close all since I wrote last and today it is cloudy and looks like wet. Have not done any gardening all the week. Cricket Match tomorrow, Marston v. Garsington. We beat them before. Have been at work all day up to now. Went to Church last Sunday – Netta was up here at night. I went down to L[ong] F[urlong] and had a long talk to Mary Holloway. She seemed pleased to see me Netta and a gang came by whilst I stood there. Tom Cooper and I had a confidential chat to ourselves about his sweetheart etc. I went and looked at the Meat for Tomorrow. There is two legs of Mutton, piece of Roasting Beef and Salt, the whole weighing 48 lb at 9d. per lb. The weather looks threatening and it will be a bad day, I think. I have had the diorrhea very bad this day or two and I feel very middling altogether. Had toothache. Plum trade awful bad now. Stored Common Flukes and Onions.

Maids taking tea at the Rectory

Sept. 18th   Monday. We played Marston last Monday here and beat them with 5 wickets to go down. We had a goodish day and night closed at 12 o'clock. Meeting next night Club night. Meeting next Thursday about Feast affair. Not many there and adjourned till Thursday next. Subscription 16s. and 6d. Sent account and scores to paper account. Weather very hot now. Wixon's wife died Saturday week. Went to Thame Flower Show last Thursday with E. S[tone], E. C[linkard], E. T[urrill], E. T[urrill], S. T[urrill], A.H., J. Hatto and enjoyed myself very much.[22]

Oct. 12th   Thursday. It has rained the day before yesterday and night before but it had been hot and dry for a long while before and we want rain very bad but today it has been drying again and now, tonight, it is bright and cold. Will be a frost I think. We had a goodish meeting before the feast and we had a capital touch at Feast. The weather was delightful, quite hot in fact, like Midsummer. Taylor and I went down and the young Spearings helped us up with the tent in good time and we got the beer down before anyone was there. I sat in the tent by myself and had my dinner and soon after the company began to arrive and after that I was as busy as I could be . . . We sold nearly a barrel. Tom Smith put the flags up about round the Course and at the entrance to the Ground. He was starter and handicapper and A. Clinkard, judge. There was printed programmes and 15 races. Wheelbarrow, flat and hurdles racing, a good steeplechase and a capital Pony race which was won by Clinkard (Bob). They had a good touch over the way at night. Entrance 1/0d. for Barrell and 3d. Whip. A capital account in the paper and a good many strangers there − altogether one of the best Feasts we have had. I did not send an account to the paper about [it]. Tom Smith told me tonight he had.[23] Martha was there and I saw her several times and spoke to her and went up to Jack's next morning and delivered a missent letter. She went away that night − have not seen her since. Went home up to Jack's with her that night, met with A.H. up there too and had a chat about our quarrel. We made it up and I went down home with her. We started at 12 and got home at 1.00. Dick Belcher was there too and lost his money and next night I had a game with A.Y. in the Bar and I hold her handkerchief now − went part of the way home with her. Fight that night with Hen[ry] Quartermain and Sam Rollins − else it has been a quiet Feast. Had a capital touch on the Wednesday night − had the whip money to come in and some beer that was left. Finished up on the Saturday night all right. Next week I took my potatoes up in Q.'s G. and have been gathering Apples, Damsons and Walnuts since by daylight and pulling up Pea sticks by moonlight. Went to Oxford on the Wednesday after Feast and to Brewers. Meant to stop to Theatre but did not. T. C[ooper] would not go. Saw Albert Godfrey, told him I was going. Came home with Alfred Clinkard and to Missionary meeting on the Friday night. A terrible row with Mother and Lizzy about being out. Jane Hedges married on Monday to W. Surman of Baldon and [I'm] told Mrs Smith, Job's Mother, died and was buried here on Tuesday. Londoner down here and buying and gathering Apples, Damsons, etc. Clinkards, Druces, etc. and waggon loads are sent to Station. Have wrote twice to B. Blageons about Portrait affair. I had my Portrait taken at Simmonds on St Clements Fair Day and he promised to send it to me but has not and I have not sent for it. It seems very cold tonight. Gales' shepherd gone today and Coster and Clinkards new Carter come. Met A.H. on Tuesday week out late and last night too. Terrible deal of the Cattle Plague and all Cattle Fairs stopped and we paid 11d. per lb for Bacon and 10d. for mutton. Walnuts 9d. per

100. Backed the big tree today. Lizzy complains of her neck, it is swelled. We don't speak again. Baldon and Sandford Club draws. Spearings going to leave over the way and going to have a sale. Our boys played Cuddesdon last week and beat them in one innings and 6 runs.[24] All my straw gone. Convolvulus blows a little and avenue looks nice now and is blooming again.

Oct. 24th   It rained all day on Sunday last and is raining now and looks like it. I began planting plants over the way last Friday and finished as far as I could today. Spearings Sale on Thursday next. Uncle Richard and his wife over here today. Richard is looking very ill and tottering. Cattle Plague at Oxford. Tom Smith sent an account of our Feast and Choir Cricket Match to Chronicle and it was put in. Lizzy and I went to Hugalls and Netta, Sunday week. He gave her some medicine and liniment to paint and we went to Aunt Wixon's to tea. I painted it and burnt the skin off and she and Leo went to him yesterday and he said that I had burnt it too much and that she was to let it be till he saw it again. It is no better. He said she was well and it would get better and well. Netta was up here and Sue and Leo, I was not very well and went off to bed and left her to supper. She brought a flower up here. I met her last Thursday night and we went in the shelter and stopped till past 10. The hounds were out that day, opening day, Middling day wet and cold – killed 2 and they were out again yesterday on J. Gales and killed 2 more. Wrote a Rate out for Baker last Sunday and had 2/6 and wine. We had bottle cheap Port for 2/8 and I had some there tonight. Had letter from Ted Watson today. He was on Board Ship as an emigrant. He is married, he says. E. C[linkard] and Leo up here on Sunday and I was over at Hattos Saturday night. Uncle James here at Gale's yesterday. Killed our pig today – the smallest. A nice pig. Sent nothing to market today. Lord Palmerston died last week and buried today.[25] Weather very cold, like autumn now. Trade very slack now. All the leaves off some of Walnut trees. We went into Mrs Harper Senr. on coming home from Stadhampton and I had some wine there and Netta had supper up here. I went part of the way home with her and back.

Nov. 7th   I bought some barley of Mrs Harper Senr. altogether 3 Qt at 28/0 per quarter. On Saturday week I went to Oxford to Brewers and fetched my portraits, 2 Vignettes, 2 full length and 2 Lizzy for 5/0. I came home with Harpers and there was a terrible row that day with G. Holloway about a horse – it is all settled though now. Cousin Sue came

The Randolph Hotel and Martyrs Memorial, Oxford, 1868, from the *Illustrated London News*

up to wish us goodbye. I bought an Ironing Table and the dung and I took one load down the Common and some over to Q.'s. It was a very dear sale – a good many people there. I planted my plants down the Common last week and brought my Parsnips up today. Mother and Lizzy went to Oxford last Monday and Mrs Hatto had a son last Thursday night. They are going to leave, he got a place at the Randolph Hotel.[26] I have had a good deal of the Bakers wine lately. Opening dinner tomorrow at Railway Hotel, Wheatley.[27] Martha and Netta was up here last Tuesday week and next day they went to Oxford and had her, Netta's, Portrait taken and it was to have come home on Sunday but she has not heard anything about them yet I believe. I was down there again last Friday night and paid Mother-in-law for some Barley and had gin and water and stopped some time. She seemed in very good humour. Saw a very old Bible, 1599. Was down there again on Sunday last with Leo and L. and went to Cuddesdon Church and met her last Monday night at 7 and home by 10/9 all right. Just been down to Sellars and ordered pair of

New Shoes, and wrote to Martha Malvern [i.e. Phipp] and sent C de V. A deal of wet weather now. Lizzie went to Hugall today, no better.

Nov. 13th   Monday. It has been a beautiful drying day today but cold. It was a beautiful day yesterday. I went to church in the morning and with Leo and L. to Littlemore to meet Netta. We went to Pattie's and to John Clinkards and they had supper and I owes John Clinkard 7½d. We all started home at a good pace and got home by 9 o'clock. I met A.H. on Saturday night, she came up here to bring her Portrait. It is a fair one but not a good one. The mouth is such a difficult thing to take well in her case. I have one. We went to T.S. and we stopped till 10.10, too late. Mother asked me next morning where I had been and I told her. She said I ought to keep better time and we must keep better time for the future. We had an interesting talk going to Littlemore last night. The Cattle Plague is spreading in all directions and is at Marston I hear. Had letter from Martha this morning acknowledging the receipt of my C de V and offering an exchange. I have lately wrote a good deal of rates, etc. for Baker and he has given me 5/0 for it. Cricket Club night tonight. No fire in parlour and nobody here. Hunt dinner at Dorchester tomorrow and shoots the Copse next day. Boiled 3 copperfuls of carrots etc. for my pigs last week and they eat it really well and appear to be doing very well . . . Deuced short of money now.

Nov. 18th   Had a new pair of strong shoes last night 14/6. I docked them 6d. for plums they owed me for. Haven't seen Netta all the week. Bother with G. Holloway about poaching on the Common. Hunt dinner at Dorchester last Tuesday. Only 5 at Club last night. Got sore toe. Saw Hatto's boy t'other day.

Nov. 22nd   Netta bought some milk up here last Saturday night and an accident took place by which a coalcart with two horses fell and went down the steep bank down against Clinkard House but wonderful nothing was hurt and next day it was a wet day and Netta came up here to tea. It rained properly and she had supper and I went down home with her and stopped late too. Rogers left their house last week – gone up in Blenheim. Been boiling carrots etc. today and got [some?] together yesterday. A wonderful rough wind today, quite a hurricane. It blew a Plum tree down over the way [at] Spearing[s] and smashed a window. Finished the sack of meal yesterday morning. Went Birding last night and several disasters.

Dec. 3rd   Sunday. It has been wet weather since I wrote last, the Foxhounds tried the Copse last Monday – nothing – and we shot it on · Friday, killed 34 rabbits. I had 2 rabbits at 2/0 – a row about it. Pitted the Mangolds and Turnips on Tuesday. Down to Nettas . . . house on Wednesday night, home 9. Mary Ann Harper died on Friday morning and Lizzy bought her New concertina yesterday. Heard about Netta's bad leg. Wednesday night told her to see a doctor before she came out of Oxford. She did not and I wrote a note to Hugall to tell him to call and see her the first time he came by there. Got the dung away over the way and Mrs Hatto churched and boy christened Joseph William today. Bill Abell and Hester Pym asked in church today. The Cattle Plague is spreading now – no cases here yet. Cleaned the hen house and pigsties out. Been a short walk with Netta tonight – her leg is better. Mother was very middling a day or two back but is better now. Steeplechase Denton, Thursday.

Dec. 18th   The weather continues very open and mild and dry now. Went to Oxford to Brewers Saturday, in today. Went to Oxford . . . last Sunday and to Abingdon yesterday to see a doctor. Saw him and was

The County Hall and Market-place at Abingdon, *c.* 1887

examined and had certificate. Home, dined and to Church where I was
took very middling – fainted. J. Harper home, haven't seen Netta for
some time now – only at Market. We have met else once a week before.
Drawed the Club. I had £2 3s. 10½d. Went to London last Tuesday to
the Giffords and Cattle Show. Got home by 12 o'clock. Enjoyed myself.
Cricket supper tomorrow night. Finished boiling for my pigs, had dancing
draw night and talk with A.Y. The Cattle Plague is spreading but not here
yet. Mrs Lowe got a boy. Pointer came home Saturday. Hugall called and
saw Mother's leg and sent some ointment. It is better. Saw the concert
show Saturday.

Dec. 27th　The weather is wonderful mild, no frost and no sign of any
yet. It has been dry since I wrote last and today it has rained a little. We
had a supper here Christmas Tuesday. A Roast Pig which Baker gave.
Fairish night. Netta was here, we had a good touch Cricket supper but
not many Cricketers here. Baker tight. They done the Ground up
Tuesday. I saw Netta on Sunday and she was in a awful way about a tale
she had heard about me and she said we must part. I wrote and told her I
was willing and she burnt the note and is willing to make it up again I
expect. Lizzy was at Leo's Sunday night and at Netta last night and
stopped all night. Netta told her Mother about our sweethearting and she
don't disapprove of it. She seemed very unhappy, A.H. about it I wrote
last night. I bought some Plumcake time ago . . . Feast today Sold my
pigs to Baker. I have sold nothing for a good while. Mother was very
middling on Sunday and has been all the week. Her eye and cough has
been so bad and she is in a poor way. A. Godfrey and Mrs and . . . here
Christmas and the London Gang and young Trump.

1866

Makes up quarrel – cattle plague at Baldon – does clerical work for James Aldworth – Professor Rogers is temporary curate – A.H. ill – exchanges diaries with Tom Cooper – becomes tax collector – sums up year and contemplates marriage prospects.

Jan. 9th   I have not wrote in my diary for some time. The weather has been wet and very rough but no frost tonight. It freezes very sharp, very rough yesterday. Netta and I made it up and go on as bad as ever. We made it up N[ew] Y[ear's] day. She was up here on Sunday night. I sold my pigs to Baker and got the money Saturday. I bought a new overcoat and leggings. Rode home with Netta and her mother. Went to Sandford Club last night. All In. Home by 2 o'clock. The cattle plague is spreading in all directions. It is at Cuddesdon and nearly all round us but not here yet. All the markets and moving horned stock is stopped altogether not even from one farm to another yard. Thousand took last week. It is spreading very fast and awful.

Feb. 10th   The weather has been very rough and on Sunday night it blew and lightened and thundered quite a hurricane. We had some snow for a day or two. Some lark shooting, not much. But no frost and I saw some potatoes growing in the open ground yesterday. We haven't had a single frost yet.[1] Netta sold their market horse and obliged to go by the carrier now. Has had a bad cold about a fortnight ago. Better now. I had a bad eye this week, better now. Have been busy writing rates etc. for the Baker lately. Got all the books up here. The cattle plague is spreading in all directions.[2] No case here at present . . . Don't dare move cattle, hay, straw, dung, skins or anything at all to do with cattle now, but it still spreads and the farmers are frightened to death about it – 10 or 11,000 a week now. Bought and planted Briars this week, 60. Done the garden up and planted it today. Was with Netta Wednesday. Aurora Borealis bright. Have had the toothache. Moved dung out of Spearings yard last Tuesday. Feb. 6th last G. Hinton owed 1/4½. Sent some greens and shallots to market today.   Mrs R. Druce died and was buried last Tuesday. Jack's wife had a son short time ago and Willgress a daughter last Wednesday and Poll Townsend a son last Friday. E. C[linkard], T. S[mith], E. S[tone] perched in bar last Sunday. Have only one night moonlight down the Common this year. Netta and I meet once a week now. Wonderful mild and wet.

Feb. 23rd It was a tight frost yesterday morning and it was two or three mornings ago but that is all the frost we have had this year. New tenant over the way up gardening today. Went to Holcombe sale yesterday. Saw Netta the night before – ugly humour. G. Holloway's wife had a daughter yesterday. Stuck notice up on church door Sunday. Tailor came back. Trade deuced slack now. Saw Hatto in his uniform on Monday. Weather very wet. Cattle Plague not here yet.

April 22 I have planted Q.'s Garden and the Garden D[own] the Common all but a bit top of the Lower piece in which the P[ea] sticks are and I began sharpening and moving them last night. My first planting of peas up in full drill and look well and the onions are up in drill and Parsnips. The ground is dry now and the weather is beautiful now and drying. Planted the row of pickling cabbage side of Lower Piece last week and K.B. last night. Got one more row of peas to plant in Common and a few potatoes and that's all. I have done planting everything then. The first planting of peas *ought not to be pressed down*. Hoed cabbage and lettuce plants yesterday, look well. Cut first cabbage in G. and Q.G. on 20th. Small but good, and pulled first lettuce in Q.G. 1 dozen, Good. Going to pull a lot tomorrow morning. Capital bit of lettuce and early Cabbage are turning in now. Stuck the peas in cabbage plants last Thursday and Friday and planted K.B. on 17th and Flukes in Q.G. on 16th. Peas and Shallotts and onions up well but rhubarb backward. Potatoes coming up and plum and damson trees out in bloom but not much this year. Plenty of greens and the broccoli is all over and I pulled the green stuff up. The briar stocks shooting well and tulips out in blossom. The flower garden looks gay now. The garden wants hoeing. Bees work well now and shudded three trees in garden and sowed celery seed . . . Cut mustard and cress. The weather, after a very long touch of wet, has set in dry with beautiful warm days and cool nights. I am very busy gardening now and collecting taxes and rates.[3] Went round last week and collected £11-0-0 and I am always writing and messing about with the Baker now. I have got a lot more to collect and shall have half the pay this year. I see Nett every now and then but she appears very uncomfortable and unsettled at home with

J[anaway]. I bought Qt of beans for £2-2-0 and half ton straw for £1-0-0
last Wednesday night. Left off wearing a cravat yesterday and am going to
Great Milton tomorrow to a sale there for Gale and Franklin. Can't buy
any pigs.

April 28th Bought 6 pigs last Wednesday 4 at 24/0 and 2 at 26/0 each.
I got 2 at 24/0 and 2 at 26/- so that I owe Baker for [my] pigs £5-0-0.
The least are the best pigs. I had them bring directly and done styes up
and put them in and with the exception of the two over the way who
cough, they are going on allright. Very clear. Went round money
hunting again last night and got some more tickets today. The weather
has been very warm this last day or two and now it rains well and looks
like it. I have sowed some convolvulus, aster and stock seed today and
stuck nearly all my peas in Q.G. and some down the Common. Poll
Townsend's baby died yesterday. Saw Netta Thursday night, it was a
beautiful night, warm, moon light and dry. The nightingales singing
lovely. We stopped and talked latish Frank Nailsman here. A good deal
of excitement and interest just now about the Reform Bill.[4] It is
expected to be settled now. Jack Thomson married last Tuesday at
Chiselhampton. Sent 17 dozen of lettuce to market and 2 dozen
cabbages. Went to Great Milton sale last Monday and had a good hard
days work of it but I didn't mind it much. The trees are coming out in
leaf and the plum and early fruit trees are out well now but there is not
much blossom this year. Onions are up in Q.G. and Common and G.
well and potatoes are up but rather straggling – growing well. Wheat
looks yellow. E. Clinkard and Liz and I sat down the garden last night
and they sang and played. Beautiful night. Mrs Harper Sen. is much
against our courting now, for what reason I don't know. Heard from
Ted Watson, he is got over there all right but can say nothing else yet.
Bought broccoli. Snows Early White, Winter and dwarf chrysanthemums,
Turnip and carrot seed today. Planted row of peas and finished potatoes
down common yesterday.

Sunday, April 29th The Reform Bill was passed on Saturday morning
at half past 3 o'clock by a majority of 5 only, 318 for to 313 against it.
Two wonderful speeches by Mr Gladstone and Disraeli. I have put my
money right this morning. It rains and looks like it. Went down to Nettas
last night and took sacks for corn and saw Nett.

Wednesday Had bats handled.

Friday, six Done Cricket Club book up. Owes Harper 10/- (paid) and
Old Tom for some Myatts. 1 peck. Mother and I out of sorts again. Mrs
Clark over the way came back and brought a little boy with her. No
cricketing of a Sunday now. Tom S[mith] and Emma C[linkard] are
wonderful thick again. See the young Slades sometimes up here. No sale
for potatoes. Things grow very fast.

May 10th The weather since has been partly wet and partly dry but not
very hot and things grow very fast now. Hoed onions and shallots and
sowed flower peas and am doing the path round pig stye up a bit. Club
meeting last Tuesday and saw Nett last night. Stopt late. Went to Oxford,
Monday, and saw Joe Hatto and got home and done Parish books up
allright in [for?] Collector.[5] This year 5 new members in Club, 2 young
Slades. John Druce was not well on Monday, had Doctor Hugall. Better
now. Threatened war with Austria and Prussia.[6]

May 14th Paid Mrs Harper for ton straw and Qr Beans, £3-2-0,
Saturday night 12th and had it home that day. Saw Netta − promised to
come to tea but did not. Went cricketing − Tom Cooper came up here
and played with us. Sent for some grains today. Moulded potatoes today.
Went to Church yesterday. Waist high . . . Yesternight the cuckoo and
nightingale sing lovely and the apple trees are out splendidly now. The
plum blossom over. The K.B. up at home but not down C. Peasticks
blown about much now and potatoes up very irregular in Q.G. Sell a
good many potatoes and cabbage out retail now, good currant bloom.
War threatened. Bank broke O.G. & Co for 60,000,000.[7] Weather very
cold and gloomy now. Sold all lettuce at home. No Carrot seed up in Q.
yet. Peas look well the last planting down Common come up well now −
all stuck. No Nobs down the common Cricketing Sundays now.

June 2nd The weather, after a spell of dry, has set in wet again. Finished
the path round the pigsty in Q.G. I made new rates out last week. Hoed
garden all over and hoed part of Common over, Saturday night. Went to
Oxford last Sunday night about keys 5/- and last night we went to
Cuddesdon to see Lary. Went on shameful there and got home 9 o'clock.

June 18th The weather has been very wet and gloomy and cold. It is
growing but not summer weather. I have been busy moulding the
potatoes down the Common this last week and doing rate books up, and
planting asters and marrow plants. The snails are a precious plague. The

carrots look well down the Common – hoed them last Saturday. Terrific storm of rain and wind blowed things about well. No potatoes took up yet – try them tomorrow. Nelly [Stone?] has been up here – got a place at Kensington and is going next week. I was took middling on Saturday but am better now – cold and rheumatic. Wrote to Ted Watson today and cleaned pigs out. Had Nett and Mr and Mrs Harper up here last night and stopped and chatted a good while. Our cricketers are gone to Watlington to play today but it has been a miserable day, so wet. I was unwell and did not go. I think they will get licked though. The peas grow wonderfully well now and there are a good many apples this year and potatoes look well but very toppy. Netta went to Letcombe about a fortnight ago and I was to have went but I did not and went to Cuddesdon and saw Joe and Lary and the next Sunday Joe came over to dinner and stopped till supper – Mother don't like it.

June 28th The weather has been beautiful lately, very hot and hay making is about now. Very busy. Oxford Match cricket last Monday – fairish day and party. Garsington got beat well. Take a good many potatoes up now. Very good they are too. Expect brewers in today. Saw Rifle Corps in Oxford on Wednesday. Budded yellow rose yesterday. Saw Netta Wednesday night – was rate collecting. Went down home the back [way] and there saw Bonny and Tiggy fishing in Jos Gales pond. We stood and watched them till they saw us and then they watched us. Home soon after eleven. Saturday Club day at Sandford. War has commenced with Italy, Prussia and Austria. Corn and bread has rose – Bread 6½ now. Bought new suit Wednesday and had my Sunday cords washed yesterday. Ben Clarke's wife died last Tuesday morning after a day's illness and buried last night. No ripe fruit in. The government resigned office on Tuesday night. Wrote and posted a letter to Ted Watson last Saturday. Taylor started off to London last Wednesday. The weather looked gloomy this morning. Pigs alright. Began the other sack of meal last Sunday.

July 1st It has rained all the day on and off and thundered very heavy but want it fine now. Peas nearly fit. Dug basket of potatoes up today to go in tomorrow – some very nice ones. Made ginger beer and washed the corks and Netta is up here.

July 8th Planted celery out last week and Saturday potatoes 3/0 bushel, peas 9d. Ripe fruit coming in. Gathered first raspberries last Friday. Kidney Beans out in bloom well. Weather this last week has [been] very wet indeed. No hay-making done at all. Netta has been up here two or three times this last week and I went over to Hugalls last Thursday night and brought some medicine and he came on Saturday and said she [Mother] was very ill and would not get any better he thought. Sent pills and cod liver oil. She seems a little better, but not much. A g up last night a good many cricketers. Last night went to Sandford club. Enjoyed myself much, had A.Y. all the afternoon. There and back with Willises. 1s. 0d. Harpers up here last night and Matilda Q. Went up to see her.

July 10th   It has been beautiful weather this week. Hot. A good deal of hay carried this week. Neddy Hurst and his horse both died in one day, yesterday. Nett stopped till 10 o'clock in Bar. Can get no buds. War over, I think. Lord Derby's government in now. Wheat up. Bread 6½. Gathered first ripe Goose[berries?].

July 22nd   Sunday. I haven't been to church for some time now. I did think I should have gone today but I have had such a bad handsting and obliged to sling him [put hand in sling]. Went to Oxford yesterday to Brewers and called at Coopers and asked Tom up to tea. He's just come up. Mother is rather better – gets up a little now. Doctor has been several times to see her and, although she is better, she will not get much better I think. The fruit is all in and all wants gathering together and the peas are all fit and want gathering too. I gathered 9 bushels for Saturday and there is as many left now. Dick Belcher and W. Harper over here today and Bella is not come. Peas in Q.G. all over and potatoes – early – are too. Weather very hot and close. We played the return match with Watlington last Monday and they beat us again but on the first innings only. Not time to play it out and they went off as soon as they had had their dinner; and in Saturday's Oxford Times they put a proper setting down for Garsington and they are going to put an answer in, I think.[8] We had to get the dinner ourselves, and Netta was up here and stopped all night and I expect her up here tonight again. She made the puddings and we got on very well. I think we play again next Wednesday 'Foresters'. Cholera is about.

July 29th, 1866   The weather up to yesterday has been dry and warm but after threatening all [day?] it poured about 1 o'clock this morning and has been showery all day and cool. I shot 5 birds N and Sth yesterday and 1 flying this morning. I got Slades double gun and a ripper it is too. Bella and Nett was up here on Wednesday night, didn't stop though and I saw

Members of the Wheeler family, who took over from the Turrills, outside the Red Lion

her last night – took notices round. Netta was up here last Sunday night to supper. I had a bad hand-sting bad for three or four days and Tom Smith wrote to and had an answer about the Watlington match but they don't give way. They gave us a awful stinger in the O. Times. Saw George's baby yesterday, grown. Going to play Foresters tomorrow – get licked again no doubt.[9] Fruit all ripe now – gathered the main of my peas now and a good deal of fruit. Had a wine bibbing touch at Slades t'other day. John's lady has been down here. Lizzy Edwards down here. Pigs alright now. Went to church today, haven't been for some time. I heard Mr Rogers for the first time today.[10] He is a bold speaking professional man – very good. A tremendous lot of apples and a good many walnuts but not much fruit. Potatoes bad sale and appear to be going off with the complaint. The cholera is about bad now and no doubt it will spread. The war is suspended, an armistice, 8 days. Riots in Hyde Park[11] last Monday night and Taylor sent Mother 2 soles down today. He was here last Sunday. Smiths carried Oat Piece rye and Holloways carried some oats in Motterills this last week. Harvest will begin this week, rather a short yield expected – Kidney Bean. Avenue just in its glory now. Began my last sack of meal last Monday. Cousin Ellen down at home. Aunt John died last Sunday. Uncle James came to see Mother last Tuesday night. Taylor sent me Bell's life.[12] Wears the new suit now. Measured for a new pair of boots last week. Onions going off – blighty – and shallots want taking up now. Some potatoes ripe, taking up flukes for eating now – good. Very few K.B. yet.

August 13th, 1866   The weather lately has been very dull, cold, gloomy and windy. The Harvest has commenced in good earnest now and Clinkard R. was carrying Saturday wheat. Finished gathering my currants and those in G., Friday and nearly all the Goo[seberries]. Had meal home Friday. Quartermain doing Clinkard's barn up. To Oxford yesterday. E. Harper fighting Saturday. Netta up here late Saturday night. Getting shallots up today and gathered first plums today.

August 17th   Took shallots up this week ought to have been up long ago. Gathered plums.

Sunday, August 19th   Fine day, warm and dry. Harvest operations in full swing now. G. Holloway carrying all night. No cricketing now. Meeting at school last Tuesday about Cholera. Cogan, Rogers etc. there and Inspectors round yesterday. No cholera cases in Oxford yet, one here.

Plums 5d. Qt. Cleaned and moulded celery yesterday. Cleaned pigs out today. Cholera better in London now. Took shallots up in roses today. Fox's party over here. Nett won't come up now. Potatoes gone off bad. Wheat carried. The war is over – an armistice now. Cholera better. Done all the Parish work now. Took some of my Myatts Ashleafs up down the Common and they are very bad. I think it will be a bad year. I sold all my potatoes the best to Baker for 4/0 per sack. The Atlantic cable is laid complete and works well. The cattle plague is at Baldon but not here yet. Jack had a row with his wife about money last Sunday. Received letter from London last week from Giffords. Rode home with Big un last Saturday week. Tom Cooper up here, came up to tea. No apricots this year and not many Plums. Peas all over. First noticed T[om] S[mith] and E[mma] about a fortnight ago – Baldon Feast. Cabbages up. Few have gone.

Friday, September 7th   The weather for the past week has been awfully wet. It has rained every day and I should think that a good deal of the white corn is damaged and there is a smart bit out yet. Mrs Harper has not cut any barley yet. Went down there last night to tell her about the Income Tax affair.[13] I have not seen or heard anything of Netta for some time and last night I thought I should. However, it appears she is very ill and has been and Dr Hugall attends her. I did not ask much about it and in fact I did not know till just as I was starting home. I shall know more about it tonight by Dinah. I felt rather down about it and I wrote a note for her by E. I don't know how long she has been ill. Tom Cooper was up here Sunday week and went to church with me and at night he left his diary with me to look at and he looked at mine and a highly interesting thing it was. It was as I expected, that there was a deeper inner life within him which the outside world never saw or suspected and veiled beneath an apparently cold and heartless exterior there beats a warm and sympathetic heart, and although in his love affairs he has trusted too much to his heart and not enough to his head, it has never led him off the path of virtue and little to regret, much less to repent of. He appears to have loved with all the earnestness and depth of a strong and abiding love, love such as a man can feel but once in his life, and if he too has found out that the loved one was of the earth, earthy, caring more for his than him, his experience has been the counterpart of many more; with perhaps much more to regret than he has. Of his first, his boyish love, I know nothing. His second – she was mercenary. Of his third no real love such as will stand the test of ridicule, sneering, adversity which will patiently abide its time; implicitly trusting the honourable word of an honourable man. Alice Hale is a mystery to me and I think that Tom himself was wanting there. If she had loved him for eighteen months all unseen or unsought by its object, it seems so strange when that love was won, that she should reject it for no apparent object or reason. Perhaps he has lost all faith in the love or word of the sex altogether and she could see that his heart was not wholly or solely all her own. Well Alice, may that be one of the few things you will never regret. Tom has loved not wisely but too well. His resolve to forsake the sex now and all is, I believe, the best if we could but think so always. His home at present is not all sunshine and roses it appears but if he steadily and sternly perseveres with his object which I suspect is to obtain a competency, always keeping a keen eye to the main chance, never turning to the right or left but straight to his own appointed end, he will yet win a loving wife and a happy home in every sense of the word and show to the world that still waters run deep. Bill [Cooper?] appears to have forgot Garsington and Garsington people. I rather suspect some of the really happiest period of his life was spent in Garsington but we are all separated now all over the world and out of sight, out of mind. Tom is about the only one who seems left or who cares about the old place or people and perhaps he soon may forget. It rained last Sunday night and he did not come up and it has rained ever since till today, 7th, and a proper lot of rain too. Went to Crown Inn, Wheatley, Thursday to [be] sworn in Assessor for Income Tax and bring papers back. There 5 hours. Delivered notices to Gale and Baker. Gale returned his back. Put notice on Church door Sunday, got to put some on tomorrow. Saw E. and someone. Sunday night was reading and writing all the evening – thunderstorm. Tom Sellar still very ill, I don't think he will get over it. Elias Woodward of the Plough died last Monday week, August 28th. Buried 31st. No alteration that I can see. Nett came up here last night for a walk. She is in a fearfully low nervous state, very middling indeed, but she tries to make the best of herself. She is better than I expected though. Talks of going to market tomorrow, Saturday. Fool if she do. Paid Baker £4.5s.0 for corn Thursday, all paid up to now. Mother still continues about the same, but a vast deal better than she was. Very little to market this week. Plums all over now.

Sept. 8th and damsons – first apples fall very much now. K.B. nearly over – potatoes bad – celery grows well now. Asters, F[rench] Marigolds and Marrows come in now. Took onions up in Q.G. this week. Turnip seed up in C.G. and weeds too. Cabbage bed very thin indeed, not many.

Lettuce gathered, some peas yesterday in Common. Apples cheap and potatoes too. A good many walnuts. Meeting next Tuesday night about Garsington Feast affair, dull go this year, I think. Harvest Home Feast come to nought. Delivered Nuisances Notices last week and the Inspector left 2 bottles Burnetts disinfectant fluid here for the use of the Parish.[14] Nearly all the Parish Noticed I think. Baker took to his mill Saturday and is very busy now with it. I wrote the contract out for him, nought for it though. War over in Germany. Peace now. Cholera getting better fast now and cattle plague. Lizzy Edwards married to Bateman of Bampton Monday week. George and Lizzy went and stopped 3 or 4 days, no chance for going now therefore and E. and C. are thick. Bother Saturday last about Watson's shooting hares on Harwell. Tiggy and Alfred Woodward entered names as policemen.

Sept. 10 Tom Cooper up here last and Dan. Did not come to tea and did not stop long. Took his diary back – did not take mine. A suit coming up Sunday. He appears to have got over his sweethearting but he must not make too sure. Saw A.H. last night, well again. No B[illet] D[oux] or word. Did not go to church yesterday. Messing about all day. Rained like fun again last night. Fox hounds at Coombe this morning. Milton men over here last night about tent. Let them have it for 5/0. Watson shaky. Nothing to do for the Parish. Taylor came down Saturday.

Friday, Sept. 14th It has rained ever since I wrote last. Rains now and looks like it. The corn is grown now and a good deal will be and is now completely spoilt. Bread rose halfpenny Wednesday, 6½. Dinah, E. C[linkard], E. T[urrill], T. C[ooper], F. W[atson] and Dad went to Thame Flower Show yesterday. Although gloomy it did not rain. They enjoyed themselves very much they said. Came up here last night and stopped and Liquored. Tent brought back last and paid for it. It don't appear hurt – one iron broke. Had confidential chat with Mrs A[ldworth] and Hattie last night . . . [15] Nett was up here on Wednesday night – had not been up for a month. She seems alright again now. Went to market Sat. Have not heard about the Income Tax yet. Sent lot of corn to Mill yesterday - Baker's mill. Mother and Nett seem alright again. Went down home with her and it rained every step of the way. Got plastered and wet. I should think she got well set down. Might see her Sunday, and then I shall know. Gathered all our damsons Tuesday, half bushel. Meeting about Feast Friday. Started well. Gathered £1.10.0 at Club. Put lists up and adjourned till next Tuesday. Tom Smith is going to put account in

Paper this week. Old Stone would not let us have the Slaughter House and I don't know what we shall do about it. Had a good party and closed about 12 o'clock. Began taking my onions up, down the Common yesterday and someone had stole some of the largest of them. Shall get really behind with the gardening. It is awful wet and keeps on so. Very rough weather.

Sept. 20th It was fine Wednesday and yesterday up till 3 o'clock when it came a drenching shower and that is about the only fine weather we have had since middle of August. There was a good deal of corn carried yesterday about and I have heard the merry cry of Harvest Home but there is still a good bit out yet and in very bad condition. Barley was 1/0, some wheat sold at 15/0/0. John Druce's pig died yesterday, I think of the lung disease and should not wonder if it sweeps the lot off about here. They stuck and dressed it but I think it is good meat, about 7 score. Ours are alright. Had meal home from the bakers yesterday, not much though. I thought he is very busy with his Mill now. Toddy [?] is Miller's man. Went off cubhunting down to Bushey Copse Monday morning. Beautiful sport and beautiful morning. Killed one at Bushey – found again in the Break and saw him and caught him in Dorchester field. Saw plenty of foxes there, went all about the Break. Saw Jacky Thompson's wife. What a little young looking thing she is. Good horsewoman too. Getting on well with the Feast affair for the amusement Fund but not very swift with the Barrell fund. Meeting again tonight about it but the weather is awful bad for athletic sports. Have not seen anything of Nett since or heard of her. I went to the Meet but she did not come and I haven't seen or heard anything about her – wonder too – or perhaps she is ill again. The onions want taking up bad now but it is so continually wet that there is no chance to. Walnuts want backing now and pippins gathering.

Sunday, Sept. 23rd It has been fine today, the only fine day we have had for a month and tomorrow is Garsington Feast. I hope it will be fine. We had a meeting last Thursday night and agreed upon the Programme, prizes etc. We got on well for subscriptions but the old cove over the way won't let us have the Slaughterhouse and that will be a licker. We have had cards of the races and programmes printed and if it should be a fine day it will be a jolly one. Tom Smith was not well enough to go to Oxford yesterday, got a bad throat, but is better today. Pointer went and Mrs Smith and bought the prizes. I went to town and to County Hall for licence and Brewers paid. Had dinner, up into the Market, saw no-one and off home. Walked to Bennet's School and then rode home with cousin George.[16] Had hair cut. Saw Tom Cooper on bridge in cart. Saw Netta Thursday night – up here to supper. Had mistook the meet. Saw her for about an hour Friday night. Might see her tonight. Tom Cooper up here again tonight. Hasn't been here for some time before. He is looking at my diary. He is the only one besides me that ever saw it I believe and he, I suppose, will be the last. However, I can trust him. Gone cricketing tonight. Harvest Home not yet – it is so wet and cold. Took my onions up yesterday and up in the garret today. Backed walnuts Friday – 3 trees very good. Bacon rank. Looks like wet. Cleaned pigs out today. Harpers going to Blewbury tomorrow, first day out this time.

Oct. 6th, Sunday The weather, after a wonderful spell of wet, has been dull and gloomy for the last few days but today it is a beautiful afternoon, bright and sunny and still, quite a treat. The bees and insects are as busy as summer but everything now wears an Autumn look about it. The leaves are falling fast and it all has a dull, dreary appearance which says as plainly as possible that the beautiful summer, with all its beauties and glories, its flowers, its song birds, cuckoo, nightingale and the freshness and bloom of the year, is dead, irretrievably gone and numbered amongst those things of which only the remembrance is left. But how short seems the time since I first heard the cuckoo this year and what a time it seems before I may hear it again. I heard the welcome cry of Harvest Home. T. A[ldworth]! But there is a good deal [left] out yet, quite spoiled. Our Feast passed off first rate this year. It rained well all the morning but cleared up about ten o'clock and with exception of one shower was fine all the rest of the day. We got the tent up and beer down allright ready and waiting and began at 2 o'clock and continued rattling away till sunset. There was plenty of racing and good too but the Pony race was a tame affair, Tom Clinkard winning easily. I [was working?] all day but went on the ground just as I was. We done about as well as I expected we should. We got Clinkards barn fitted up and the evening meeting there and a jolly one it was. There was a good company there and a good many nobs there. Professor Rogers was there – Chairman – and very jolly and pleased he seemed too Dr Hugall and some more and in fact it was a first rate party. They had plenty of beer there and had a Kilderkin to come in on the Wednesday night and on that night there was quite another muster down on the ground again where there were more races and a match with Murphy's pony, and John Yates, Rogers and daughter was there, on horseback, and Evans and Beck, and a jolly party

School children round Garsington cross, 1902

they were and no mistake. Such fun and cheering. I saw Netta up here on the Monday night and I was standing outside talking to her when who should come up but her mother, Mrs Harper and Harper and caught us standing there. I never saw Mrs Harper . . . up street before in my life and they would have come in but there was no room and I went down part of the way down home with them but soon back and at it till 2 o'clock in the morning. She came up the next night and helped us a bit and stopped to supper. Dinah was raking about somewhere and I have not seen her since. Aunt Susan up here now and Mother is not so well again up late etc. Bad. Tom Cooper up here. Diary searching. Earthed celery up this last day or two, it wanted [it] too, and backed a lot of walnuts and a proper bad trade they are too, about 2/6 per thousand. Dad is bad now. Hudding and doing about. The Potatoes are awfully bad, more than half. Mistake about the meal with Baker last Thursday week, done with his meal. Had straw home from Mother-in Laws Monday. Joe Clark paid me his rent last night. Lot of Christening Feast Monday. Counted the people at Church today. There was 139 beside school children. It was for the Bishop. Wet today. Rogers was there still and will keep on a little longer. I think he was hunting with our harriers here on Friday last. They killed one but a short run. And in the Feast week we had a day on the Hills but could not find till we got to Buswell's field. Had a short sharp run of half an hour and killed on Osborne's hill. But we are fearfully short of hares this year. Haven't put a plant out this year. Apples want gathering. Harper taking his potatoes up and planting plants. Tom initiated into the Order of Foresters.[17] Cattle plague nearly all over but sheep plague increasing. Cholera stationary – some days up and some days down. Bennet got Dicky Wheelers house and Jack Tradesman got Daniel Dai's allotment down the Common. Have not seen the Baker's party all the week. A long but somewhat faulty account in this week's Chronicle about our Feast affair.[18] Tom Smith's doings and of course he and his party get all the praise – so be it.

Nov. 5th, Saturday night   Just saw and had a long confidential chat with A.H. Took her book, church service, down. She was up here last Sunday to tea according to promise. Stopped to supper and straight down home. Had wine. No. 1 fairish. Had thought about going to Oxford to T. C[ooper] else. Shocking affair at Little Milton. A young man Hurst committed suicide.[19] Shot himself about his sweetheart. A very sad affair indeed. His mother kept his letters and caused it, it appears. Done the Parish books last night and tonight. Baker is gone down to Joe Gales to get them signed. I hope he will too – as they are. Old Charley Pym and cousin Brooks Turrill died short time back. Old Druce had a sale up at his old place. Has left it and gone to live with Bob.

Nov. 11th, Sunday night The weather after a few days fine has been wet again. It poured last night, a good one. I finished getting my potatoes up yesterday, a moderately fair lot. I sold my two pigs over the way last Thursday to Baker and he killed them. We led them out with a string onto the road and up to the Butchers and killed and weighed them there. 10–18 and 10–11. Very dear to me. I moved the other two with them in the afternoon and killed one of our pigs the day before – a nice little pig too – and I salted them and last Tuesday Baker and I went to the Workhouse to meet the Auditor. He was fearfully late and Baker went off to Thame Market and I got through all right and to Wilgress's to see him about Rates and Taxes – not at home. Down to Oxford with Fletcher to Brewers meet and T. C[ooper]. Paid owed and to T.C.'s. Stopped a little while and to Halls for Rates and Taxes – got them. Off home. At work till late and off again to Wheatley on Friday to pay the Assessed and Land Tax - got through allright and met Uncle Richard there. Got home at two. Paid £65 and have finished taking my p[otatoes?] up and began taking coley [cauliflower] up. Began Saturday week. Very good and very cheap. Have been busy Collecting lately and Baker and I have not settled up yet. T. Cooper has been up here tonight with Dan. He did not seem in the best of humour, he said Bill was come up to Garsington but I have not seen anything of him as yet. It was a sharp frost yesterday morning and looks like it now. Wood hunted. Short of cash. Met A.H. t'other night and we had a long talk about things – home in good time. No trade for apples. Trump's girl's got a son. 8.30 o'clock – fine.

Sunday night, November 18th The weather has alternated wet and dry all the last week and yesterday morning and night it froze very sharp indeed but wet this morning and all day. I finished getting all the potatoes up yesterday – boiled some little ones. These appear full and very good ones too and the pigs eat them and are doing well now. I gave them the last of the beans yesterday and I shall give them no more. Took up 5 doz. of celery for Saturday – wants going now. Apples awful bad trade – no sale for anything and our Markets are up again and bread will rise again no doubt as there has been so much wet that there is no chance of a good crop next year. Had our coal home last week. It cost £2.10.0. Paid. Baker and I settled up last Friday. He done me as usual but I will have it straight

with him now if he don't look out. Saw A.H. at the meet on Wednesday
night and she just came up here now but didn't stop and I went down
home with her and back again. I went down to Sellars last week, had
shoes . . . and saw Tom. He is better but still very bad, a awful leg and the
result is doubtful yet, I think. Rogers preached a good sermon today. Not
many there. Finished sorting the apples. Pigs very cheap indeed £10 6/2
each. Nice pigs. Very little hunting now, shooting stays however.

Nov. 25th Sunday night. Tom hasn't been up tonight. It has been fine,
or nearly so, for a whole week – what a wonder – but still the Markets go
up and the bread is risen in price, 7½d. now.[20] All sorts of corn and stock
is rising and the prospect is high prices. There has been tremendous floods
in the north of England – much damage done.[21] Had a deal with Murphy
last Wednesday, sold a good deal of [coley?] this last week and two sacks
of potatoes to Harpers for £1.0.0 and they gave me a bad sovereign. I
took it back just now. I have been looking potatoes out over the way and
doing carrots by moonlight all the week. Took all my carrots up and
topped them and shall take the Parsnips up tomorrow I think. A very
sharp frost on Tuesday and Wednesday but none since. Saw Nett Friday
night. Was behind the meet [arrived late?]. Neighbours Clarkes went
away to Frilford [?] Wednesday. Income Tax meeting at Crown Inn
Wednesday next. Combe wood sale Monday – did not go cheap this year.
Dressed my pigs today and cleaned them up a bit. Lizzy Aldworth, or
rather Mrs G. Holloway, came up to tea Monday night and stopped some
time and I armed her home and stopped up there to supper but I would
not go in.[22] How things change. Watson sold everything and sacked his
men.[23]

Sunday, December 9th The weather has been wet and cold and
rough but not very wintry at present. Nothing of importance has occurred
since I wrote last. I have been busy getting my carrots etc. up together
and pitting them and boiling potatoes and yesterday I boiled carrots and
tonight my pigs got out of the stye and led me a chase about the gardens
but I got them in. Mrs Harper and I fell out last Tuesday about a sack of
potatoes and I have not been there since. I expect I have done there. Sold
Murphy some apples t'other day and wrote Income Tax book out and
been rate hunting and last Saturday I took our clock to pieces and put him
up again. He goes very well but does not strike right. Took nearly all my
shallots up. Grand Trades Union demonstration in London last Monday.[24]
Had a capital touch hunting here last Monday. The fox ran from the

copse up through the Grounds, through our yard and ½ way to Combe, and back, and lost him in Tom Aldworth's field. Harrier hunting Thursday here but not much of a run. Dinah went to Oxford Saturday week. Looked my potatoes all over in the cellar over the way. Was very middling last night, a fearful headache. Markets here up very high – wheat £17 per load and bread is now 7½ pence a loaf and wages 10/0 and less. It makes trade very dull indeed. Joe Clarks party is not come back yet. Rogers here today.

Sunday, December 16th The weather for the past week has been wet, dull and cold but no frost, and up to now the winter has been very mild but excessively wet. A dreadful colliery accident at the Barnsley colliery, 400 lives lost. Another in Staffordshire, nearly 100.[25] A fearful and appalling affair. They were nearly every one killed that was in the pit and some of the workings extended for two miles underground. Subscriptions about for the relief of the widows and orphans. John Quartermain of Gotham [Farm] died last Tuesday, I think buried yesterday. He was ill only a very short time – rapid consumption. Not a very gay account of his son John. The cattle plague appears to be breaking out again fearfully in various parts of kingdom and I am afraid it is going to spread again. If it do it will be a very bad job indeed. Market is looking up again. Wheat crop promises so bad, so much wet. French troops withdrawn from Rome. Fenianism about pretty much in Ireland, expects a rising there. Haven't done much gardening this week, so wet. Began hoeing the garden. Mended pig sty and pulled pea sticks up by moonlight. See Nett every now and then – am going down there tomorrow night. Mrs Harper gave me a good rating Saturday about potatoes to her. Haven't been there since. Went to Sandford to Club Monday night and paid Freeborn money. Cash in hand £128. 17s. 8d.

December 23rd, Sunday night The weather has been wet, dull and mild. Some mornings frosty and one day a beautiful day. Today has been mild and last night foggy. I boiled carrots Monday night. G. Hinton came up about the apples and they stopped – drank till 12 o'clock.

Friday Jack Brown came up and bought the apples. Paid and took them away and bought my Flukes at 10/0 per sack for the best and 7/0 for the setts and paid 1/0 to bind the bargain. He seems a straightforward, keen, hard dealing cove. I called at Harpers Friday and asked them if they wanted any – no – and a good job too. I have sold nearly all my celery

now, all the parsnips and some of my pitted carrots. Last Tuesday we had
the wind-up supper with the Cricket club. There was 18 to supper
including cousin F. Turrill Stadhampton, Dr Hugall, Bamforth, Sturges
Cuddesdon, etc. a very good party indeed and all passed off quietly about
12/30. And the next day we had a capital run with the harriers. Found in
Horseshoes garden and, after a capital run, killed him in Buswell's close. I
went on round to Harpers, Netts, and saw Mrs Harper about her Income
Tax. I took a note and went to Oxford next day to brewers – Good many
there – and back home. Bought a ticket in the Art Union but I'll be
bound I shall get nothing.[26] There was about 355 persons killed in the
Barnsley Colliery and they got out 85. And they are filling the pit up now
so that they will not be able to get the other bodies out for a long time, if
ever. I don't know for certain how many there are killed in the other.
They are getting up subscriptions for the sufferers. I went to Baldon wood
sale Thursday and stopped about there all day but did not buy. I thought
it dear. I saw the ruins of some old ancient building with tomb and effigy
of some of the Pollard family 1577.[27] There are traces of a large building
and some stone coffins by the large pond. It was years ago since I saw it,
perhaps in my Nuneham days.[28] I thought of it as I crossed the rickety old
bridge over the water to it. It is all enclosed now. Lent Taylor a shilling.
Tomorrow night is to be another pig feast, two roast pigs and fixing at 8d.
each, just for a frolic, so I dare say we shall be busy this time tomorrow.
T. Smith is the chairman. Saw Nett on Monday evening for a short time
but it was so wet and cold. Promised to meet last night but either I or she
was too soon or too late, I did not see her. Went to church today, a good
many there. Rogers still here officiating. Watson only comes home
Sundays now. Nothing settled yet. Got beef for Christmas in. Young Jack
Yeates' son christened today. Dinah gone off somewhere tonight. Confab.
at Bakers Friday night, scandal. I was down the common digging –
trenching by moonlight. I stuck to it till past 11 o'clock and I had enough
of it. Haven't heard of any parties this Christmas time yet. Rogers was at
the Tithe Feast – chatted away – a good one and sang several songs.
Neighbour Clarkes not come back yet. Had the fox hounds at Brake last
Monday, killed.

Dec. 30th 1866 As perhaps this is the last time I shall write any more of
my notes in this book this year, it may be as well just to take a retrospect
of the past year so soon to be numbered with the years that are gone; so
soon to be one of the years that are irrevocably beyond our control with
all its follies, its pleasures, pains, anxieties and hopes; so soon to be one of

the years that to all intents and purposes is as far removed from us as the days of Adam, for what has been done in the past year can never be undone. What was meant to be done that year and was not done, never can be done now. The time, lost in the year that is past, can never be regained; only the time that now is is our own; that which was and is to come is not ours. It has struck me very often that if all that we meant to do, all that we have left undone in the past year had been done and if all the hopes and wishes had been fulfilled would it really have been better for us or not? For my part there are many things that I meant to do, many things I wished would happen that now I am glad did not happen and was not done and vice versa. The past year has been an uneventful one to me; nothing particular has happened that will at all, as far as I can see, influence my destiny, either for good or evil, but it is impossible to tell. I have known a few strange things happen in my time that have worked for someone's good or evil and from apparently trivial causes. We don't know what fate has in store for us and it is, I suppose, better that the future be hidden from us. I don't know that I am any the poorer and certainly I am not much richer than I was on last New Year's Day. I have, thank God, enjoyed good health and without that the rest is worthless. Give me my health and strength and I am the equal of the rich. I can enjoy what I have; they can do no more, and without it we are equal still. The rich can't buy it and the poor can't sell it. In the beginning of the year I commenced the rating for Baker. How that will answer I don't know. Of all the artful downy coves that ever I knew, he cops all. I have learnt more of him without his knowing though than ever I did before – whether it will be good for me or no remains to be seen. He is too artful for me and sometimes I have a good mind to have nothing to do with it but I will try it a twelvemonth and then see. By some of my ventures I have made money and some, lost it and altogether I think it will be a middling year financially for me. I have had quite enough to do to keep things going and I have not been out to any pastimes in all the year for in the summer and spring I have no time and in the winter it is no pleasure. By the by, I don't care so much about pastime and pleasure as I used to do. I don't seem to want to go out to any of the fun that I used to. I have seen nearly all of pleasure that I care to see and I am content to jog along as I do at present. I am doing very well and I'll let well alone. I eat, drink and sleep well and enjoy myself when I can and if I don't save money I must see my way clearer than I do now if I alter it just yet. Mother was very ill during the summer and I thought, and a good many more, that she would not get about again, but thank God she is again and is now at the present time better than she has been for a good while and I hope and trust she may long continue so. The summer was exceedingly unfavourable for gardening operations and garden produce of all descriptions has been unsaleable. Dinah has on the whole been on fairish – rather afraid once of T.S. [Tom Smith, or could it be Trysting Stile?] but as she gets older she may know better *perhaps*. Sometimes I think that I should like to be alone in the world, to have no relatives, brothers, sisters, mother, father nor no-one to trouble or care a fig about you, and no-one to care a fig about, for half the trouble and care and anxiety is about someone belonging to you; so that I could do exactly as I please about things concerning myself and no-one to ask me why or when or how. I believe I could please myself if I had only myself to please but what is, is for the best, at least I hope so. I am now a full member of a Benefit club and entitled to sick pay and medical attendance. I am Collector (with J. A[ldworth]) of assessed and Income Tax and have wooed, won and promised to marry when circumstances either compels or admits of such a course. I am 25 years old, old enough to be a great deal better and, although I admit I have done wrong in promising marriage, I will fulfill it when it is claimed. I began courting my fate years ago and although I have tried to shake it off times and times, and we have fell out and quarrelled times we was sure to come together all the better friends again. It seems inevitable and I can't help it now. There is many a slip between the cup and the lip and we might never after all be married. There are lots of chances and changes in life and things may happen which may finally separate us for ever. I am well aware of all that. I know that such and such things might happen to one or both of us, and our day dreams be all swept away. But just now she seems my destiny and come weal or come woe, I must abide by it. She is neither good-looking, good scholar, or the best of temper, but then there are qualities which balance these defects which are nothing serious in my eyes, although I am not an impartial judge. She is not the one I should have thought would have taken my fancy years ago, but I have seen the falseness, the unreality of my ideal more than once since then. I have looked behind the scenes, seen the tinsel and the beautiful and good and true I confess I have never really seen yet or even hope to. I have found out that human nature is human nature but my experience, limited though it has been, has shown to me that the standard of excellence of both women and men is a good deal lower than I thought in those days. There may be some good, fine, high and true-minded women in the world and I know there are some cold, heartless and introverted ones who think self is first no matter what is in the way, and it is, in a more or less degree, with us all. I have been told times and times that I shall make a bad job of it if I do marry her but then nine tenths of these are interested and the other is mere idle meddling gossip which will pick faults out that there are and find faults out that are not. Those who can do best without marrying at all are undoubtedly best off, but those who can't must shut their eyes, jump in and swim if they can. That's just my idea of what it is. You will never find a woman out till you have married her and then you must put up with it. It is all very well to say you should have found it all out before marriage – we may think we know it all but we don't. However, I have made up my mind and I'll chance it some day *mayhap*. A mutual interchange of confidences with Tom Cooper in the summer when he showed me his private notes of events in the last few years of his life and I mine. His was a very full and minute account of his love affair which occupies nearly the whole of his diary. Was extremely and, at times, almost painfully interesting and, to a certain degree, instructive. He is more of a sentimentalist than one would think. He has had some narrow escapes I think but happily for him he is now fine. That I think brings my retrospect of the events in the past year to a close. I have much among other things disheartening, to be thankful for and I look forward with hope to the year that is coming. Farewell 1866. Christmas has been rather dull, the weather was dull and foggy and wet and trade is slack and nothing going on. We had a pig feast on Christmas Eve – a tidy party and dancing on Wednesday night and Ringers but not much and last night we had a party in the parlour – noisy, no dancing but done as well. Nett was up here Christmas evening. Stopped to supper and enjoyed ourselves, first rate. Rained going home. Stopped at her house a while. Dinah is gone down there tonight to tea and Friday I was shooting at the copse. Killed 13 couple. My last go there I think – no sport and at night Magic Lantern at school.[29] Rubbish. Had a capital day's hunting here with our pack Wednesday. Rogers out, killed two.

Memories

Years ago when I was a little boy I can remember being out all day of a Saturday at play and I and Ted Watson, Coopers etc. We were down Smiths Common where the great Elm trees used to stand at foot of Shepherd's Hill, with their great gnarled roots projecting out in the old ditch there. Old nooks served us as a house and home for play. We were racing about sliding and pretending to be hunting and shooting. The large rank grass there grew to such a height we could lie down amongst it unperceived. We enjoyed ourselves then as only children can. It was a bitterly cold winter's day with snow on the ground some thickness and yet, strange to say, we were perfectly happy and contented and remained down there all day long. I can remember our sitting there, and it frightened us and sliding on the ice that was in the old and wide ditch. We were all very young then but I question if ever we shall in future can be so perfectly happy as we was then and how the actors in that days sport are all gone, some to their last long home – others all are over the world. The very ground itself is all altered, the old Elms are gone and the ditch filled up.

Memories and thoughts 1867

I can remember some years ago when Tom Cooper and I were great chums then. Went off down below with our tin whistles. It was our favourite pastime. There of an evening to meet and play about the grounds below. Of an evening we went and sat on the top of Shepherd's Hill and played Annie Laurie and other tunes. Old W. Holloway came to us and said 'Well done boys' What I should call the second stage. How things change. Where are we all now?

1867

Very cold winter – snow in March and frost in May damage garden – becomes introspective – goes for long, solitary walks – on bad terms with A.H. who 'disobeys' him – he tries to control the company she keeps – ends diary considering himself to be (reluctantly) engaged.

Sunday, January 6th 1867   This is the first note in the Book this year and I wonder what it may be my lot to note down in this Book before another New Years day comes round. The weather was cold and dry and on Sunday last it began freezing and it has been a fearful severe frost up to last night and it has thawed since.[1] It froze upstairs. Water in a cup was froze solid within a foot of my head in bed. Split the washing jugs all to pieces and froze everywhere very sharp. On Wednesday morning the ground was covered, to the depth of a yard in places where it drifted, with snow and it snowed and froze properly. The carriers were obliged to walk to Oxford and the next morning it was a fearful sharp rhime – that was a cold one and no mistake. I was out shooting and you could not see ten yards before you – a dense fog. I have been out shooting a good deal but haven't shot much. There are so many out at it. I saw a wild fowl in Birds Brook yesterday but Pitman and I could not get him up. It is all Felp shooting – no larks and I expect they are all smothered in the snow. On Monday I began helping Baker do his Christmas accounts up. I was at it for a day or two at [a] time and done a lot of bills up and delivered some for him.

Sunday, January 13th   The weather began thawing last Sunday. Thawed rapidly and was all gone in a day or two and was very mild and warm but it has froze very sharp this last day or two and snowed a little last night and freezes fearfully sharp now and is bright and clear and looks like it. We killed our pig last week – a nice pig, 14 score I should think. Nett walked to market Saturday week in the snow. Got home – just called – fearfully tired and was up here last night and stopped till 10 o'clock and I went down home with her and a jolly rum walk that was. It snowed all the way and blowed well. Bother about Teddy shooting hares in Gale's field. Finished boiling all my carrots up Monday and looked out all my onions ready for market at 1/6 per bushel. Pump froze. Joe Clarke came home Friday and payed me his rent. Owes Mother for two bundles straw. Went to church today and saw our new Rector, Mr Wayte. He is a fat curious looking man, very dull and mumbling. He is going to get up a choir and do something grand here. Began doing my shallots and seed peas. John Slade still very ill and Tom Sellar now better.

January 20th, Sunday night The weather has been fearfully cold and frosty all the week and it freezes just about it now. It is got in the ground a good depth and everything is frozen up and all ground work is stopped and trade is fearfully dull now in everything. It has froze all the week and freezes now with a bitter cold wind and a little snow. The rivers are all frozen and flooded, and consequently there is an immense deal of skating going on and on Wednesday last there was a fearful accident on the Regent's Park water in London when all at once the ice broke and immersed 200 in the water.[2] It was a fearful sight and one not to be forgotten for some time by those who saw it. 40 lives were lost and it is supposed there are some more in now. I have been shooting nearby all the week and storching [stonching?] about the fields till I am tired of it. There are a good many blackbirds and felps in our garden and I have shot a good many. I had a touch of lark shooting one day but I could not get at them they are so wild – wants more snow. An immense number on the hills. Shredded trees and began tying up. The new choir has started last Thursday – a good many in it – and I heard them today for the first time. They sang very well. Nett did not come to the meet that night. Awful cold up here now. Haven't seen her all the week before. Sold all my onions to Murphy and all gone. New hymn books at Church. Joe Clarks party came back Monday. Mary Harper came back – married I think, rings on. Bought the last meal for my pigs.

Sunday, Jan. 27th The weather was extremely cold and wintry all the week up till Tuesday night when it rapidly thawed and has been very wet and mild since. It was a beautiful day today warm, bright and still. Put notice on Church door in morning and to Church this afternoon. A fresh clergyman there. A mild man. A wonderful lot of people there and tidy singing. There were 41 persons got out of Regents Park water and they are going to drain the lake and see. I cobbed a dozen felps and blackbirds for Wednesday. I pulled the avenue up in Q.'s Garden Friday, and yesterday I planted rose trees up both sides. I looked potatoes out Wednesday. Was down at Netts Thursday.

January 28th I sold all my potatoes today to J. Brown of Cowley at 10/0 and 7/0 per sack. I had the money and he the potatoes and I sold him all the carrots at 2/0 per cwt and he is to fetch them this week. First heard about the Wheatley affair with E. and R. last Monday. R. C[linkard] about taking Watson's farm. A good many potatoes frozen about now. Can't sell any pigs nor shallots. Owes old Dickey Townsend 2/0 for poles and he owes me one pole. Cut my rose trees today and done Rates out and Cheque book up tonight and notices on the Church door yesterday.

February 10th, Sunday It is mild weather now and very wet. It was a fearful hurricane on Tuesday night; another Wednesday evening about 2 o'clock. I never knew of such a storm. It rocked our house fearfully and woke me up. I thought the old place was coming down and it has been very rough all the week since. And last Friday it thundered and lightened and was very rough. Been to church today, not many there. The Great Reform Demonstration in London tomorrow.[3] Rogers there and reform programme tomorrow night in Parliament. I sold my pigs to Birt of Cowley at 10/0 per score – they weighed well. Had the cash and went to Capps Clerk to H.B.G. [Headington Board of Guardians] about Mrs Harper's appeal case. Had hair cut. On to T.C.'s – not at home. To Oxford yesterday to Brewers. Ordered, dined and paid and to County Hall. Heard several cases. Alfred Clinkard's not settled yet. A.C., J.C. and I went to Chequers and stopped some time. Jack went to P. & B. his wife like to have another. Met T.C. coming home – promised to come to tea – wet day and he did not come. Had blocks split up and stacked and done with the pigs and done a little hoeing and went to nearly all the Parish rate and Taxhunting. Was down at Mother in Laws Tuesday night to see about her appeal job. Stopped till ten o'clock, Nett and she and I looking over old account books etc. Did not see anything of any Garsington people at Oxford yesterday. Brown owes me 4/0 for shallots. Paid Baker off. I went down to see Tom Sellar Wednesday night and he went off to the Infirmary Thursday. I went down and helped him off this morning – he went off in good spirits and better than I expected. Escorted cousin Sue home Wednesday. Met Nett last night, would not stop. Rained. Mrs Aldworth and all that lot have been bad. Better now. Was up at Horseshoes Sunday night, T[om] S[mith], strong job there. Planted cherry trees in Q.'s Garden last Friday week. They were fairish ones, cost 6/6. Brown has not fetched the carrots yet. Gooseberry buds swelling out now – slushes the plants now. Taylor and gang doing Harper's well now. Took dung down Common Thursday.

Tuesday, Feb. 19th The weather since I wrote last has been open, mild and wet. No frost and no sign of any. Have had one night down the Common digging and done the borders up a bit down there and set Tom Phipps on digging down there. It is awful wet down there though yet. I bought some seed peas yesterday by Howard and planted some of them today. Cabbage plants in Q.G. and G. and began digging the piece up again the same. It digs well and I finished pruning Saturday last, apricots and all, and I shall begin planting quick now. Sold all my turnips today to Murphy for 1/9 to get them away.

Friday Went down to Nettas Sunday night about the appeal case and I suppose I must go to prosecute the appeal Thursday but it will be no go I am thinking. Old Stone drunk up here Saturday night and upset the baker about the tax affair. Ranting tea meeting tonight.[4] A good many there. Joe Ruffles baby died t'other day. No trade for shallots. Tom Sellar better. T. C[ooper] did not come up Sunday. Been and had a confab with Bakers Party tonight. Pruned young apricot trees Friday. Drains burst on my ground in Common. Gooseberry trees out in leaf now and everything is getting out in leaf much now. Very mild and damp. Potatoes very dear. Very little hunting going on now with our pack. Saw E. S[tone] with A.G. Sunday. Had bill and receipts from mother in law's. Seldom go to H's now. Fenian outbreak[5] in Ireland last week and Reform meeting and programme out.

Monday, February 25th The weather still holds fine and although threatening it has not rained. A slight frost this morning. I dug and planted the piece in Q.G. nearest lane last week. I planted it Friday with peas and potatoes and it was dry enough too. I went down the Common Saturday and opened a drain down there. It was awful wet there and a good deal of water got away. A little digging but not much; it is so wet. Sold Murphy the turnips and he has cut some of them up, I see. I went down yesterday and the drain still runs. My plants look very bad but lettuces look fairish at present. I have not dug much down there yet. I have finished digging in our garden and Heborn has been clearing the trees. It is nicely dried now. I went to the Headington Board to prosecute the appeal for Mother in Law. Got there in good time and got through alright and home by 3.30 and sent the potatoes off – John Browns – and drawed 1/6 to bind the bargain on the shallots. He did not seem to like it much but I don't care much about that. Business is business. Can't sell shallots at any price. I have the red carrots on hand still. Did not see anything of T. C[ooper]

Sunday – did not go to Church last Sunday either. A new parson there, a Mr Bowles the new one that is coming I hear. Mrs Williss is very ill today. Went down to M-in-L's yesterday at night to see her about the Rate. Was at home by herself. I sat and talked about things and one tale on to another for a good while till Mary came home and then I came away. I did not see Nett nor have I seen her all the week. Taylor has done the cricket ground up last week and I went and saw it last night and it looks capital now. The roads are dried up a bit now. Bother last Saturday night with Navvy and Baker and Saturday he told me that he would pay it but he have not paid it yet. The gooseberry trees are out in leaf but no bloom yet. The red early potatoes are shot well. Trained young plum trees up. Rhubarb not shot up much. Crocuses out in bloom. A rackety party indoors now. Wind rough. It took about 2 bushels seed potatoes to plant the piece in Q.G. Planting cuttings out Saturday and have transplanted lettuce plants out last week and P.C. [Purple Cape?] plants. I planted nearest the house in piece, this side of Dr Tanner's Premier next Veitches Perfection and next Ne plus Ultra and in piece Ne plus Ultra and Green marrows last and all Miatts potatoes. It is light and the birds sing till after 6.30 now and mild with it. No moon.

Sunday night, March 3rd   The weather has been very clear and very cold with very sharp frosts at night and bitter wind from the N.E. It was intensely cold last night and the frost was not out of the ground at noon today although the sun has been shining all day. A singular and brilliant appearance of the sun at sunset tonight. It seemed as if a column of fire rose from the sun and continued bright some time after the sun had set. I was going part of the way home with T. C[ooper] and O.B. who came up and just stopped to tea and off again back directly. He was looking well. Dinah goes flowing about with her hair all round her shoulders. Looks such a guy. Mr Francks was up here Friday night at school. Did not go. Not up to much I heard. Met A.H. t'other night and gave her a good lecture about G.W. She did not like it and I have not seen her since. She was not at the school it seems. Fan came back. Went to church today. New Clergyman, a tidy one too. Navvy paid his tax and rate. Government withdrew their resolution and promised to bring in a Bill next Thursday. It is all reform in Parliament now. Our pack was out Tuesday and had a good day about here. Ran to Sandford and Dorchester, did not kill though. The foxhounds killed 3 Monday. Young Fred Morrell married last Thursday. Baker's daughter christened today and Jack's wife got another daughter and her mother died Tuesday and buried

Friday. Saw Emma Wheeler at church today and Lottie too. I finished digging and planting the garden last Tuesday and Heborn finished Friday. I finished the celery piece yesterday and planted a row of peas, marrows and Wards Thursday, and I finished cabbage plant piece and forked it up and filled the plants up down the Common and planted two rows of peas down there – Q.G. seed. Wednesday afternoon. I dug a trench in my ground yesterday week and Friday morning I went down and bushed it and filled it in. Tom Smith gave me the bushes and I think it will stop it a bit now. Tom Phipps has finished digging it up and it looks well now and the land is drying nicely now and I saw dust flying about today. Some of the plants look well about and some don't. I bought a 100 of the Navvy for 8d. and mine look but middling. Dad's look well. He has put his peas in – I see 8 or 10 rows on stale dug ground – and put his P.C. plants out. He is gone to Hampshire now with some sheep. Now the weather looks a little duller but a cold wind. Navvy and Barty doing their place up. Planted onion seed in G. Tuesday. I hope the frost has not hurt the potatoes in the ground. Got some seed to sell. No bloom out yet and this cold wind will keep them back – a good thing. Put earth side of flower border in Q.G. The hard winter appears to have killed the bay trees and all the gillie-flowers. No sale at all for shallots.

March 14th The weather has been very cold since my last. A bitter Northeaster and on 12th, Tuesday, last it froze very sharp indeed and I went down the Common and finished my digging. It had snowed a little and last night it snowed and nearly all day today and it is over your shoes today. But it has melted today. It looks very wintry out now. I began digging the Upper Piece last week. It digs very tough and wet but I stuck to it and done it all up. It is all dug now and trenched last Wednesday 6th. I planted all my peas below the plants down the Common. It was got nice and dry and I wish now I had put my seeds in. The day before there was a steeplechase at Baldon. I did not go and I planted the celery piece that day – flukes, onions and Asparagus. No peas in sight yet. Castle done the ditch out round Common. Plants look but middling. Very little gardening done yet down the Common, the ground has been so wet. It was got nicely dug before this snow but now it is a licker. I have finished digging everywhere now and I shall plant as soon as I can. I have planted all at home but the bit nearest Blacksmith's shop. The gooseberry trees are nearly out in leaf but no bloom out yet. Began doing it up behind the Q.'s House yesterday. Last night John Slade died about 8.30. I helped carry his sister to the grave a month or two ago. He was ill then and has gradually

faded away. He broke a blood vessel and was always a delicate subject.
Ted courts cousin Emma – Horseshoes – and he does not appear to take
the slightest notice of John's death or in fact when he was alive. Fat pigs
9/- per score. Have not seen Nett for some time. Have been indoors
nearly all day today. Looked seeds out and labelled them. Some of my
rose trees dead. Baker has had the new paling done round the front of his
house and the old trees cut down. It looks better. Old Stone gave them
another rattle up at the Horse Shoes Saturday night, Jem Clinkard. Three
of the Conservative government resigned.[6] Would not agree about their
Reform Bill last week and the new bill is to come out Monday next, I
believe. I expect it will be of a Liberal character and if the House of
Commons really desire to pass a bill at all they will this. Went down to
Sandford Club Monday. J.F., J.C. and I all agreed to shift the money from
the Savings Bank to the PO Bank at Oxford. We got home about 11.30.
It snowed all the way home and Cricket club night the next night – all
there. Cousin Sue Sellar went off to Leo's to service in London last week.
Tom is getting on nicely now. Our new Parson, W. Bowles, visits about
well now and at Church, Sunday, he sang the first part of the Chant and
goes down to the Belfry to put his surplice on. He is a drawler but a good
preacher. Sent Tom Aldworth two pecks of seed potatoes for those we
had of him last year. Joe Clark gone to St[anton] Harcourt to work. John
Druce having his house thatched. John Cook doing it and Taylor is doing
the hedge all round. Store pigs very cheap. Works . . . garden.

Sunday night, March 17th   The weather during the last week has
been excessively severe and wintry, more so than has been known in
memory of the oldest inhabitant, and it froze fearfully last night with a
keen North Wind and it is gone in ground some little way. I am rather
afraid the potatoes will get froze now for it freezes nearly all day long and
the snow lies about makes it look very wintry indeed. It has, of course,
stopped all gardening and what has been done had better been left
undone. I staked the rose trees yesterday and raspberry canes but all early
bloom although not actually bursted will be more or less injured by the
frost and sunny days. I cleaned and hooped the cider kegs Friday and had
paint home yesterday by Howard's son – he was unwell himself – and
shall paint them tomorrow. Put Parish notices on Church door this
morning. Sent Baker's meat back Friday. Alfred Clinkard's child [Lizzie]
christened Friday. There was a Fenian rising in Ireland a week last
Tuesday night. They attacked and destroyed a few Police Barracks, etc.
and there were a few shot but it is all weared out now. Freezes.

March 24th, Sunday night The weather began to change Friday and today the snow is all gone except in the distant hills where it shines like long strips of white ribbon. It was a fearfully snowy, frosty week. All the week an immense quantity of snow fell and the ground is awful wet now. I went and helped carry poor John Slade to church last Tuesday. The road to the church was obliged to be swept all the way and it snowed at the grave. He was a nice gentlemanly young fellow. His sweetheart was much cut up at the grave. How all her hopes are blighted, which so short a time ago seemed so promising. They were just going to be married. I don't think any of the planted tackle is hurt after all. The Apricot trees are out in bud. They look brown but not in bloom yet – I think they will stand it. I have finished the water butt. The Christ Church steeplechases came off at Denton yesterday. There were five races. We had a good many rough ones up here at night but all passed off quietly. I went to Oxford to Brewers and bought Carrot Intermediate and celery white and red. I met T. C[ooper] we stopped and just spoke and I came on. Nett caught me just against Cowley and I rode home with her. We were very cool. I had not seen her for a long time before and I suppose it is wearing out – well and good. I went to Capps about the Rate and he was not at home. I shall not trouble anything about it now. I have to go to Wheatley tomorrow to pay Income Tax and Thursday. The Reform Bill comes on tomorrow for second reading. Is £15 rating Counties and Household suffrage in Boroughs and fancy it will not pass as it is.[7]

Wednesday, April 3rd The weather has been very dry and at times very rough, but still the ground is very wet and works bad. I have finished doing Q.G. up altogether. The first planting of peas is just coming up and the peas done. Common coming up too. The cabbage plants look very bad indeed. No bloom out at all except Apricot and that looks well. No sign of shooting in the lower cherry tree but the upper tree is. Done my flower beds up. Put my seeds in down the Common on March 30th. Mice works the peas down the Common, and I sooted and poisoned some tack for them. Lettuce down the Common look well, but a good many are dead. I went down to Wheatley with Baker and was sworn in Assessor of Assessed Taxes for this year. I delivered notices and today I had receipt books come by post to me. Ted Slade is going on very pretty now. He and Tradesman, Pitman and Bobby had yesterday a shooting touch and all got as drunk as Bibo[8] and last Sunday old Mrs Woodwards and Sam Hilsdon's daughter died and both buried today and the underbearers are now indoors drinking and singing away a good one.

Pitman and Jack got fighting last night. Jack C. up here. Saw Nett one day last [week]. Mary was very ill and had Cogan – bronchitis – better now. Billy came down and saw her Sunday. The Reform Bill was read a second time and I suppose will pass now. The Fenians are quiet now – all over I suppose. Lots of babies born again now. Dust blows. Gooseberries out well now and tonight I heard a thrush singing in the dark at 8.15. We had a capital finishing days hunting with our pack last Wednesday. I put one up on Rooster [?] Hill and, after a capital run, lost her up in Blenheim Piece. Ran 2 or 3 more but did not kill. Been down the Common tonight and began drawing the drills out for potatoes. It is very wet though. Luke Clarke done the thatching up. Done the hovel and pigsty and all up.

Friday, April 12th   I finished planting all my potatoes last Tuesday night. I have finished all but 3 rows on 6th and that day I put the early ones in Common, and they are just peeking through at home. The first plantings of Peas are up in full drill but look very weak and bad. I have limed them several times. The cabbage grow a bit now. I filled the row up in Q.G. Wednesday in plants. They look but middling. The apricot bloom is nearly over and the early plum blossom is just coming out in bloom but not much this year. The gooseberries are out well now and the tulips soon will be. The upper cherry tree is shooting but the lower one don't seem to move yet. I gathered some hoptops[9] tonight and covered potatoes up and forked the garden about and been tax collecting and doing about. Cripps has altered the Rate Book. I saw the first swallow today. I was looking carrots out and I heard him overhead. It was a frost last night and so it will tonight, I think. I had a letter from David [Stone] N.Z. – this week I think. Done flower beds up and the borders down Avenue. I went up by the brake to Baldon last Sunday by myself and the Sunday before. It was dry and pleasant and, being the first this year, I did enjoy it. I read a paper after I got home last Sunday. I found Nett up here by herself, didn't know she was coming. Stopped to supper. The first night Cricket down the Common. There was a good muster considering how cold the wind was. I had the R[ate] B[ook] and notices by Book Post from Surveyor. Done the garden bank and hedge up this week. There was a fire at Baldon last Friday.[10] It began about half past 12 and it burnt two cottages and Clarks farm down. I heard of it soon after one, but did not go till past 3. It was of course all down but there were 3 engines at work there. The new cottages there look nice houses. It is supposed to have been the work of a child. Fat pigs 8/6 per score. Baker is having the old washouse and all that row of buildings completely demolished today, preparatory to commencing the new slaughter house, storeroom, kitchen, etc. in its stead, and has had the new windows put in the front of his house and door. Coopers won't know the old place again. Tom called in about three minutes before I got home Sunday night. Did not see him at all. I wonder where he had been to. Might know someday. The weather is dry but cold. The wind is now shifted to South and I think we shall have it wet. Potatoes very dear, bread 7½. Owes old Tom for 5 pecks of flukes 5/- and he owes me ⅓ peck of Myatts. The onion seeds in G. coming up. The people down the Common are very busy. What a troop I met tonight. Castle broke in Oxford. Holloways caught Gunners. What a gang goes off every day. I saw a troop of Hussars come along the Lower Road last week. They were a fine body of men and horses. The only ones I ever saw on that road. Plants K.B. on 15th or thereabouts. Moonlight. Nett did not come to the meet. E. S[tone] goes on very pretty. Sowed some flower peas and gilly seed Wednesday. Rhubarb shooting but very late and rose trees shooting now – some killed though. The forest trees

Queen Street, Oxford, *c.* 1885

are as bare and leafless as winter. This has been the first Spring day but it has been a fearful rough wind nearly all this week and the night before last and all day yesterday it was just about rough. We are all pretty well and, as for politics, I haven't heard a word all the week. The Reform Bill was to have been in Committee Monday. The French Exhibition opened 1st April but not finished yet.[11] 9 o'clock.

Wednesday night, April 17th   Today has been the first day of Spring. It has been a beautiful warm growing day and now it is beautiful and moonlight and still – else it has been fearfully rough and windy and I daresay there has been a deal of damage done by it. I planted some Brompton seed yesterday in pots and Saturday in boxes and borders and today I sowed the celery seed. It was old seed. The onions are up in full drill now and the lower cherry tree is shooting at last. The apricots are setting well, I think a good many, but not much plum bloom. The early ones are out now and the potatoes are coming up. I stuck the peas in plants and began in G. today. The peas look bad this year. Last week I went down the C. and filled the 2 rows up in C. plants. They are very ragged. The vine moving. It rained and blowed a good one Sunday. I went my favourite walk as usual, it was very rough but sheltry under the wood. I enjoy these quiet walks now more than ever I did any. The birds sing delightful and the pheasant crow reminds me of bygone days; and above all I am perfectly and securely by myself. No chance of meeting anyone up there and you cannot read and talk too. It seems a rest and relieves one from so much incessant thinking and in a manner you lose your personality, you forget yourself and all the hurry and hurly and at least for once in a week you feel at liberty to forget and be quiet. Sometimes I do a little castle building, sometimes I think of old times and old playmates and brothers and sisters[12] and think of what might have been and what is now, of the old loves, hates, plans, etc. and it may be, lives over again the happy days of boyhood, its free and careless enjoyment of the present and what is; but no thought or care for what might or will be. It may, and to some undoubtedly it is, foolish and unworthy a man to think or let such childish fancies and remembrances occupy any, even of our leisure moments. But at times and when out alone and unobserved, such thoughts and retrospection of the days of Auld Lang Syne will come and drive the stern, matter of fact, everyday planning and thinking of living out. And very often the knowledge of what you are and what under different circumstances you might have been tends to open your eyes to many a fault, many a shortcoming and perhaps many a sin which perhaps at no other time you can get such a vivid and clear perception of. You can, when you are thus musing and remembering, all unconsciously perhaps, then see where and when you first began going wrong or right, as it may be, and can up till now see and know what its consequences are or, in all probability, will be; and it would be well for me if the backslidings of bygone days and which at such times you feel are such, would act as a strong and deterring cause of preventing a repetition. I suppose I was cut out for a quiet life. At all events I know of but one I would care to have with me at such times at all, and then perhaps we should be thinking or talking of the past or our future and old (at least to us) times. As for the empty senseless rattle and talk of all the rest, I prefer a quiet walk alone by a quiet wood with my own thoughts or a book and I am happier then than all the week. There I have jotted down in my rambling way some of the thoughts which in my Sunday evening rambles occurred to me. May I never be worse employed. I have been very busy collecting taxes lately and serving notices and filling them up. Mother in laws rate is reduced. Went down this Monday for T.T. We sat round the fire chatting and joking till 10 o'clock and then Nett and I strolled over the grounds by moonlight home. She was in a good humour. No cricketing Sunday last, so rough and wet. Baker goes on with his building. Have not got the roads or trade quite yet. All over with Ted and cousin Emma. See swallows now and took a bird's nest and four eggs today.

Tuesday, April 30th It was a most beautiful day yesterday, quite like summer, so warm and sunny and, what is quite a treat, still; and today it rained in the morning but fine since. And I have been busy today making a pigsty gate and this afternoon I planted my last row of peas down the Common and filled up the other in Lower Piece and filled up the onion bed and planted pinks. The potatoes are up in full drill and look well and in the garden they are nearly fit to mould. I trod the onion beds in Q.G. and G. yesterday and they cut a very sorry figure indeed. It was a beautiful day Good Friday. I did not go to Church till night. Was hoeing potatoes and sticking peas. Finished all in Q.G. that day. The cabbages are growing now well and lettuce will soon do. The Rhubarb fit to pull and rose trees shooting well. Trained bay tree up and sowed flower seed Saturday – Blue flower. French and German and dwarf chrysanthemum, Asters, Indian pink, imported 10 week stock everlasting flower and the Brompton seed coming up well but slugs work it well and the apricot trees too. No K.B. up. Second planting of peas down the C. up well, and the seeds are up

well down there. Most of the plum and damson trees are out of bloom
and the apple trees are just coming out now and the hedges and trees are
coming out in leaf very fast indeed now. I first heard the cuckoo for
certain last Wednesday and the nightingale a day or two before and now
they are to be heard all day and night long. There is some talk of a war
with France and Prussia and I rather think they will have a turn too.[13]
The Reform Bill goes on alright and will pass now, I think. There was a
grand division on the Rating clause but Government won by 21 votes.
All sorts of corn rising in Price now, especially wheat. Got no pigs.
Doing the styes up. I have stuck the framework of my peas up in C.
today. The early potatoes are coming up down there; and there are
getting some tidy-sized gooseberries. Tulips out in bloom. Transplanted
spring flowers roots 10 days ago. Our choir get on well now. They all go
down in the belfry and march out up in the Chancel just before the
Parson. Nett was up here to tea Easter Sunday and we went to Baldon
Church. It is a very pretty church inside and it was decorated up to the
door with candles and flowers – and so was ours. The altarpiece was
decorated very nice indeed – a thing which never was known before. I
went down and collected M-in-Law's rate last week. Primrose Hill
steeplechases last Wednesday. It was a miserable wet day but a good
many people went from here and it rained all the afternoon and today
was Wallingford Pony Races. Tom Clinkard's pony was trained and got
ready for it and today it went off to the Wallingford races and ran in 2 or
3 races but I have just heard that he has not won. Emma [Turrill] and
Tom [Smith] went and our sporting party. We had an opening match at
Cricket, a very tame affair and a whip party at night. A good many here
and a proper quarrelsome party there was at night. They was all up for
fighting and in putting J.C. out he hit me. I had a good mind to pull
him. There was a good fight outside with J.T. and H.W. On the
Saturday night before I was behind time and got a good setting down
and Tom S. was put in my office and P[arish?]. Treasurer and they
collect 2d. out of a 1/0 Sunday night. Ted Cooper up here last Sunday
night. Was down the Common. Lost his dog. Haven't seen anything of
it. What a fop. I took my favourite walk and down into Common and
up with Cricketers and off to bed. Did not go to church at all. Was
middling in the morning but better at night. Fan Woodwards got
another beau now. Baker nearly got the walls of his buildings up. We
had a dancing party up here Saturday night. Jack the Tradesman has
moved from the Hill to old Woodwards whose wife died a short time
back. Alfred Quartermain's wife comes up for Relief Mondays now. Fan

is very ill. Alice Sellar is at home – Invalide. Dinah has been over to Milton last week. There was a Confirmation here last Friday (Good) not many though. Work till 9 o'clock now. Haven't seen T. C[ooper] for some time. Bought some slabs of Druces [carpenters?] last week. S. has been here today, clearing up. Grass is growing fast now. Nance Rogers is at home now. Lower cherry trees not much shakes now. Put the geraniums and Calceolarias out – Dinah has. I planted the K.B. in garden about ten days ago and the etc. down Common, last Tuesday. It is still very wet down there. Onions just shooting. It is rumoured that Watson is going to leave and have a sale. Assessment day Friday. Midsummers are earlier than Myatts. Peas grow now. 12 o'clock.

Monday, May 6th The weather since I wrote last has been lovely. It has been beautiful, still and bright and sunny and it is lovely now. The cuckoo and nightingale sing nearly always and it is beautiful Spring weather. Sowed flowers out in borders, Harpers and Snows [superb?] early white broccoli last Wednesday and row of peas in Common. Finished sticking all my peas Friday and hoed all my seed beds in Common and C. plants – early potatoes up well in C. and moulded potatoes in Garden Thursday, and Q.G. Saturday. Hoed peas today and tied lettuce in Q.G. and Common Friday and Saturday a few.

Sunday night, May 12th I have not been to Church at all today. It rained all the morning. It began raining Friday and it thundered very heavy with lightning and it has been wet and growing since. I put my geraniums out last Friday, a poor lot, and sowed lettuce and onion seed and turnip seed in onion bed. It is coming up now. Some of the seeds are up well. I moulded my early potatoes down Common Wednesday night, and adzed the lower bit of flukes up Thursday night. It worked pretty well. The peas are awfully thin and look bad. Onions moderate. Pulled 2 dozen lettuce down there, tidy ones, cut no cabbage.

Sunday night, May 12th, 9 o'clock Since I wrote last I have been out for my usual Sunday evening walk and I have been in nine villages since half past five. It is rough and cold and quite unlike last week which was beautiful and summerlike. Oh, how beautiful this merry month of May is and how soon it steals away. How soon the beautiful May is out of bloom and the fresh bloom of Nature is faded. It is a question if I see it looking so beautiful as it did tonight. The very birds and insects seem to know that it is the first fresh Spring from the cold and dreary winter, and

sing and warble as I only hear them in the bonnie month of May. All
nature's treasures are displayed in their glory in this month. The May,
violets and all other beautiful and sweet scented, simple and lovely
flowers. Perhaps it is because we have not seen or heard it for such a long
time; but however, I think the month of May the Queen of the Year. At
no other period of the year are there such beautiful bird music, such
flowers and such bright green and fresh looking leaves; at no other period
of the year do I love my country house and a quiet walk with Nature's
songsters and Nature's beautiful woods and fields and flowers. There are
no flowers in all the gardens and conservatories of the wealthy that can,
for simplicity and pure beauty, rival the unnoticed, unthought of wild
flowers. Where I was tonight I could hear the triumphant crow of the
pheasant secure in his woodland home, could see the timid rabbit
scampering off to the cornfields, could hear the nightingale warbling in his
solitary thicket and such notes as only the nightingale can utter and which
is only to be heard in its glory in May. Of a certainty, there is something
even in this life worth living to see and dismal indeed must be the lot of
that misanthrope who cannot see anything of enjoyment in the beautiful
month of May. In other lands there are mighty and majestic aspects of
Nature which from their very sublimity strikes the beholder with awe
and, perhaps in some instances, fear. But for all that a good old English
landscape in May is unequalled, I think, but then tastes vary. But I at least,
for one, do enjoy the May Month. Tom [Cooper] was up here Sunday.
He promised to come up to tea but he did not. Came up time after –
down to Cricketing and bided awhile and off home. Looked at my diary
and cricketers came up and he went off home. He left me his diary to
copy some songs out of. Not much of consequence in it this time – well
for him, I think. I can't think how he can remember conversations so well
as he does do for a special pleader. I rather think somewhat of C.A.
Lumo. K.B. up.

May 14th   Sowed onion and carrot seed yesterday in C. Broccoli
coming up and celery I think. Tied lettuce in yesterday and done pigsties
up day before and sowed own aster seed . . . No peas out yet. Hoed flukes
C. and filled peas up with K.B. Nance Rogers married and . . . asked in
Church. Reform Bill not passed yet. Weather very cold and dull. Had a
long walk and interesting talk with Nett last night by moonlight. The net
draws closer. Collinson the photographer here with a beautiful coloured
vignette of Dinah. It was a beauty, a show speciman. He took a good
many here.

Sunday Night, May 26th I have just been to Church, had not been for some time. The choir do not improve much I think. The weather ever since I last wrote has been unusually cold and, on the morning of Thursday and Friday last, it was a most extraordinary sharp frost for the fourth week in May. It froze everything up, killed the Early and all other potatoes too that was up, and mine was out in bloom. K.B. and all done up down C. Some gardens up town not hurt and some spoilt. I never remember such a frost so late and I hope never shall see another for it has done me pounds damage. Tom [Cooper] was up here Sunday to tea. He stopped and looked at my diary and then off down the Common to Cricket. He went in once or twice I think. Saw his Alice and party in horse and trap going along the Lower Road. I went along to the C[ommon] G[arden] and had look round and then back when I met A.H. and Alice. I just spoke and asked them where they was going to. Would not say and off to Common again. Stopped till was over. T[om] would not come up but went off along L[ower] R[oad] I came up with Gang, waited and then went outside and met my star and gang when she and I went for a walk. It was beautiful weather, warm and moonlight, and for the first time we set to and had a straight talk about where we are and what we mean to do and when. What our prospects are and likes and dislikes and of course planned the future out as so many may have before, forgetting that Man proposes and God disposes. I told her just what I thought would be best, what my prospects and circumstances were and we agreed on some things and some we did not. We agreed not to get married this Cuckoo and left that question open. Sometimes I think that I should like to have a wife and live as miserable as married people do, especially when our Dinah is so awfully awkward and won't mend my things or do anything and then sometimes I can see very plainly that it is best as it is. However, it would not take much to persuade me to it even now, for married people always live somehow and we does no more. I am fully determined to be married before many months are over if I can, however, get anyone to have me. I am almost tired of single misery. I should not mind it so much if I had someone to mend and keep things tidy. What we did say, however, was straight to the point and if we was to be married before leaves [appear] again I should not wonder. I have often spoke about these things to her before but she always said time enough yet. But I think if couples before marriage was to discuss ways and means a little more than they do, it would be better. If I could see my way clear into everything outside, don't know but what I should be then. I have been busy doing about in the Gardens. Hoed G. all over and done my seed beds up a bit down Common. Have cut no cabbage yet of any account, 1½ down C. Watsons sale Thursday. Bought paint and logs not a good sale. Was there for Mother-in-law. Done Parish books up. Tom C[ooper] here now . . .

Sunday night, June 2nd   The weather for this last day or two has been beautiful and today it has been bright, warm and like summer and things grow a bit now. I sowed some celery seed and cabbage seed yesterday and put some lettuce plants out down Common and trimmed the paths up a bit down there, and at night I have been down there adzing potatoes up a bit. I planted some more K.B. down C. last Saturday, and some are left up now. The potatoes cut a very sorry figure indeed about in places, the turnip seed in onion bed in Q.G. and lettuce are coming up a bit. I planted some Brompton plants out and some calceolarias in flower border in Q.G. last week. I cut some cabbage and pulled nearly all my lettuce in C. yesterday. I finished doing the Parish books up and Baker and I went to the Workhouse to meet auditor, Tuesday – we got £2 10.0. allowed us by Overseers for Highway Rate but he would not allow it. I went on to Oxford, called at T. C[ooper], asked him to call for some cups that I was going to buy. He said he would. I goes on to Brewers and then meets J. Y[eates's] cart so I went and bought them and sent home by them. I then went back to Brewers into the house and had dinner and settled and off to Tom's again but it was now too late for him. He was gone and I did not see anything of him that day. I tried to buy a straw brim but could not get one to suit. Bad go with the auditor. The Reform Bill drags its slow length along[14] and it will eventually pass but as it stands now it is a much more liberal bill than it was originally. Household suffrage in Boroughs and 12/£ rating in Counties. The Compound Householder is abolished and altogether it is a satisfactory measure.[15] Bread is still at 8d. the loaf, and wages 11/0. The threatened war about the Luxembourg question is all satisfactorily settled and the Exposition in Paris is attracting an immense number of visitors. Princess Teck confined of a daughter.[16] Burke the Fenian reprieved.[17] Jack Tradesman's child died this morning but I have not heard the particulars yet, sudden though I think it was. The baker's new built [building] progresses towards completion now, nearly all roofed in. I wrote a contract out for him Tuesday night and he got it accepted for the roads.[18] I mean 275/£ he makes a good thing of it I believe. Fanny Quartermain very ill now. Mother went up to see her Thursday. Singing two or three times a week getting ready for Dorchester, 20th June.[19] Our Bowles out and out singer. No sign of another cousin George yet. Baker's wife and Hattie burnt their photos – such frights. Six o'clock.

Whit Monday, June 10th Twas a beautiful day yesterday and today it
has been a most lovely day, bright warm and still, one of the most lovely
days I ever remember in my life. The band is now playing beautifully on
the Hill, I suppose just coming home from going their round of the
Village. They are at the moment playing a waltz tune I heard at Malvern
and the remembrance of that day comes back as fresh as if it were only
yesterday. That was a lovely day too, one I shall not easily forget. I am
sitting here, have just seen the band and the people go by into the Club
room. There was somebody up in a chair carried on men's shoulders – old
Wigs perhaps. The sun is setting gorgeously in the west and the air is as
clear and calm as ever an English atmosphere ever is. I am glad that it has
been so for although I have not enjoyed myself, still I am glad that the
weather has not hindered others from enjoying themselves. They sang the
Anthem at church this morning and they sang very well too. I did not go
and Mother and I had our dinner together. Dinah and Nett was gone to
church, I had a good mind to go but I did not – if I had known that the
Anthem was going to be sung I should certainly have gone. Nett was up
here Saturday, Sunday and today up to dinner. She and me went down
the Garden and gathered Gooseberries till the band came up here and
then she went upstairs, and when the band went round she and Dinah
must needs go off staring after that all over the town. I wanted her to stop
at home with me but Dinah persuaded her off. I did not like it and I told
her so. She said that she was going home to see her mother who is not
quite well it appears – if so well and good – if not, I shall have something
disagreeable to say to her if I see her presently. The beauty of the day is
now all over and of the summer too. The May is all over and I seldom
hear the Nightingale now, or in fact never, but the cuckoo is still about all
day long. The roses are just coming out in bloom and my one row of
early peas are out in bloom well now. I sowed some celery seed last
Saturday week but I do not see any of it coming up. Baker had his
housewarming last Friday night, and a good touch too we had. Joe
Cooper was up there and he did sing too and no mistake. Broke up about
12 o'clock and then I took our traffic down to Harpers for market. It was
about 1/30 when I went to roost – took 12lb of potatoes up. It is past
8 o'clock now and the sun has set and the calm twilight has set in and the
moon is now shining beautifully and bright. We have nothing hardly to
do and I am sitting upstairs writing at the open window. There is a party
– young Trump and his side and they are all crying. Whatever is the
matter I don't know but I have just been down to them and it appears
that the police had took him down at the Plough for the poaching affair

2 years ago. They took and handcuffed him and were taking him off [to] Oxford when John Yates paid the fine and now he's free once more. It was a terrible disappointment to his young wife who he has brought down with him, and there is a very bad feeling about the police tonight and I expect there will be something done tonight with them. I hope not though, for it will spoil their pleasure perhaps. There is a good deal of excitement and angry feeling tonight. Past 9 o'clock I went and spoke to young Trump and I hold some money for young Jack Yeates to repay him, I suppose, for lending him the money. Well, I hope it will be a warning to him and for the future to let poaching alone. There are not many here at present but I suppose we shall be on presently allright. The moon is shining splendid now and I hope the few remaining hours will pass off all quiet and peaceable. There has been no cricketing at all today and in fact those old pastimes are wearing out and no harm either. Boswell is fiddling down below but not much dancing going on at present. There are a good many couples walking about tonight, but then it is the only holiday of the year to a good many. One time, not many years either, how I waited and wished for Whitsuntide to come. How much I thought of that day, how much I planned and expected to enjoy myself and I suppose I did too. How it is all changed now. I don't seem to feel the slightest interest in it and there is no pleasure for me in that day, and while all the rest of the village are enjoying themselves my lot is to sit at home and work or stand still and see other people enjoy themselves. Well, every man to his mousetrap. I have not at present seen anything of Nett so I suppose she is staying at home for the evening. Nearly all my chums have left now, there are hardly any left who I was flirting with last year. Haven't seen anything of Billy or his party yet and last night, when I was down at Netts, I heard him coming up the road and he went into supper but I suppose he is offended about something. I wonder where Tom [Cooper] is now. We went for a walk last night up to my old spot, Sandford Brake, but we did not stop and got home before the Cricketers and I waited on them and then off home with her. We went up into her garden and had a look round and I [came] back. What awful swearing there is going on below and I can hear the report of the pop guns on the hill and crackers now. It is now past 9 o'clock. I should think I made 6 and 3½ and tonight 6 dozen of G[inger] B[eer]. K.B. up down Common and peas coming out in bloom, seeds look well and potatoes look better now. It is getting quite chilly now and I should think the band will soon come out again and off home. I should think they are well drunk by this time. Tom [Cooper] was up here Sunday week. He was down the

Common Cricketing and he came up here with them and stopped a short time and then off home. Did not see anything of him last night so I suppose he was not up here and perhaps he is now thinking of the old place and people, of the many happy and unhappy Whitsuntides we have seen together and of the old faces and forms who have passed to their last long rest but are not forgotten yet. How the years roll on, sometimes in joy, sometimes in sorrow but still resistlessly rolling on, and now the Whitsunday of 1867 is all over and will soon be forgotten and so the world goes on.

Tuesday morning, 7/30 I seem very sleepy and tired this morning. Did not go to bed till nearly sunrise, the birds were singing beautifully and it was quite daylight. It all passed off quite peaceable up here without a bit of a row with Crabb and Old Stone. Rogers got up too but I don't think he did hit the old man. There was not much doing this year. Nett came up here and stopt till we closed or just before at least and then she and I and A[lice?] S[ellar?] and G.W. went down home together. We had not been out so late before for years, however here I am all right. I did get a lot of Brandy and water out of our party, though young Harper was up here. We had a fine lark going home but all's well that ends well. I wrote the foregoing at intervals on Thursday night, sometimes upstairs writing and sometimes down doing about.

Sunday Afternoon, 4 o'clock The weather is rather cold and gloomy and we have had some rain during the week. I am just returned from the Churchyard where I have been to hear our Choir sing the Anthem which they have been practising for Dorchester next Thursday. They sang it very well, their Organist was over here Wednesday night to hear them and he said they done it very well. Have not been to Church today. Must get the tea. I have finished moulding all my potatoes everywhere now and last night I finished cleaning my seed beds up a bit and trimmed paths. The peas, although thin, are looking well and those in Q.G. are all out in bloom. The Turners are some strong looking and good bloomers, the Celery seed is just coming through in places. I planted a lot of plants out last night in flower borders and I cut some good roses Friday for Market. The Cherry tree is looking better now and K.B. are climbing up the sticks. Cleaned pigs out today and bought half bushel beans yesterday. Asked bigun for some rosebuds, no go. Put notices on church door this morning, was late. This Whitsuntide has passed off all right and quiet so far as I know. I got 34/- for young Trump and he is going back today. I hear he started Wednesday night but of course was too late, nearly 2 o'clock Wednesday morn when we broke up and last night we had a very quiet civil party and dancing but altogether it has been a dull go this time. The weather was lovely, cut nearly all my cabbage down Common and lettuce all gone. Gooseberries are turning ripe now but potatoes are not fit yet. What a awful plague the snails are. Carrots want thinning out in C., cleaned Broccoli bed yesterday and measured for pair new shoes too. Went round Sellars Garden with A. and there I heard a little about the Baldon Club affair. It was rather a wet day and I was knocking about at home in the morning and down C. afternoon. When I came home Dinah was gone, as she said, down to Netts to tea. Well I rather suspected that it was a Baldon Club go. I did not say anything but in the evening I was to start Rate Hunting and just before I started, Cousins Sarah and Emma came up here and we stopped and chatted a good while up here, and then I started off collecting. I went nearly all over the parish and then down to Mother-in-law's as that finished my beat, expecting to find A.H. at home. When I got there Mary and her mother was having supper. I gave her the notice and she asked me to stop to supper. It was nearly 10 o'clock and I was hungry and so I stopped and had a good supper. Then Mary and I went out in the Garden and looked at the roses and then I came home and off to bed. Mother asked me whether I had had my supper and where. I told down street and she wanted to know where Dinah was and who was gone to Baldon. I told her and she said they were all agreed and I could see they were too. Ma did not like it nor I neither. However, I wrote Saturday to tell that I should not come down Sunday, as I had promised her I should, and that I was determined to part as I did not like her goings on at all. I had given her a good setting down on Tuesday about it and she seemed rather pert about it. However, I was not to be trifled with, 'Hearts are not Playthings' and I soon told her so. Me, or not me, one or other, now or never. I had an answer back at tea time begging me to go down and all would be explained, and then I could please myself whether I would or not, rather cool I thought. I hesitated a good while before I started. I only wish Tom [Cooper] had been here and then I should not have gone. I had nothing to do and nowhere to go so fool like down I goes. Walks boldly in, nobody at home but Miss Harper. After a little parlying I walks into my business quick and sharp, not in a good humour either. I questioned her about what I wanted to know and she answered me fearlessly and apparently unconcerned whether we parted or not. We was on a good while, then J[anaway] came in and we had a rest and talked about weather, crops. He soon left us though and I told her that what she said had considerably qualified the tale I had heard. That although things looked better than I expected, still I thought that she had acted wrong, very thoughtless, very, and if she really meant what she said, that it had better be all over and she be free. Her Mother then came in and we sat there and chatted a good while with her and then Nett suggested a walk out in their field. She went and got ready and off we went. We walked sometimes in silence, sometimes cuffing things over as I was determined to know whether she cared for me or not. We sat on the old [k]noll by the side of the Beans till it was nearly or quite dark and talking, complaining and explaining. Now I did not want to break it off but I meant to make her think so, because when I heard her tale I was satisfied that it was a mere girlish flirtation, what I had done times myself. What I did not like was her not telling me all about it. Well, I says, it's no use our arguing away here, we shall be here all night. If you mean to consider yourself as my sweetheart or as engaged to me, which way you like, you must do so and so if not, Goodbye. We came off towards her home. We kept on talking till we came to the gate to part for home and where we had kissed and said 'good night' scores of times before. Well, I says, here we are, which way is it to be? Part or not, part for good and all? Well, you keep on finding fault of me, if you don't like me, well enough, we had better part, but as I find no fault of you it is for you to decide, I don't care. 'Oh well', I says, 'if it is come to don't care we will part, so Goodbye'. I took her hand to shake hands, I was half way outside the gate. She clasped my hand in hers, she was crying and said 'Well, Joe, from the bottom of my heart I'd rather not part, we cannot part so'. I turned round and said, Will you promise me to do as I told you? Yes, I will promise so far that I cannot give up all and all at once my old playfellows and companions, but I will go on better. I told her that I did not want her to forsake her companions but to be a little more select. To think more of me and mine and do as I says, not as other people do. She said she would if I would not leave her. The long and short of it is that we are just about as foolish as ever. We stood and promised and planned as any other young foolish lovers do. We were very happy and certainly I came back in better spirits than when I started down but it was now nearly 11 o'clock. Off I came home. Mother asked me next morning where I was the night before. I told her. She said, well you need not have been so late. Ah but I says, we had a good deal of business to settle last night. She did not say any more, I wonder what she thinks about it. The weather has been gloomy and warm and some of the early grass is cut and carried and Haymaking will soon begin. Our Cricket Club has died a

Garsington cricket team

natural death of old age.[20] There were only 3 here last night and they won't play anybody or club I mean. I took bushel potatoes up yesterday, very good too, they are just getting over the frost now. Celery seed came up thick, pulled all my Lettuce up. Mother and Dinah gone to Oxford today and just came back now, 6 o'clock.

Wednesday, June 19   Fany Quartermain died Sunday morning, June 16th, and is buried now, the bell is tolling now. Some Roses out, not gathered bottlers. Have not spoke to Dinah since Baldon Club job with Ted Slade. Just had a confab with Baker about sweethearting and a deal of chaff with E. S[tone?]. Mary and I fell out t'other day. Going to thin carrots out by and by. Can hear the Cuckoo now, but the beauty of the season is over. Planted 10 week German stock out 3 days ago, early peas out in pod, they need rain.

Sunday Night, June 30th   The weather has been most beautiful and lovely. Bright hot and still and more like summer than we have had at all this summer season. Haymaking is about now general, everybody is busy now and cricketing is all over in our Parish now, I think. I planted some Cauliflower plants in our G. last Wednesday and in Q.G. and I transplanted some celery plants in Q.G. last Wednesday, tidy plants at 8d. per 100. Cauliflower 9d. I am taking a good many Potatoes up now, they are fetching 8/6 but they come out bad. K.B. out in bloom in Q.G. Nearly all Cabbage gone, no peas fit, they all want rain now and the ground is cracking fearfully down the Common. Things look pretty well down there, peas are blighting at home. They are mowing Betty Craft now. Holloways got a Mowing Machine at work below. Was at Oxford yesterday to Brewers and on B with Nett. Called at T[om's], not at home, left word to come up to tea, haven't been though. Went to Church this morning, had not been for a good while before. Was at work nearly all day last Sunday, tatoring, then went down to Netts. She and her mother at home. We sat and talked some time and then we started off to the Wixons for a walk. Twas a beautiful night, party bathing [in River Thame]. Back home and gathered flowers, it was Commemoration week and then down home with Nett.[21] I saw her once or twice this last week and had a long chat Thursday night. Mary Holloway died that night at 10 o'clock, buried yesterday at Abingdon. I think many a game I have had with that young girl. She was a merry light hearted girl years ago, gone on a long journey now, poor thing. The measles are about here now a good deal. Baker has nearly finished his new built [building], killed his first sheep last night there. I have got to the last page in this Book. I wonder what it will be my lot to note down in the next, if any. Haven't seen anything of T[om] C[ooper] for some time. Courting somewhere I expect. Bought new pair of strong shoes last night of Sellar 11/6. Trade dull. Our choir went to Dorchester Choral Festival. They had 7 or 8 carts and had 2 breakdowns but nobody injured. A good many went, they had a good day's enjoyment and gave satisfaction. But it is getting slow now and will when Bowles leaves, I think. Ripe fruit coming in fast now. I gathered first ripe fruit Friday. I saw plenty in Market yesterday. I have some beautiful roses out in bloom now and I have put some buds in. Mother in Law and Clinkards finished haymaking I think, not much fruit this year. Tidy sized tankards on the tree now, wheat out in bloom well. Hoed the garden last week. Tom [Smith] and Emma [Clinkard] still very thick. Druces crew in here to tea now, very warm. The Reform Bill creeps along but the excitement has died out now. Sweet Peas coming out in bloom and some of seeds too. Brompton plants want planting out. Sandford Club tomorrow, I don't know whether I shall go or not. I rather think I shall though. 5.30. Tom C[ooper] is just come this evening, there is no cricketing I think. How I wish it would rain, all the Lettuce gone. I have promised to meet my fate at 6 o'clock so I must now conclude or I shall be too late, so farewell Old Book, I have sat down and jotted away for many an hour and perhaps I might have been worse employed.

J.T.
June 29th, 1867

Carrying water from the Gizzel

Notes

Abbreviations used in notes: JOJ = *Jackson's Oxford Journal*; J.T. = Joseph Turrill; OC = *Oxford Chronicle*; VCH = *Victoria County History*

1863

1. The Sandford lock-keeper confirmed that there is an obelisk in the middle of the weir but it is not possible to read the inscription. Sandford Local History Society gave three sets of names recorded on the obelisk in 1843, 1872, and 1912. They were all Christ Church undergraduates who were drowned while swimming near the weir. The two names seen by J.T. were William Gaisford, son of the Dean, and Richard Phillimore, son of the Regius Professor of Civil Law. Their deaths were reported in the OC on 24 June. The two students drowned in 1912, were Rupert Buxton and Michael Llewellyn Davies, who was J.M. Barrie's ward. The *Oxford Times* reported their deaths on 19 May. The pool by Sandford Weir was evidently notorious when Jerome K. Jerome wrote *Three Men in a Boat* in 1889. He said it 'is a very good place to drown yourself in' and 'the steps of the obelisk are generally used as a diving board by young men now who wish to see if the place really is dangerous' (chapter 18).

2 The Volunteer Rifle Review took place on 24 June. It was announced in the OC on 20 June and reported on 27 June. The historical background, mentioning battles fought at Oxford, was included in a long description. The last similar event had taken place in 1798 when the Duke of York reviewed 20,000. The *Chronicle* reporter said it was a 'splendid gathering on Port Meadow'. There were between 8,000 and 9,000 riflemen from 'the middle ranks of society and therefore of slender means'. After an arduous field day a general holiday was recommended by the mayor, whose idea it was to stage the event. Many sightseers arrived by train and a stand was built on Port Meadow for spectators, who paid 2s. 6d. or 5s.

3. A sharp frost on Sunday 19 July was reported in the OC on 25 July. Elsewhere, e.g. 29 July, J.T. seems to use the word frosty to mean very cold but not necessarily below freezing point.

4. Ranters were Primitive Methodists.

5. GWR Widows' and Orphans' Annual Rural Fete held at Nuneham Park on Tuesday 28 June. An announcement in the OC on 25 July included a list of entertainers – French clowns, patter singers and acrobats. There was also dancing and archery and the Quadrille Band and the Paddington Rifles band played.

6. The line from Thame to Oxford was built between 1862 and 1864. It opened on 24 Oct. 1864 and finally closed to passengers in Jan. 1963. J.T. records several accidents in the diary and a number of people killed.

7. A leading article in the OC on 5 Sept. described the bad effect of the dry weather on the harvest, but it was less serious in the north than in the south.

8. This was a very high price for a pair of handmade shoes. There might have been more than one pair but he does not say so. The average price was about 14s. per pair and he actually paid 14s. 6d. for a pair on 18 Nov. 1865.

9. J.T. was probably referring to an early seventeenth-century tomb of three members of the Dormer family. Pevsner's *Oxfordshire* comments on the high quality of the carving.

10. The report on Garsington Feast in the OC published on 3 Oct. was by J.T.

11. The fire at Grimbly Hughes and Dewe, grocers, started next door at Verey's the tailors and spread to a wine merchants on the other side. All three premises were destroyed and other buildings in Cornmarket St. damaged. The fire was discovered by two University policemen. Two fire-fighters were killed according to the OC report on 3 Oct. Grimbly Hughes was rebuilt and opened again in Oct. 1864.

12. A County and Borough Police Act was passed in 1856 making professional rural constables compulsory. This replaced the old, unsatisfactory voluntary system of appointing someone in the parish for a year.

13. The earthquake was reported in the OC on 10 Oct., but Oxford was not included in the list of places affected. A letter from J. Turrill of Garsington on the subject of earthquakes was published on 31 Oct. It referred to earthquakes which, according to an old History of England, took place in the reigns of Henry I, Henry II and Elizabeth I.

14. A report in the OC on 7 Nov. gave names of places badly affected by the gale. English vessels were among the wrecks off the Dutch and Danish coasts. Stock-carrying vessels on the Thames and along the coasts were sunk and all the animals lost.

15. 'London Journals' appears to be a general reference to magazines from London rather than the name of a particular periodical.

16. Village church bell-ringers usually had a set of handbells which they rang as well. They toured their own village and sometimes other villages at Christmas in the same way as carol singers, with similar rewards.

1864

1. A report in the OC on 16 Jan. said that 'the Princess of Wales was unexpectedly confined with a Prince at Frogmore'. This was Prince Albert

Victor, Duke of Clarence, who died in 1892 just before he was due to marry Princess May (Mary) of Teck. She married his brother, later George V.

2. This was probably the ferryman's thatched cottage by the river. It is marked 'The Cottage' on a contemporary map.

3. This refers to the dispute between Denmark and Prussia over Schleswig-Holstein. The British Government had given advice and some encouragement to the Danes, and Britain was expected to support them in their fight against the combined armies of Austria and Prussia, especially as the father of the Princess of Wales had recently become King of Denmark. However, the government, worried about the large numbers of Germans living in Schleswig-Holstein and the fact that no support would be forthcoming from France, refused to send troops and the Danes were left to struggle alone. They finally surrendered on 18 July. This war is referred to again on 7 Feb.

4. Legislation in 1853 had made infant vaccination compulsory, but it was not yet effective despite the possibility of parents being taken to court for failing to comply. Many were still reluctant because the methods used had serious side-effects. The disease was greatly feared not only for its possible fatal effects but for the permanent scarring on the faces of those who recovered. During the epidemic in Garsington there appears to have been a determined attempt to take whatever precautions were then considered necessary and the people were certainly aware that smallpox was highly infectious.

5. One of the first things to be done after a death was to toll the bell but the sexton had to be paid, so presumably the poorer families would sometimes leave out this part of the funeral ceremony.

6. This was reported in the OC on 13 Feb. A mutinous crew (Malays and Greeks) on a ship called *The Flowery Land* killed the captain and his friends. Seven were condemned to death and two reprieved.

7. The murder was reported in the OC on 5 Mar. Wm. Stevens, aged 24, lived next door to his victim, aged 17. He had threatened to kill her because she would have nothing to do with him. He was sent for trial at the July Assizes in Aylesbury.

8. Richard Newell, wheelwright and carpenter, was living at the Malthouse.

9. The Queen's College and Magdalen were landowners at Denton and the Earl of Macclesfield was lord of the manor. Lord Parker was probably the first earl's son.

10. The reservoir at Bradfield near Sheffield burst its banks on the night of 11/12 Mar. 1864. The OC gave a detailed report on 19 Mar. of the devastation caused, with trees, bridges, farm houses and villages submerged. The writer of the leading article compared the disaster with a similar one at Holmfirth in 1852 and took the opportunity to point out the folly of the 'long contemplated project of a reservoir on Headington Hill' for Oxford.

11. Thomas Stonor, Lord Camoys, was Lord-in-Waiting to Queen Victoria between 1846 and 1874 and his daughter-in-law, Elise, daughter of Robert

Peel, was lady of the Bedchamber to Princess Alexandra, the Princess of Wales. A picture of a meet of HM Staghounds at Stonor House on 18 Apr. 1875 appears in the guidebook. Only the monarch was allowed to keep hounds for deer hunting.

12. The case of 'Damaging Flowers at Garsington: Wm Druce v Thomas Druce' came up at Bullingdon Petty Sessions on 2 Apr. 1864 and appeared to be the result of a family row over the non-payment of rent by T. Druce to Priscilla Druce, wife of William. The rector gave evidence saying that the property was part of the glebe and that all the rent had now been paid. The case was dismissed, with a caution.

13. This must have been a spontaneous action on the part of the men employed by Gale. Perhaps they objected to the new mowing machine. Garsington workers did not form a trade union branch until 1872 and this had declined by 1875 when 'the branch was found as sheep without a shepherd, the secretary having left them'. At least one labourer had been sacked for daring to join. See *Agricultural Trade Unionism in Oxfordshire 1872–1881*, Oxford Record Soc., 1974.

14. Garibaldi's visit to England was well covered in the OC on 23 Apr. He had a packed programme which was said to have exhausted him because he was already in bad health. This led to the cancellation of his provincial tour and his visit was curtailed. However, he did spend two days in Cornwall with friends before sailing from Plymouth to Caprera in the Duke of Sutherland's yacht. A leading article discussed suspicions that the Emperor Napoleon and/or the French Government had demanded his return. This was denied by the British Government.

15. May be hugged and kissed. J.T. was rather coy about these matters when putting pen to paper. The meaning of 'x' is for the reader to decide.

16. Regular reports on the war over Schleswig-Holstein and the American Civil War were appearing in the OC. A conference on the former was held in London and included English and French representatives, but it failed to settle the dispute.

17. Princess Alexandra had recently married the Prince of Wales and was much admired for her fashionable clothes, so her favourite styles were in demand. However, efforts to trace an 'Alexandra coat' have so far failed to identify one known by her name which would also be suitable for men. The 'Alexandra jacket' designed to wear with the crinoline is well documented.

18. '53' seems to be a person. (See also entry for 18 July.)

19. According to the *Agrarian History of England and Wales*, Vol. VI, ed. G.E. Mingay, Oxfordshire was relatively slow to make use of horse-drawn mowing and reaping machines. They did not appear in sale notices in the county until about 1860 and only became common in the 1870s although Bernard Samuelson, a Banbury agricultural engineer, who was to establish an international reputation for reaping and mowing machines, had founded his business in the 1850s.

20. The Royal Oxfordshire Horticultural Show held in the gardens of New College. Reported in the OC on 11 June.
21. A well-known Oxford photographer's shop at 26 High Street. Henry Taunt was employed there in the 1850s and 1860s before he started his own business and became well known himself for his photographs of Oxfordshire.
22. A vote of censure on the government's foreign policy was introduced by Disraeli. He described it as 'a policy of meddle and muddle'. The government was defeated in the Lords, but won by eighteen votes in the Commons.
23. Mr Thomas Briggs, aged 70, was murdered in a first-class carriage on the North London Railway. His body was thrown out of the train. He worked for bankers in Lombard St. His gold watch and other personal possessions were missing but his hat had been replaced by that of the murderer. See also reference below to arrest and trial of Franz Muller (entry for 14 Sept.). The case caused a great sensation and was fully reported on 16 July in the OC. A similar type of hat to that of the murderer, which was a cross between a bowler and a top hat, was afterwards given the name 'Muller cut-down'.
24. This fete in aid of GWR Widows' and Orphans' fund was held at Aldermaston Park on 5 July. It was announced in the OC on 13 June. A special train from Oxford via Abingdon, Culham and Didcot linked up with the Cheltenham train.
25. *Cartes de Visite* were introduced from Paris in the 1850s. They were cheap, usually full-length portraits approximately 3½ in by 2¼ in, pasted onto a slightly larger card and were originally intended to illustrate calling cards. Queen Victoria and Prince Albert and their family were photographed in 1861 and after that the craze spread to all classes and was known as cartomania. People exchanged portraits with friends and relatives and put them into specially designed albums. Photographs of royalty and other famous people were also collected. The photographers were able to give details of their services on the backs of the *cartes*, so it was an effective way of advertising. Surviving collections are now valued as a fashion archive (see e.g. Robert Pols, *Dating Old Photographs*, Federation of Family History Societies, Birmingham, 1992).
26. Ballast train is an expression which seems to relate to the railway. It is possible that some wagons drawn by horses or a steam traction engine were taken through the village to the new railway lines.
27. This was reported in the OC on 13 Aug. It recommended viewing through an ordinary opera glass. The comet was near the Pleiades and could be seen 'as long as starlight lasts'.
28. Robert Surman jun. was tenant of the small farm in Southend, which then belonged to Christ Church. His occupation in 1861 was beer retailer. An undated letter from Revd Wilgress to the college reported complaints about the beer house causing a nuisance and said that Surman would have to leave and had nothing to pay his creditors (see note 19 for 1865).

29. James Legge, journeyman upholsterer, took his wife and three children from Tunbridge Wells to Reading and abandoned them at an inn. In despair she threw them into the river and jumped in after them. Reported in the OC 13 Aug.

30. In the nineteenth century steam gradually took over from other sources of power. It had been used in corn mills as a supplementary source since the end of the eighteenth century. There is no record of a mill in Garsington in the nineteenth century, but there were two at Wheatley not far from the parish boundary. It is unlikely that George Fruin owned the steam ploughing machine he was using as they were usually hired. Their use was widespread in the midlands and south from c. 1854.

31. This was held on 30 Aug. by the Banbury Horticultural Society in the grounds of W. Munton Esq. at West Bar. It was a fine day but windy and one marquee was blown over onto some of the exhibits. There were prizes and a concert was held in the evening. There were two bands, the Orpheus Glee Union, solo songs and piano pieces. 5,000 visitors attended and profits were £128 6s. 1d. for the show plus £69 for the concert. Reported in the OC 3 Sept.

32. *The Hunchback* was performed at the Theatre Royal in the Town Hall and a report appeared in the OC on 27 Aug. It referred to 'Sheridan Knowles' fine play', but was critical of Mr Henry Irving's performance. *Belles* was not mentioned.

33. This probably refers to St Lawrence Church, Toot Baldon. There were reports about the state of disrepair of the chancel from 1765 until 1808, when 5 guineas was allotted for repairs. It was during the incumbency of Edmund Peel (1860–71) and his two successors that the church building was restored so it is likely that the chancel, traditionally the responsibility of the incumbent, was given priority (see *VCH*, vol. V).

34. J.T.'s account of the match against Headington appeared in the OC on 10 Sept. He praised the destructive bowling of James Aldworth and A. Clinkard and the fielding of R. Turrill.

35. The OC had a very long account of the drama surrounding this case. Franz Muller was arrested in New York for the murder of Thomas Briggs (see entry for 18 July). It described his conduct during the outward voyage and gave his case for the defence. Although there were no photographs in the paper normally, a large portrait of him was printed on 17 Sept. He was a tailor, aged 23, and his trial and conviction took place in Oct. On 10 Dec. the OC published his last letter, written before his execution to his parents, in which he declared his innocence and said he had been convicted on circumstantial evidence.

36. J.T.'s preliminary announcement appeared in the OC on 24 Sept. and the Feast took place on Monday 26 Sept. His report on it and on the cricket match was printed on 1 Oct. The teams were captained by R. Turrill and G. Holloway, A. Clinkard was judge, John Aldworth starter and T. Smith

secretary. In the evening there was an assembly in a large room near the Red Lion which was lent by Mr J.B. Spearing. The large room was probably the slaughterhouse which he mentions elsewhere in the diary. Sports were held in Mr Smith's close.

37. The two plays were reviewed in the OC on 15 Oct: 'On Monday evening the drama of *Don Caesar de Bazan* was presented for the first time this season, the leading characters being entrusted to Mr. R. Souter in the delineation of which he displayed his usual ability and tact. Mr. McLean played the difficult part of Don Jose in an excellent manner and Miss Eburn performed Martina with quiet discrimination. Mr. Morgan and Mrs. Clifford Cooper as the Marquis and Marchioness of Rotunda were quite equal to the occasion. This was followed by the capital farce, *The Clockmakers Hat*, in which the clever acting of Miss Wood kept the audience in a continued roar of laughter.'

38. *Grimaldi or The Life of an Actress* by Dion Boucicault, the Irish playwright, was advertised on 17 Sept. in the OC. 'Two celebrated actors from the Theatre Royal, Drury Lane' (unnamed) were making their first appearance in Oxford.

39. 104,000 lb of gunpowder exploded at Erith. Report in the OC on 8 Oct. gave details of the injured. There were five dead and five missing.

40. There was an eating-house in Oxford at 6 Queen St. called Maltby's.

41. Animals in rural areas in 1864 were still likely to be doctored either by local amateurs or by their owners and the methods used would often have been similar to those applied to human ailments. A tenant at Guidens Farm, who had been described as a farmer in earlier censuses was, at the age of 59, a 'veterinary surgeon' in 1861 but was no longer living there in 1864. His skills had probably been acquired 'on the job'. From 1844, when the Royal College of Veterinary Surgeons was established, there was a very gradual increase in the study of veterinary science and by the end of the century there were many more professional vets.

42. J.T. must have left out a vital word here e.g. it could be 'mother's friend's daughter'. He also seems to be confused about the date of the wedding.

43. These are said to have been built with surplus wood from the railway.

44. This was reported in the OC on 31 Dec. Most of the farm buildings and machinery and three pigs were burnt, but the cattle were rescued.

45. It was announced in the OC on 17 Dec. that William Hedges Cooper of Oxford married Miss Sophia Tanner of Farnborough at St Michael's, Belgrave Square but there was no such church in Belgrave Square. There was a St Michael's church not far away in Chester Square.

46. A case of poaching.

1865

1. In the Tithe Schedule (1843) George Holloway was the owner of the cottage now called Lanesra. Mrs Druce may have been living in a separate cottage on the Malthouse site.

2. The old cottage next to the Red Lion later rebuilt and called Fern Cottage.

3. The Radfords had owned several cottages. This one was probably 23 Wheatley Rd.

4. An article in JOJ on 1 May said that a false rumour had been put about that Oxford Savings Bank had been robbed. This was quickly refuted and on 1 July a letter from a trustee of the bank was also published explaining the bank's affairs.

5. The four couples, whose initials are given, appear to be friends or relatives of the bride and groom arranged in pairs and walking to church in procession in the traditional way. It is not possible to identify everyone, but it seems as if the bridal pair, George and Lizzy, may be included in J.T.'s list, George with his sister Harriet and Lizzy with one of her brothers, John or James.

6. On 29 Apr. JOJ published an account of the surrender of General Lee's army to General Grant, which virtually ended the Civil War, and also announced the assassination of President Lincoln at the theatre in Washington on Good Friday. Wilkes Booth, brother of actor Edwin Booth, was the assassin and he was also murdered. Reports continued to appear for many weeks.

7. It was customary for the bride and groom to return to the church on the Sunday after the wedding dressed in their wedding finery again, for the benefit of the congregation. Sometimes the whole wedding party went too.

8. Booth was the murderer of President Lincoln.

9. The report in OC on 29 May said that the Wheatley Club had only recently been established and therefore it was an easy victory for Garsington. After the match they adjourned to the Crown Inn, where 'Host Bushnell served up a plentiful repast in first-rate style'. David Stone was in the team. J.T.'s announcement for the forthcoming match published in the OC said that 'The two clubs are supposed to be composed of the first bats in the county'.

10. Dr Mark's concert was announced on the front page of the OC on 3 June. Grand concerts would take place for two days in Oxford Town Hall, with afternoon and evening performances by Dr Mark's pupils and students from the Royal College of Music, Manchester. All performances were in aid of Dr Mark's Great National Enterprise, which was the encouragement of native musical talent.

11. Industrial School Cowley was listed in the 1864 PO Directory. Industrial schools were established for deprived children who might otherwise have become criminals.

12. The annual meeting of parish choirs from the county was reported in JOJ on 8 July. Choirs and clergy assembled in Christ Church Hall and, wearing surplices and carrying flags and banners, formed a procession. They marched round Tom Quad singing a psalm on their way into the Cathedral. There is a long description of the service, sermon, lunch, speeches etc. Four hundred choirs attended, including Garsington.

13. R.C. coat is difficult to identify. He may have used the word coat for jacket in which case it could be a reefer jacket. These were common at the time.

14. A freehold cottage residence was advertised in JOJ on 15 July. The auction was to take place at the Red Lion on 26 July. The description and location appear to refer to the house which had belonged to Richard West until his death in 1858. He left it to his daughter Mary Ann Clinkard, wife of Richard Clinkard of Guiden's Farm who mortgaged it, with her consent, in 1862. The mortgage was transferred to the Oxford Building and Investment Trust in 1868. Mary Ann's relatives were determined to keep the house in the family and eventually paid off the mortgage so that it became the property of her niece, Frances Jacks. Frances was married to Thomas Clinkard, Richard's nephew, who also worked at Guiden's Farm. Presumably the auction sale was not legal under the terms of Richard West's will.

15. A rough draft of J.T.'s unpublished article is in his notes. The chairman made a speech saying that they hoped David Stone would be as successful and well respected in New Zealand as he was in Garsington. A large number of people attended the meeting at the Red Lion.

16. A fault appeared during the laying of the cable and seemed to be quickly repaired. However, the cable broke and the attempt was abandoned until 1866 when a second cable was successfully laid and the first one repaired. Reports on the whole operation with a good deal of technical detail appeared in JOJ and the OC in July and Aug.

17. Cattle plague was usually known as rinderpest. There was a bad epidemic in the eighteenth century when drastic measures were used to prevent it spreading. Diseased cattle were killed, contacts put in quarantine and farmers compensated at half the market value. An Act passed in 1850 enabled similar measures to be taken in the epidemic of 1865/6. Reports appeared regularly in the press from Aug. until the end of the year. It had been imported from Europe and there were not many local cases so far, but J.T. refers to it again in Jan. 1866 when there were cases at nearby Cuddesdon.

18. According to the diary, four girls, dressed in white with black mantles and white cloaks, carried the baby's coffin. Children or young people carrying a child's coffin appears to be an old established custom. In *The Diary of Thomas Turner 1754–1765* (ed. David Vaisey, Oxford, 1985, p. 216), Elizabeth Porter, aged 4, had died on 2 Jan. 1761. The entry for 7 Jan. reads 'In the morn went and invited the children to support Miss Porter's pall'. A picture by Frank Holl called *Her Firstborn*, painted in 1870 (Dundee Art Galleries and Museums), shows the funeral procession of a baby whose pall is being carried by four young girls.

19. A surveyor's report on the Plough in 1850 said that the roof needed extensive repairs, so perhaps nothing satisfactory had been done until 1865. The indoor licence appears to refer to its rise in status from beerhouse or shop to a fully licensed public house. Crawford, who had been competing for trade with the Red Lion, had worked at a large farm in Cowley and was a tenant of the farmer, Richard Clinkard. The entry on 28 May 1865 which reads 'Bob Surman out Crawford in' suggests that Crawford took over the tenancy

of the Christ Church house in Southend and obtained an indoor licence
there. By 1871 he was no longer in the Garsington census.

20. The Witch refers to the Wyche, an old cutting through the Malvern Hills
reaching about 845 ft. Malvern developed rapidly as a spa town in the 1860s
when the railway made it accessible and three stations were built: Great
Malvern, Malvern Link and Malvern Wells.

21. A hot-air balloon would have been used for the entertainment of the large
numbers of visitors to the town. James Sadler (1753–1828) who was born in
Oxford is said to have been the first Englishman to have made an ascent,
which he did from the Botanic Gardens in 1784.

22. Thame Flower Show was part of the Thame Horticultural Show reported in
the OC on 16 Sept. It took place in 'beautiful grounds belonging to Mr.
Seymour' and was 'a show of cut flowers [i.e. asters and dahlias], fruit and
vegetables, all of a very superior quality'. The Band of the First Life Guards
and 'Captain Wykeham's Own Corps of Drums and Fifes' played alternately.

23. Tom Smith's report in the OC on 14 Oct. agreed with J.T.'s verdict that the
feast held on 26 Sept. was well conducted, having been organized by the
Cricket Club with J. Aldworth as chairman and T. Smith as vice-chairman.
They adjourned afterwards to a large room lent by T.B. Spearing which
would have been the old slaughterhouse at the Kennels.

24. Garsington choir v. Cuddesdon choir. Their return cricket match was
reported in the OC on 14 Oct. Tea was provided by the Revd King
(Cuddesdon) and the Revd and Mrs Wilgress.

25. Death of Lord Palmerston, the Prime Minister, was reported in the OC on 21
Oct. He died in office on 18 Oct., aged 80, and was buried in Westminster
Abbey.

26. The Randolph Hotel had just been built on the corner of Beaumont St. in
the centre of Oxford. Pevsner's *Oxfordshire* gives the date of the building as
1864. J.T.'s friend, Hatto, must have been among the first employees to be
taken on when it was ready to open.

27. The Railway Hotel at Wheatley has survived the disappearance of the railway
and is now one of several pubs in the village. It stands at the bottom of
Ladder Hill opposite the site of the old Wheatley station and is the last visible
evidence of the station's former existence.

1866

1. J.T. is rather confusing about the frosts which they had at the beginning of
the year 1866. On 9 Jan. he refers to a very sharp frost but says on 10 Feb.
'we haven't had a single frost yet'. Again on 23 Feb. he says there was a
'tight' frost on two or three mornings around that time but that was all they
had had that year.

2. Cattle Plague had now become serious in Oxfordshire and Berkshire. The
Act of 1850 was invoked at Reading Assizes and Oxfordshire Quarter

Sessions enabling the justices to initiate the necessary measures. Articles about the progress of the disease continued to appear regularly in the OC from 6 Jan. until Aug. when the ban was lifted.

3. On collecting taxes and rates J.T. at first says he is working for James Aldworth but it is not clear exactly what their individual responsibilities were. The Oxford City Directory of 1868 lists 'Assessors and Collectors of Land and Assessed Taxes' and 'Assessors and Collectors of Property and Income Tax' for each parish. Usually the same two people collected both. In Sept. 1866 he went to the Crown at Wheatley to be sworn in 'Assessor for Income Tax' and in his summing up of the year 1866 he says 'I am collector (with J. A[ldworth]) of assessed and Income Tax'. He went again with James Aldworth in Apr. 1867 and on that occasion was sworn in as 'Assessor of Assessed Taxes' which seems to be the same as Assessor and Collector of Land Taxes. Returns of the total valuation of land in the parish were made by the local assessors who were nominated by specially appointed commissioners, usually JPs. Each parish was assessed on this valuation to produce an appropriate amount of tax. The rate for obtaining this was then fixed by the local assessors whose duty it was to display a copy of the assessment on the church door so that objectors could appeal. The rates tended to remain the same over a number of years so J.T. was probably carrying out the well-established routine of putting up the notice and collecting the money.

4. After the death of Palmerston, who opposed reform, Russell and Gladstone had proposed a moderate extension of the vote to about 400,000 people. This was enough to bring down Russell's government, which resigned in June. Disraeli, the strongest man in Lord Derby's Conservative cabinet, then brought in a Reform Bill which, after various amendments, eventually became law in 1867. It enfranchised over 900,000 by household suffrage, almost doubling the electorate. Household suffrage in this case meant occupiers who were responsible for paying rates of £12 or more. There was a leading article in the OC on 20 Apr. and one reprinted from *The Times* and continuous coverage of the subject from then on.

5. The 'Collector' must refer to James Aldworth.

6. There was a report in the OC on 12 May that Austria was expecting to be attacked by Italy. In June/July Bismarck's Prussia defeated Austria in a seven-week war and went on to lead a unified Germany. After that war Venice was joined to a unified Italy, which was now freed from the prospect of a war with Austria.

7. There were articles in the OC on 19 May on the 'monetary panic' resulting from the failure of Overend and Gurney's Bank, with a deficit of £19m. Several other banks also failed and the bank rate was raised to 10 per cent until Aug. G.M. Young, in *Victorian England, Portrait of an Age*, wrote of the failure as a major disaster: 'The new system of Limited Liability had brought into the area of speculative finance thousands of quiet-living families who had

hitherto been satisfied with the Funds or a few well-established Railways or Foreign Loans. They were now the chief sufferers and the contraction of their expenditure and the loss of their confidence weighed on the country for years' (see ch. XIX).

8. The return match between Garsington and Watlington Temperance Club took place on 16 July. On 21 July the *Oxford Times* report criticized the behaviour of the Garsington team, especially G. Holloway and R. Quartermain, implying that they were drunk, but praised J. Aldworth for his batting and bowling and A. Clinkard for his batting.

9. Garsington v. Foresters on Magdalen College cricket ground was played on 30 July and reported in the OC on 11 Aug. The game ran out of time when the Foresters, needing 110 runs in their second innings, were 42 for 5.

10. The name Rogers appears frequently between July 1866 and Feb. 1867 as Mr Rogers, Rogers, or Professor Rogers but all refer to the same man who was acting as temporary curate after the departure of the Revd G.F. Wilgress. Although he was Drummond Professor of Political Economy at the time, James Edwin Thorold Rogers (1823–90) had been familiar with the duties of a curate after he graduated, first at St Paul's Oxford and later at Headington. Details of his life from the *Dictionary of National Biography* reveal a little of his character and explain his interest in the lives and labours of agricultural workers. (See also note for Feb. 1867).

11. A demonstration in favour of the Reform Bill was due to take place in Hyde Park. The Home Secretary decided that the park could not be used for this purpose and the gates were closed before the crowds arrived in the evening. The organizers, after protesting that he was exceeding his powers, diverted the meeting to Trafalgar Sq., but some more unruly members of the crowd stayed behind and managed to break into the park. This resulted in stone-throwing and many arrests. Reported in the OC 28 July.

12. Bell's Life may have been *Life and Labour of Sir Charles Bell* by A. Pichot published in 1860. Sir Charles Bell (1774–1842) was a famous surgeon and neurologist who did pioneering research. He was an attractive and flamboyant character who would have appealed to J.T.

13. J.T. appears to be acting for Mrs Harper, his future mother-in-law, in an income tax dispute. She had taken over Southend Farm after her husband's death in 1861.

14. An Act passed in 1866 compelled local authorities to appoint sanitary inspectors and it became mandatory to insist on the removal of nuisances, i.e. anything which was known or thought to be a danger to public health. The provision of disinfectant was a practical way of ensuring that the notices were taken seriously.

15. Mrs Aldworth and Hattie were probably James's wife and their servant Harriet Moreton.

16. 'Bennet's School' was either St Clements School listed under Parochial Schools in the Oxford directory for 1863 (the master was William Bennet) or

Cowley College established by the Oxford Diocesan Board in the old manor-house, Temple Cowley (headmaster J.M.C. Bennett).

17. Order of Foresters is a friendly society for insurance purposes.

18. The OC report by T. Smith, which J.T. calls 'somewhat faulty', is perhaps more interesting than usual, mentioning many names of participants and of some of their ponies and horses.

19. This suicide was reported in the OC on 10 Nov. Paul Hurst, aged 17, son of a blacksmith/publican, had 'blown his brains out' in Mr Matthew's field in the village. His parents had refused to give him a letter from a young girl and, after asking for it three times, he said they would hear something before night. They thought he was too young to have a girl-friend.

20. Price of bread, the staple food of the poor, was used as an indicator of the rise and fall in the cost of living. It reached 10d. in London in 1867 and was about 10 per cent of the average labourer's wage. Prices gradually came down in the last three decades of the century. There were articles in the OC on 24 Nov. 1866 and 20 Apr. 1867.

21. Long reports appeared in the OC on 24 Nov. Approximately fifty lives were lost, including some in Leeds, Halifax, Manchester, Preston, Wakefield and the W. Riding, and much property was destroyed.

22. A contradiction here. Perhaps he meant to say he was asked to stop up there for supper, but did not accept.

23. J.T. refers to Watson's sale again on Thursday 23 May 1867 when he went along and bought paint and logs. This first report saying everything was sold and the men sacked must have been a rumour, heard in the bar perhaps.

24. This demonstration was reported in the OC on 8 Dec. It was part of a campaign for the enfranchisement of the industrial workers.

25. At Barnsley an estimated 340 had died, as reported in the OC on 15 Dec. On 22 Dec. the OC said that the number of dead in N. Staffordshire was 355.

26. The art unions, societies whose aim was to distribute works of art, ran the only legal lotteries after state lotteries were abolished in England in 1823. J.T. also said he received lottery tickets from Glasgow (see entry for 13 Mar. 1865).

27. The medieval church at Nuneham Courtenay was pulled down by Lord Harcourt in the eighteenth century after he had moved the village to a new site on the Oxford–Henley Road. The monuments were scattered and the Renaissance tomb of Anthony Pollard was removed to the grounds of Baldon House, where it remained until it was returned to Nuneham in the early twentieth century (see *VCH*, vol. V). A postcard photograph of the tomb at Marsh Baldon was in the collection found in J.T.'s house and was probably taken by him.

28. No definite connection has been established between the Turrill family and Nuneham, but it is possible that he went to the school there in the 1850s. His elder cousin Joseph from the Three Horseshoes was being encouraged to become a qualified schoolmaster in about 1850 when he was 25, and a letter

from the former curate, the Revd W.J. Copeland, to F.J. Morrell suggested
that he should be sent to Nuneham away from the 'noisy alehouse' for extra
teaching experience. The teaching at Nuneham school at that time was
thought to be particularly good.

29. The magic lantern was an early method of projecting enlarged pictures etc.
onto a white screen. They were drawn or photographed on glass slides and
slotted in in front of the lamp.

1867

1. Severe weather was reported in various parts of the country in the OC on 12
Jan. There was a leading article on the 'Fickleness of the Climate'. It had
been 20° below freezing and then there was a rapid thaw.

2. A two-column account in the OC on 19 Jan. gave graphic descriptions of the
drowned and reports on some of the inquests.

3. This was the Reform League demonstration reported in the OC on 16 Feb. An
estimated 20,000 marched in orderly procession to Trafalgar Sq. headed by a
band and a troop of farriers. Tradesmen were taking part as members of the
Reform League but threatened to hold their own demonstration at Easter if
they discovered that the government's intentions were not strictly honourable.
A meeting was held afterwards in the Agricultural Hall and Professor Rogers,
who was on the committee, moved the first resolution which ended in a
demand for 'residential and registered manhood suffrage'. (See Disraeli's
Reform Bill, 1867, referred to in the note on 29 Apr. 1866.) Professor Rogers
ceased to be the curate at Garsington at the end of 1866. In 1867 he stood for
re-election to the chair but failed owing to his 'advanced political views' and
'his habit of speaking on political platforms' e.g. at the Reform League meeting
in London in Feb. 1867. He held appointments at London University,
campaigned for an Act which would enable clergymen to resign from Holy
Orders and, as soon as it became law, took advantage of it himself in 1870. He
served as MP for Southwark before returning to Oxford in 1883 as lecturer at
Worcester College. He had a distinguished academic career which ended with
two more years as Drummond Professor before his death in 1890. His books
include *A History of Agriculture* in 2 vols., 1886, *A Student's Manual of Political
Economy*, 1868 and *Six Centuries of Work and Wages, the History of English
Labour*, 1884. He also edited Adam Smith's *Wealth of Nations* in 1869. He had
seven sons and a daughter who is mentioned on p. 107.

4. On ranting tea meeting see note 4 for 1863.

5. The revival of the Fenians reached Ireland from America. An account in the
OC on 23 Feb. says they were led by an American, Colonel O'Connor.
Telegraph wires were cut before the attack and a mounted policeman was
shot. There were rumours that eight hundred men were involved but it was
thought more likely to be about a hundred. The leaders, who came from
America, escaped by boat from Dingle Bay on the west coast.

6. A leading article in the OC on 2 Mar. discussed the reform resolutions which Disraeli, as Chancellor of the Exchequer, had presented to the House. On 9 Mar. three Secretaries of State were reported as having resigned after disagreements about the Bill. They were Cranborne, Caernarvon and Peel and were described as 'ultra conservatives' but also 'the ablest members of Lord Derby's Cabinet'.

7. He was right. The Bill was amended.

8. Bibo meaning a tippler or drunkard comes from the Latin *bibere* to drink.

9. Hop-tops or hop shoots were eaten in April/May as a delicacy and were sometimes called mock-asparagus because their flavour is said to be similar. J.T. may have sent some to the Oxford market. Hops were more widely cultivated in England in the nineteenth century and used not only in beer-making but also as a herbal remedy for liver and stomach disorders. Wild hops (*humulus lupulus*) from the hedgerows were also used. Elizabeth David in *An Omelette and a Glass of Wine* (Harmondsworth, 1986) wrote an interesting article on the subject and included an eighteenth-century recipe for hop-top soup.

10. A fire at Marsh Baldon was reported in the OC on 6 Apr. Cottages occupied by Barrett and Currell, labourers, and other thatched buildings were burned down. The report was corrected the following week in a letter from a resident who said that the fire-engines mentioned had arrived too late and that the fire had been tackled by two engines from the Nuneham estate.

11. This was the Paris International Exhibition similar in scale to the Great Exhibition of 1851. It was sited on the Champs de Mars and surrounded by pleasure grounds and gardens and was not completely ready until about a month after the opening on 1 Apr. The emphasis was on art and industry, especially the use of machinery, and on agricultural and horticultural displays. Working men's excursions were organized from London and the French authorities provided accommodation for 200 at a time. Articles were published in the OC on 6 Apr. and 18 May and in the *Illustrated London News* on 6 Apr.

12. This was J.T.'s only reference to his three brothers and three sisters who had died, presumably from TB, or consumption, as it was called then. The rector in 1853 noted that 'this family all have a tendency to consumption'. His parents were first cousins, which probably increased their children's chances of contracting the disease. His three sisters all died in 1858, aged 19, 20 and 21, when he was 17. Lizzy died soon after he married A.H. in 1869.

13. France and Prussia were quarrelling over Luxembourg. The OC had an article about this on 27 Apr. and another leading article on the Reform debate.

14. This echoes a line in Alexander Pope's *An Essay on Criticism*: 'That, like a wounded snake, drags its slow length along'. J.T. was interested in poetry and copied a number of sentimental poems into his notebooks, and also songs from Tom Cooper's diary. Some came from magazines and not all are

attributed. It is possible that he tried writing some himself, but there is no evidence of this in the form of rough notes whereas there are notes for letters and for his OC articles.

15. The rates of the Compound Householder were included in his rent.

16. Princess Teck's daughter was the future Queen Mary, wife of George V.

17. Burke the Fenian was presumably Thomas Bourke who was sentenced to death in Dublin in May and reprieved, with six others, on the day before the execution after a campaign by public figures. It was thought that the executions would be counter-productive since the Fenians were no longer regarded as a serious threat.

18. J. Aldworth's contract seems to have made him responsible for the upkeep of the roads in the parish.

19. Dorchester Choral Festival was held on 20 June and reported in the OC on 22 June. Choirs participating were Dorchester, Wantage, Garsington, Horspath, Little Wittenham, North Moreton and Coleshill. Luncheon was in a large marquee provided by Mr Minchin and the list of Reverend gentlemen accompanying the choirs included Mr Wilgress as well as T. Bowles. All the choirs were praised.

20. The Cricket Club, which had been well established from the early nineteenth century, revived and was still flourishing in the 1870s and 1880s. Mr Muscott, in the school log-book, frequently noted that the school had a holiday to attend a cricket match locally. However, the club's early records no longer exist and have only survived from *c.* 1890.

21. J.T. was probably gathering flowers to send to Oxford market. Demand would be high in University Commemoration week which traditionally takes place in June and includes the degree giving ceremony, the Encaenia Garden Party, and the college balls.

Glossary

Adzing	Earthing up potatoes with a tool called an adze.
Again	Against.
Backing Walnuts	Probably collecting them.
Bottlers	Plums for bottling.
Bud	To insert a bud under the bark of another stock plant to raise a different variety. Sometimes used in the diary to mean dis-bud, i.e. removing some buds in order to improve the quality and size of those remaining.
Cheap John	Cheapjack.
Churched	After childbirth the mother attends a church service when thanks and prayers are offered for her safe delivery. She is then said to be churched.
Cobbed	From *cob* to strike or hit.
Cock/s	Used in skittles. Can be the target or the object thrown or a throw.
Cuff	To cuff things over, meaning to discuss and examine.
Cuff boxing	In which all blows are aimed at the face.
Culls	Rejected produce.
Drag	A long open carriage with transverse or side seats.
Dray	A heavy goods cart.
Felps	Fieldfares.
First	In church. First banns called.
Flats	Broad shallow baskets used for packing produce for market.
Flukes	Kidney potatoes.
Handle	Provide with a handle.
Haulm	Stalks and other dry vegetable remains used like straw.
Hovel	Originally a movable shed without sides.
Hud	Collect or gather together.
Kilderkin	A small barrel or cask containing about 18 gallons.
Landrail	A bird which is almost extinct in the British Isles owing to modern farming methods. (Also known as corncrake.)
Middling	The meaning varies with the context but usually in indifferent, poor or very bad health.
Missly/Mizzly	Drizzly.

Moulding	Earthing up (potatoes).
Out-asked	Last banns called in church.
Pit	To store root vegetables in a hole or pit.
Quarter	28 lb or 8 bushels.
Score	Weight used for pigs (20–21 lb).
Shrudded	Probably *shrouded* meaning lopped (also shredded and shudded).
Slushes	Waters (watering early in the year was a method of destroying pests).
Stick	1. To push rods into the ground for peas to climb.
	2. To kill a pig by stabbing.
Storcking	May be J.T.'s spelling of stalking.
Straw brim	Straw boater.
Tack	Food.
Tankards	Dessert apples (although this usually meant turnips or swedes).
Tatoring	Digging potatoes.
Vignette	Photographic portrait with shading round the head.
Whip	Money collected by subscription, especially for drinks.
White corn	So-called because it changed to a lighter colour as it ripened. The clay soil in which it grew was called white soil.
With/e	Tough, flexible branch, especially willow or osier.

Some People and Families in the Diary

Much of the information on people mentioned in the diary is taken from the 1861 and 1871 Garsington Censuses and occasionally from the 1851 Census, but usually it is not possible to tell exactly where people were living unless there is information from other sources. The censuses do name some houses, e.g. farmhouses, pubs, the rectory etc., and names of roads are sometimes given or areas indicated, e.g. 'Centre of the village' or 'North End', and this can be a help in locating a family.

Abell	William Able, a labourer aged 23, m. Esther Pym, aged 20, in Dec. 1865.
Aldworth	James the baker. His daughter was bpt. Mar. 1867.
	John the butcher, d. 1865, aged 28.
	Lizzy, or E.A., m. George Holloway, 27 Apr. 1865.
	Sarah, m. Alfred Clinkard.
	Thomas, farmer at Hill Farm. In 1861 he farmed 110 acres and employed 5 men and 2 boys.
	All the above were children of William and Sarah Aldworth who both died in the 1850s. Sarah was J.T.'s aunt.
'Baker'	James Aldworth.
Belcher	George, a widower, labourer aged 70, in the 1871 census living with his daughter, Maria, aged 32, and grandsons William, 14, and Henry, 5. All born at Nuneham.
	Dick may be related but does not appear in a census.
Bennet	William, a carpenter, b. Clifton Hampden, aged 28 in the 1871 census.
Bishop of Oxford	Samuel Wilberforce.
Boswell	Joe, son of George, labourer, b. Garsington c. 1845 after the family moved from London.
Bowles	Revd Thomas, curate at Garsington between Feb. and Aug. 1867.
'Bruiser'	Seems to be a nickname for T. Smith. See p. 83.

Buswell	Richard, a farmer at Cuddesdon.
'Butcher'	John Aldworth.
Castle	John, aged 58, a land steward in the 1861 census. His daughter, Ann, only appeared in the 1851 census, aged 15, a servant.
Cherry	William or 'Paddy', aged 25, m. Maria Humphreys in 1864. Both their fathers were labourers.
Clark/e	Benjamin, agricultural labourer, aged 47 in the 1861 census; and Kezia, his wife, aged 40, d. 1867.
	Eliza was living with her widowed mother and brother James in 1861. She was baptized in 1838 and had an older sister, Ellen, who may have been known as 'Nancy'.
	Joe, a ganger on the railway, who was J.T.'s tenant, is not identifiable from the information given in the diary.
Clinkard	Richard (1786–1869), a tenant farmer who was living at Exeter College Farm at the top of Clinkard's Hill with his second wife, Mary (1795–1865). He farmed 130 acres and employed 5 men and 3 boys in 1861.
	James, their son (1826–70), a seedsman, m. Harriet Turrill (1826–80), daughter of Mary Turrill at the Horseshoes.
	Alfred, their youngest son (1830–1912), a farmer, m. Sarah Aldworth. Worked on his father's farm.
	Richard (1819–86), son of Richard by his first wife, Ann. Tenant farmer at Guidens Farm, owned by Wadham College.
	Thomas, son of James, bpt. 1853. Worked at Guidens Farm.
	Emma, daughter of James, bpt. 1848, m. T. Smith 1873.
	Ernest, son of James, bpt. 1865. Later became a pupil teacher at the village school but had to give up owing to bad health.
	Lizzie, daughter of Alfred, bpt. 1867.
	John, publican at the Golden Ball, Littlemore. Son of Richard and Ann, bpt. 1815. He left Garsington with his family in 1851 and his wife Elizabeth d. 1852. They had five children, Ann, John, James, Sarah and Richard.
Cogan	Two doctors, brothers, lived in Wheatley.
Cooper	In the 1851 census William Cooper, baker, was living at the Old Bakery, near the Red Lion, with

his family. His son William was 9 and the twins Thomas (Tom) and Edward (Ted) were 6. They had moved by 1861 to Oxford and J.T. was a regular caller. In the 1864 PO Directory there is a William Cooper, shopkeeper and beer retailer, at 1 Temple St., Cowley Rd, which was close to the Cape of Good Hope. In J.T.'s rough notes there is a reference to the Garsington cricket team being served at 'Temple Bar' by 'mine host Cooper'.
Joe, the singer, appears to be a newcomer.
Fanny and Sophia, see Smith.
William, aged 31 in 1871, b. Bampton, worked for the widowed Harriet Clinkard, farmer.

Coster	H., owned a threshing machine at Stadhampton. (Coster was also the name of the occupant at the Red Lion in 1824.)
Crawford	Joseph. In the 1861 census he was a farm bailiff at Hurst's Farm, Cowley, aged 30, and living in the Oxford Rd, where he became a beer retailer. He had left by 1871.
Cullam	William Cullum was a wheelwright and carpenter at Wheatley.
Currell/Currill	John, agricultural labourer, d. Dec. 1864, aged 78. James, his son, d. Nov. 1864, aged 33, after the accident described in the diary. James's elder brother, William, had a son, Mark, aged 11 in 1861.
'Dad'	A nickname. J.T.'s father had died in 1853. May have been an uncle or other relative.
Dinah	Who helped at the Red Lion. She could have been a relation or a family friend from Great Milton where she went to stay.
Druce	John, blacksmith and shopkeeper, lived next door to the Red Lion. Aged 55 in 1861.
	William, a carpenter, lived in the Wheatley Rd. Aged 37 in 1861.
	Robert, who kept the village post office, next door to the Horseshoes. In 1851 he was unmarried but in the 1861 census he was 49 and his wife, Elizabeth, was 72.
Fletcher	Vincent. Gardener/groom at the Rectory. Lived at Rectory Cottage. Aged 39 in 1861.
Fortescue	Robert (1849–64). Grandson of Robert Surman, farmer/contractor who lived at Well Barn Farm, Southend.

Sophia (Sophy), bpt. 1850, granddaughter of Robert Surman.

Gale
Joseph, who succeeded Richard Quartermain as tenant at Southend Manor (now Garsington Manor) in 1853, b. *c.* 1815 at Orsett, Essex. His wife, Mary, was born at Cuddesdon and in 1861 they had three young children. He farmed 490 acres, employing 20 men, 7 boys and 2 maids.

Galpin
William, a butcher at Cowley.

Gifford
Elizabeth, a widow who died in 1862 leaving three children, is mentioned in J.T.'s rough notes. She was Elizabeth Greening before she married and was born in Garsington in 1824. Her father was a farmer. Her mother, Harriet, was Rebecca Turrill's sister.

Godfrey
James, a baker, lived with his widowed mother next door to Hill Farm. Bpt. 1834. Albert and John ('Jack') were his younger brothers.

Levi, son of Thomas, a labourer, bpt. 1832. Lived on the Wheatley Rd next door to William Yeats.

Vincent, a labourer, was his younger brother.

Goody
James/Jim, hurdlemaker, son of William, hurdlemaker. Bpt. 1846.

Hall
Susannah, a retired farmer, aged 66 in the 1861 census, living at or near Kiln Farm with her sister, brother-in-law and lodgers.

Hanks
Ben. There was a Benjamin Hanks living in part of Library Farm cottage in 1824, but the family may have moved to another village soon afterwards for they do not appear in the censuses.

Hall & Tawney
The Oxford brewers who owned the Red Lion and Fern Cottage.

Harper
Mrs Mary, a tenant farmer at Southend Farm, which still belongs to the Queen's College, and widow of William. J.T.'s future mother-in-law.

Ann, (1845–1930), called A.H. or 'Netta' in the diary. Daughter of Mary, m. J.T. 1869.

Mary, Ann's sister, bpt. 1841. In service.

Mrs Anne, who died in London and was buried in Garsington on 17 Apr. 1864, was a widow aged 54. In 1851 she was living at Southend Manor House with her father, Richard Quartermain, and two of her children, Mark aged 16 and Mary aged 7 (both born in London).

Lizzy, who lived in London. Richard Quartermain jun. died at her house in Nov. 1864. She was probably related to his sister, Anne Harper.

Eli was aged 52 in the 1861 census, an ochre dealer. Lived in Southend, next to Home Close with his wife, Caroline, and son, Eli aged 12 and grandson, William aged 4, who was born in Paddington.

John, aged 55 in 1861. Ann Harper's uncle. His wife, Ann, was 52 and sons, William, a carpenter, 23 and Moses, 10. He also had a daughter, Ann, bpt. 1841 and a son, John, bpt. 1845.

Mary Ann (1825–65), daughter of Moses, labourer, and Phoebe. School teacher at the village school.

Thomas, a journeyman baker, b. Wheatley, aged 25 in 1861; and his wife, Mary. His brother, William, lived with them near the Horseshoes.

William, b. Chelsea. Aged 33 in 1861. Lived in the last house in Southend with his wife Rebecca.

Harvey	Ann. See Joseph Turrill.
Hatto	Joseph and Ann, who lived at Littlemore, and their son, William Joseph, bpt. Garsington Dec. 1865.
Heborn	Giles, b. Garsington 1802 and d. Radcliffe Infirmary 1873. A declaration by George Fruin in 1877 said that he had been a shoe-maker and, for thirty years, had occupied a cottage and garden in Garsington for which he paid no rent and was entitled to the freehold. In 1851 he is described as an agricultural labourer. He does not appear as a householder in later censuses.
Hedges	Jane, aged 14 in 1861, was the daughter of William, a carter, m. William Surman of Toot Baldon in Oct. 1865.
	Charley was not mentioned in the census but may be related.
Hillsden/Hilsden	Ann, d. aged 20, Apr. 1867.
	Ben, a sawyer, aged 43 in 1861.
	James, agricultural labourer, aged 17 in 1861.
	John, agricultural labourer, and wife, Sarah; both 66 in 1861. Sarah d. 6 May 1864.
	Sam, agricultural labourer, 47 in 1861.
Hinton	George, aged 63, and son George, 25, were market gardeners from Horspath living near the Red Lion in 1871.

Hollys   Probably Joseph and Richard Holley, millers at
                      Cuddesdon.
Holloway   George was tenant at North Manor Farm (then
                      called Upper Farm) and Great Leys Farm, i.e. the
                      North Manor estate. In 1861 he was 55 and his wife
                      43 and they were living at Manor Farm. His son,
                      George, was 19, son, Mark, 15 and daughter, Mary,
                      17. When George jun. married Lizzy Aldworth in
                      1865 his parents moved to Great Leys so that he and
                      Lizzy could live at Manor Farm. George sen. was a
                      Roman Catholic, b. at Lidstone, and farmed 300
                      acres employing 12 men and 4 boys. His nephew,
                      son of brother William, was also George Holloway,
                      a carpenter, who was living with his maternal uncle,
                      William Druce, near the Horseshoes in 1861.
Howard   An Oxford carrier who lived at Cuddesdon. He
                      called at Garsington on Mondays, Wednesdays and
                      Saturdays, setting out from the Post Boy, at 139
                      High St., Oxford.
Hugall   Dr Thomas John, MRCS LSA, who lived at
                      Stadhampton.
Humphries   James, son of Abel, aged 17 in 1861.
                      James, aged 48 in 1861. His son, Thomas, was
                      16, and his daughter, Maria, 18. Maria m. William
                      ('Paddy') Cherry.
Janaway   William, brother of Mary Harper, a farmer. He was
                      a wheelwright, aged 50 in 1861, already living with
                      his sister and her husband as a worker on the farm.
                      The family were Dissenters but some appear in the
                      Parish Registers.
Johnson   Tom, son of John, dairyman, was 10 in 1861.
King   Mary, daughter of the vicar of Cuddesdon, m. the
                      curate, Revd G.F. Wilgress, at Cuddesdon in April
                      1864.
Lady Slack   Nickname for a Dickensian type nurse who had
                      probably been imported to cope with the smallpox
                      victims.
Lizzy   J.T.'s sister. See Lizzy Turrill.
Mother   Mrs Rebecca Turrill.
Mother-in-law   Mrs Mary Harper.
Morrell   Fred. Frederick Parker Morrell, son of F.J. Morrell
                      of Oxford, m. Henriette Anne Wynter in 1867.
                      Their son, Philip, and his wife, Lady Ottoline, lived
                      at Southend Manor House between 1915 and 1928.

Nelly	Ellen Stone.
Netta	Ann Harper.
Newell	Dick, a wheelwright living at the Malt House, Pettiwell. b. Stanton St. John, aged 32 in 1861.
Phipps	Simeon, aged 60 and son Simeon, 25, b. Headington, brick-makers at Kiln Farm in 1861.
	Jane (1808–65). William Hedges' sister-in-law.
	John, who was shot. Unmarried agricultural labourer, aged approximately 55.
	Tom, also an unmarried labourer, 73 in the 1871 census.
Pym	Charley, d. Nov. 1866. Lived in Southend. In 1861 he was living with his parents, Joseph and Sabina, brother Jem and sister Esther, a servant, who m. William Able in 1865.
Quartermain	Richard, 'old Mr. Quartermain', d. May 1864, aged 80, was the former tenant at Southend Manor Farm. His widowed daughter, Anne Harper, bpt. 1810 Chiselhampton, had died in April and her death was mentioned in his will. He was b. in Little Milton and his older children in Chiselhampton. His son, Richard, who was living with him in 1861, d. Nov. 1864, aged 38. The census places them next door to the Red Lion and it is clear from the diary that they were the tenants at Fern Cottage who gave their name to 'Quartermain's Garden'. J.T. says that Quartermain's sale took place in July 1864. 'Poor Dick' who was left with an empty cottage must have been Richard jun. who died in Hornsey.
	John was another son of old Richard, named in his will, a farmer at Chiselhampton. He handed over the keys of the cottage.
	Fanny, d. 1867 aged 24, was the daughter of Alfred, another son of Richard. Her younger brother was also called Richard.
	Another Richard, labourer, bpt. Garsington, 1798, was lodging at Southend Farm in 1861.
	(There were several other families named Quartermain in Garsington in the nineteenth century descended from those recorded there in the sixteenth century. The family at Southend Manor came from Chiselhampton.)
Radford	John, a carpenter, sold his 'newly built house' to F.J. Morrell in 1862. His brother, Thomas, had

emigrated to California but it is not clear from the diary whether John and his family had also emigrated.

Rogers
John, a farmer, aged 32 in the 1871 census.
William, whose name appeared in the Parish Register when his child was baptized in 1869.

Ruffles
Joseph, whose son was born in 1864, was a carter in the 1871 census, aged 27, with his wife, Martha, four children and father Joseph. They married in May 1863.

Rymel
(Should be Ryman.) Mrs Howard Ryman was Ann Harper's sister, Harriet (1827–65), who had married a Cowley shoe-maker.
William, or 'Willie', was their son, b. 1 Aug. 1851. He lived with his grandmother and worked on the farm. After she died he became the tenant.

Sellar/s
William was a shoe-maker living near Home Close, Southend. Alice and Susan were daughters, bpt. in 1846 and 1848 and Thomas, his son, bpt. 1850, was a groom. J.T. refers to 'cousin Sue Sellars' so presumably her mother, Mary, was a Turrill.

Sheldon
William was a butcher, aged 32 in 1861, b. Shotover, m. Ann Turrill, who died after their son, George, was born in 1851. Ann was J.T.'s cousin. In 1853 m. Mary Ann Aldworth, daughter of William and Sarah.
Another George was a blacksmith at Littlemore in 1864.

Shepherd
Francis, aged 45, agricultural labourer, and his sister Caroline, 41, a pauper, were both in the 1861 census.

Slade
John Fryer, aged 27, and his sister, Elizabeth, 33, both d. 1867. J.T. mentions another brother, Ted, but they are not in the census. A farmer, William Slade, was in the 1863 directory for Sandford.

Simmonds
Photographer at 36 Cornmarket St., Oxford.

Smith
Thomas Slatter, bpt. 1810, tenant farmer at St John's College Farm, living at the farmhouse in Pettiwell (now Pettiwell House). He farmed 155 acres and employed 5 labourers in 1861, m. J.T.'s aunt, Maria Turrill, 1844 (d. 1846).
Thomas, his son, bpt. Jan. 1845, also a farmer with his father.
Job, aged 50 in 1861, farm labourer, b. Hinksey; and his wife, Elizabeth, aged 49, b. Alvescot, an

infant schoolteacher. Elizabeth was formerly married to Richard Cooper deceased, who worked for the curate, and they had two children, Fanny and Sophia, bpt. 1852 and 1857.

Stone
Ellen Sophia, ('Nelly'). Aged 15 in the 1861 census and living with her grandmother, Mary Clinkard, at the farm.

David, her brother, aged 17, also living at the farm. In 1865 he went to New Zealand, probably with Richard and Mary Clinkard's eldest son, Thomas, and his family, who departed that year on a ship called *The Siam*.

William, son of Richard and Mary, bpt. 1816, d. 7 July 1864. (Mary Stone m. Richard Clinkard when widowed.)

Sturges
George, b. Wheatley, was aged 30 in the 1861 census, married with two children. He worked as a shepherd and general labourer and in the 1870s became a market gardener and owner, briefly, of Pettiwell House.

Dick, aged 12, was his son.

Surman
Robert moved to Garsington from Horspath and became Lord Macclesfield's tenant at Well Barn Farm in Southend (now demolished). In the censuses he was described as butcher/dealer or contractor. Died 1877, aged 84.

Robert, his son, aged 33 in 1861.

Betsy was probably Elizabeth, granddaughter of Robert sen., aged 21 in 1861 and living in his house.

William from Toot Baldon m. Jane Hedges in Oct. 1865 when he was 21 and she was 19. Farmers named Surman in Garsington today are their descendants.

Tawney
See Hall and Tawney.

Taylor
Tom, J.T.'s friend whose wife d. at Baldon in Mar. 1864. She may have been a servant at Baldon House. (There were two servants named Taylor in the 1861 Baldon Census.)

Townsend
There were several families with this name. Joseph was a carrier, aged 41, in Southend in 1861. Probably the carrier listed in the local directory who was operating from the New Inn, St Aldates.

Jim, son of William, labourer, aged 19 in 1871.

Dick, son of Richard, agricultural labourer, aged 25 in 1861.

Tradesman　　Jack the Tradesman. May be a nickname for John Clarke, a smith, aged 26 in the 1871 census. His wife, Emma, had a baby son Mar. 1866, d. June 1867. A daughter was bpt. 5 May 1867.

Turrill　　Rebecca (1807–71), mother of J.T. and widow of William, her cousin, d. 1853. Licensee at the Red Lion. Her father was Richard Turrill, Parish Clerk.

Mary, widow of Rebecca's brother, John. Licensee at the Horseshoes.

Joseph, Mary's son (1825–67). A carpenter who became Parish Clerk and schoolmaster, m. Ann Harvey, daughter of a Drayton bailiff, 14 Jan. 1864. Catherine Harriet, their daughter, was bpt. in Jan. and d. Aug. 1865.

Joseph, the diarist, son of Rebecca and William, b. Garsington, 15 July 1841, buried Garsington 14 May, 1925.

Lizzy/Elizabeth or 'Lizette' (1848–69) was J.T.'s youngest and only surviving sister.

Eleanor/Ellen, bpt. 1834, J.T.'s cousin at the Horseshoes and Emma, her sister, bpt. 1841. Emma did not marry and was still living there in 1881, housekeeping for her brother, William, who had become the Licensee.

Sally. J.T. had three cousins called Sarah. One was Ellen and Emma's sister, bpt. 1838.

Henry, J.T.'s paternal uncle, who was a farmer at Great Milton.

Elizabeth, daughter of Henry, aged 24 in 1861.

James, a paternal uncle. Poulterer in Oxford.

John, a paternal uncle. Butcher at Stadhampton, d. 1865.

Richard, a paternal uncle. Farmer at Great Milton.

Brooks, J.T.'s cousin who died in Nov. 1866, was probably a son of Henry and Susan. Brooks was Susan's maiden name.

Fred, J.T.'s cousin from Stadhampton. Son of John? Rowland, son of Henry.

Watson　　Edward (Ted), b. Portsmouth 1841. An orphan brought up by his uncle, John Druce, and family, next door to the Red Lion.

Fanny, helper at the Red Lion. There is no clue to her identity and it is unlikely that she was related to

	the other Watsons in the village.
	Josiah J., tenant at City Farm described as a coal and corn merchant in 1861.
Wayte	Samuel. The new rector, Jan. 1867.
Wells	Robert, a farmer at Chiselhampton who probably held the lease of Magdalen College land on the Watlington Rd, near Southend. Thomas Wells was their tenant in 1843.
Wheeler	Richard (Dicky), aged 22 in 1861 census, a mason/bricklayer. Son of Damaris Wheeler, a grocer.
White	James, b. Cowley, aged 45 in the 1871 census, a market gardener.
Whitmill	Maria, farmer at Chiselhampton. Young Whitmill's death was noted on 3 June 1864.
Wilgress	Revd G.F., curate 1857–66.
	Mrs Frances, his mother, d. May 1863, aged 60.
	Mary, his wife, daughter of the Revd King, vicar of Cuddesdon, m. 1864.
	Mary Frances, his daughter, bpt. Apr. 1866.
Willie	William Ryman.
Winspurr	William, a tailor at Chalgrove.
Wixon	William, a butcher at Stadhampton.
	Elizabeth, his wife, sister of J.T.'s father. Kept the Bear and Ragged Staff, d. Sept. 1865, aged 64.
Woodward/s	Elias, aged 42 in 1861, d. Aug. 1866. Shoe-maker and beer-seller who kept the Plough with his wife, Sophia.
	Fanny, his daughter, aged 14.
	George, his son, bpt. 1842.
	Elias, his cousin, bpt. 1838; and wife, Elizabeth, d. 10 Apr. 1864, aged 24.
	Mary, aged 80, was buried 13 Apr. 1867.
Yeats/Yates/Yeates	There were several families in Garsington, often using the same Christian names.
	James (Jim), agricultural labourer, aged 40 in 1861, living near the Red Lion. His cart was used to deliver pigs to Thame.
	William, agricultural labourer, aged 25 in 1861, living with his wife, Elizabeth, in the Wheatley Rd. Son of John, agricultural labourer.
	Robert, aged 39 in 1861, living with Matilda Quartermain and their children.
Young	Joseph. Butcher at Cuddesdon.

Index

Abingdon, 20, 93
Aldermaston, 45, 47
Aldworth's pond, Hill Farm, 7
Aldworth's common, Oxford Rd, 30, 74
American president (Lincoln,) 78
Ascot cabbage seed, 84
Aurora Borealis, 95

Baldon, *passim*
Balloon, The, 23 Queen St., Oxford, 54
Banbury, 52, 53, 54
band, village, 135
bell ringers, *see* ringers
Bettycraft, *see* Bury Croft
Blenheim (Wheatley Rd houses), 31, 58, 66, 77, 84, 92
Blenheim apples, 11, 62, 63, 70, 72, 73
Botanical Gdns, Oxford, 41
Bowles, Revd (curate), 122, 124, 134, 141
Brachers (Oxford photographers), 41
Bracknell Pippins, 62
Brasenose Wood, Shotover, 14
Brompton stocks, 128, 129, 134, 141
Bury Croft, 82, 141

Cape (i.e. The Cape of Good Hope, east of Magdalen Bridge), 57
Cartes de Visite, 48, 50, 53, 86, 92
cattle plague, 85, 86, 89, 92, 93, 94, 95, 96, 103, 105, 109, 112
Cattle Show, London, 94
Chadlington, 60
Chalgrove, 6, 10
Chiselhampton, 17, 21
cholera, 51, 54, 86, 100, 102, 103, 105, 109
Christ Church cathedral, 82
Cogan, Dr, 22, 24, 26, 27, 48, 51, 79, 102, 126

Combe Wood, 16, 17, 30, 64, 76, 78, 111
comet, 50, 51
Commemoration, Oxford University, 141
concert, Dr Mark's, 80
concertain, 67, 72, 73, 74, 93
Cowley, 19, 31, 76
cricket matches, 3, 6, 9, 11, 41, 44, 46, 55, 58, 77, 78, 79, 80, 82, 84, 87, 90, 99, 100, 102, 130, 140
Crown Inn, Wheatley, 30, 79, 104, 111
Cuddesdon, *passim*
Culham, 20, 21

Denton, 17, 29, 72, 73, 93
diary, Tom Cooper's, 103, 105, 116, 132; 107 (sees J.T.'s diary)
Didcot, 47, 48
Dorchester, 19, 21, 27, 29, 77, 92, 122, 134, 141
Downs, Wheatley Rd, 17, 37, 48, 70
Drayton, 19
drought, 50, 51, 53
Dr Tanner's Premier peas, 122
Duckland (Smith's farm), 41

earthquake, 11, 13

fairs, St Clement's, 89; St Giles', 53, 54, 56, 57
falling star, 17
feasts, 10, 11, 50, 51, 58, 88, 89, 103, 105, 106, 107, 109
flower shows, 41, 54, 82, 88, 105
Forward potatoes, 50, 51, 73
Fraser Wards peas, 8
funerals, 26, 31, 86

Garibaldi, 32, 36

Gizzel/Giswell spring-fed pond (one of village's main water sources), 37, 53, 58, 83, 142
Great Milton, 9, 22, 67, 97
Grimbly Hughes, 11, 12

harriers, 14, 15, 17, 22, 27, 65, 69, 72, 109, 112, 113
Headington, 46, 53, 55, 56
Holcombe (farm at Newington), 96
hoptops, 126
Horspath, 15, 24, 30
Horseshoes, the Three, 28, 53, 76, 120, 124
Hugall, Dr, 27, 28, 80, 90, 92, 93, 94, 98, 100, 103, 107, 113
hunting, 13, 14, 17, 21, 27, 61, 63, 74, 76, 90, 93, 105, 106, 111, 122, 126

Ladder Hill, Wheatley, 16, 28, 79
Lemon Pippins apples, 11
Letcombe, 99
Little Common (opp. King's Copse), 16
Littlemore, 15, 19, 49, 66, 67, 92
Littlemore Asylum, 2, 7, 8
Littleworth, 10
lottery tickets, 74, 79, 113

Mallam (auctioneer), 43, 46, 59
Malvern, 86, 87, 135
marriage (views on), 115, 116, 133
Marsh, Cowley, 64
Marston, 83, 84, 86, 87, 88, 92
May (month of), 131, 132
measles, 141
medical insurance, 27, 115
Midsummer potatoes, 27, 28, 131
monthly rose, 14
Morrells, brewers, 19
mowing machines, 41, 42, 43, 141
Muller (murderer), 58, 62
Museum, Oxford, 82, 86
Myatts Ashleaf kidney potatoes, 76, 85, 98, 103, 122, 127, 131

Ne plus ultra peas, 122
Nineveh (farm at Nuneham), 40, 48
Nuisance notices, 105
Nuneham, 6, 16, 20, 22, 54, 113

Old Berkshire Hounds, 14
Osborne's Hill, Chiselhampton, 24, 109

Palmerston, Lord, PM (death of), 90
Parker, Lord, 29
Parks, University, 83
Phipps Well (next to bakery), 53, 74
Plough, The, 31, 77, 86, 104, 135
polecat, 11
police, 9, 11, 26, 30, 44, 57, 77, 80, 105
potato 'complaint', 7, 81
prices (market food), 85, 86, 99, 100, 105, 111, 112, 127, 130, 134
Primrose Hill, Newington, 30, 31, 77, 130
Purple Cape broccoli, 122

railway, 8, 10, 16, 17, 20, 22, 23, 24, 27, 28, 29, 30, 46, 48, 53, 54, 60, 62, 64, 66, 67, 75, 76
railway bridge, 14, 15, 16
Railway Hotel, Wheatley, 91
Railway Tavern, Oxford, 48
Randolph Hotel, Oxford, 91
rates and taxes, 92, 95, 96, 98, 99, 103, 105, 110, 111, 114, 120, 121, 122, 125, 126, 129, 134, 138
Rifle Corps, 99
ringers, 18, 19, 21, 31, 37, 38, 68, 116
Ripstones (i.e. Ribstone Pippins), 11
Rogers, Prof. (temp. curate), 102, 107, 109, 111, 113, 116, 120

sales, 16, 57, 63, 64, 90, 96, 97, 111, 134
Sandford, 1, 14, 95, 99, 112, 122, 124
scarlatina, 29, 63
Shetfords lettuce seed, 78
shooting, 70, 72, 73, 84, 93, 100, 105, 111, 116, 118, 119, 125
Shotover, 14
smallpox, 22, 24, 25, 26, 27, 28, 29, 35
Snows early white broccoli, 97, 131
South Oxfordshire hounds, 14
Stadhampton, 9, 19, 24, 27, 43, 57
Staghounds, HM, 31
Stanton Harcourt, 124
St Clements, Oxford, 6
steam thresher, 7
steam plough, 54
steeplechases, 28, 29, 38, 72, 73, 77, 93,

123, 125, 130
Stokenchurch, 3
Stonor Park, 31
strike (at Gale's farm), 32
suicides, 51, 109

tailor, 79; *see also* Winspurr
tankards, 141
tax assessor, 104, 125
tax collector, 115
Teck, Princess, 134
Thame, 88, 105
theatre, 52, 54, 60, 89
Three Pigeons, Tiddington, 3
Trinity College men, 73
True Wards peas, 28, 32, 123
Turners peas, 137

Veitches Perfection peas, 122

Volunteer Rifle Review, 5

Waggon and Horses, Culham, 20
Wales, Prince of, 20, 29, 53–4
Wallingford Rd Station, 48
Wallingford pony races, 130
Wantage, 52
Warborough, 40, 41, 44, 68
Watlington, 99, 100, 102
Wayte, Revd (rector), 119
weddings 21, 31, 37, 50, 51, 78, 79
Wheatley, 6, 10, 15, 23, 26, 30, 31, 32, 61,
    62, 66, 76, 79, 83, 84, 104, 110, 125
White Hart, Cornmarket St., Oxford, 57
Willgress, Mrs F., 4
Wilgress, Revd J.G., 24, 25, 26, 27, 30, 31,
    37, 40, 62, 96, 110
Wilgress, Mrs Mary, 37, 73
Winspurr (tailor), 14, 36, 43.